WHAT'S HAPPENING TO
THE AMERICAN FAMILY?

WHAT'S HAPPENING TO THE AMERICAN FAMILY?
Tensions, Hopes, Realities

SAR A. LEVITAN,
RICHARD S. BELOUS,
and FRANK GALLO

Revised Edition

THE JOHNS HOPKINS UNIVERSITY PRESS
Baltimore and London

This study was prepared under a grant from the Ford Foundation.

The Johns Hopkins University Press, 701 West 40th Street,
Baltimore, Maryland 21211
The Johns Hopkins Press Ltd., London

The paper used in this publication meets the minimum requirements of American National Standard for Information Sciences—Permanence of Paper for Printed Library Materials, ANSI Z39.48-1984.

Library of Congress Cataloging-in-Publication Data

Levitan, Sar A.
  What's Happening to the American family?

  Bibliography: p.
  Includes index.
  1. Family—United States.   2. Family policy—United States.   3. Social change.   I. Belous, Richard S.   II. Gallo, Frank.   III. Title.
HQ536.L48   1988   306.8'5'0973   87–46304
ISBN 0–8018–3702–2
ISBN 0–8018–3658–1 (pbk.)

CONTENTS

ALL IN THE FAMILY— WHAT'S LEFT

American families are besieged from all sides. The divorce rate is close to record heights; marriage is being postponed, if not rejected; fertility rates are below zero population growth; increasing numbers of children are being raised in poverty by their mothers only, either because of divorce or because their parents never married; and mothers are rushing out of the home and into the workplace in record numbers. The traditional Ozzie and Harriet family (a breadwinner husband, homemaker wife, and children) constitutes only a tenth of all households.

Sanctions on disapproved behavior, imposed in the past by governmental fiat or community mores, are weakening or being discarded. Religious authority retains at best a tenuous hold on American hearts and minds. The radical changes in family structure that have taken place during the past few decades of upheaval have resulted in significant and varied societal effects. Some have clearly improved the economic and social situation of families, while others have had deleterious effects on millions of adults and children and continue to threaten social stability. Taken as a whole, these changes have had a more profound impact on society than a host of public programs and technological innovations.

The optimism reflected in the first edition of this book, that the conservative national turn would affect family stability, did not materialize. Social behavior apparently is not responsive to election results. Exhortations by political and religious leaders to adhere to traditional virtues have had little impact. President Reagan and his allies in the self-proclaimed "Moral Majority" were successful at the ballot box, but not in the bedroom.

Freud called families the germ cells of civilization, and many social critics warn that a virulent disease threatens the vitality of these cells. If the family cannot function, who will raise and socialize the next generation? Society has created a vast array of institutions and programs to provide many of the services and goods that were formerly the sole province of families, but they have their limits. Schools may teach reading, writing, and arithmetic, but many lessons are best learned within the home. The evidence is mounting that, lacking the necessary cooperation from the home, schools may be powerless to accomplish even their basic functions. Widespread family breakdown is bound to have a pervasive and debilitating impact not only on the quality of life but on the vitality of the body politic as well.

In the not-too-distant past, the predominant household structure consisted of a husband in the workforce, a full-time housewife, and several children. In contrast, today's families are highly pluralistic and likely to remain so. The predominance of working wives challenges the traditional role of husband and father as provider and acknowledged head of the family. Women are contributing an increasing share of the family income and are demanding not only a more equitable division of household chores but an equal voice in family decisionmaking.

Such developments should be applauded, but high divorce rates, increasing out-of-wedlock births, and the prevalence of poor children threaten family stability. There is some comfort that the 1980s witnessed a halt in the rising divorce rates chalked up during the 1960s and 1970s, but the absolute number of divorces and the divorce rate remain near record highs. More disturbing, out-of-wedlock births have continued to increase at a rapid pace during the 1980s and, if current trends continue, will soon become a more important cause of female-headed families than divorce. More than one of five births now occur out of wedlock. As a result of these changes, a growing number of children are being raised in single-parent families, and the number of female-headed households has climbed. One of every five American children—and half of children raised by only their mothers—grows up in destitution.

The loosened marriage knot and the pluralistic American family structure have generated new discontents and anxieties. Whether or not society is better off because of the new sexual and household freedoms depends, in large measure, on religious and personal preferences, but the unsettling impacts of the new behavioral patterns cannot be ignored. Thus far we have neither stemmed the tide engulfing the family nor found a suitable alternative institution for rearing and socializing the next generation.

Despite some of its bleak findings, this book is not intended as an obituary for American families. Before we mourn the family, it would be wise to look beyond the disturbing statistics.

Numerous governmental and private efforts have measurably improved family life. These endeavors include income support, family planning services, prenatal care, child care, education, school lunches, and assistance to battered wives and abused children. However, much more can be done to improve family life. All levels of government in cooperation with private institutions can and should play a role in such efforts. Unfortunately, in the current decade the federal government has abdicated much of its responsibility in this partnership. Events during these years indicate that a strict laissez-faire policy is no better for families than it is for the economy. The problems engulfing an institution as pervasive as the family are crucial to the welfare of society.

To sum up, the family should not be placed on the endangered species list, although some changes in family structure are deeply troubling. Clearly, it would be neither possible nor desirable to turn the clock back to an earlier era. American households will remain highly pluralistic, but we must realize that along with the emerging new family structures and sexual freedoms there is a new and growing list of discontents with ominous implications for American society.

Tensions stem from the need to provide a stable family for the rearing of children and for preserving the vitality of American society without infringing upon personal freedoms. There are no simple or easy solutions to these conflicting and sometimes irreconcilable goals.

The first edition of *What's Happening to the American Family?* envisioned a more sanguine scenario than does the present book. Burgeoning out-of-wedlock births, slower but continuing growth in the number of female-headed families in all social and economic strata of society, and the disturbing rise in the number of children living in deprivation—to mention three of the more unsettling developments—have contributed to the bifurcation of society into haves and have nots. The problems contributing to the erosion of the family have not abated in the 1980s:

	1960	1980	Most recent available year
Divorce rate per 1,000 existing marriages	9	23	21 (1987)
Births out of wedlock	5%	18%	22% (1985)
Children living in poor families	27%	18%	20% (1986)
Families headed by single parents	12%	18%	20% (1987)

"Women and children first," a chivalrous precept in days gone by, assumes a grotesque meaning when it is applied to the widespread destitution among female-headed families.

In the past, economic expansion and a variety of federal social programs opened opportunities for upward mobility. These bridges have deteriorated in recent years as a result of federal negligence, slowing economic growth, and the failure of many impoverished children to acquire the basic competencies necessary to obtain a good job or even any job. The present debilitating trends may still be reversed, but exhortations by political, religious, and community leaders have had little effect in rehabilitating the family. We can still hope and pray that public attitudes and personal behavior will change and that the leadership needed to help shore up the crumbling family structure will surface in the not too distant future. Recent bills have been introduced in Congress dealing with parental leave, child care, health insurance, welfare reform, a boost in the minimum wage, and mandatory child support; they offer promise, but little has yet been accomplished.

What's Happening to the American Family? focuses on the changing family and its implications for both individuals and society. The book examines factors that have led to the erosion of the traditional family structure, including divorce, out-of-wedlock births, single parenthood, fertility patterns, premarital sex, and cohabitation. The influx of women into the workforce and government policies affecting the family are also emphasized, including the transferability of European policies to the American scene. The final chapter discusses the suitability of alternative family structures and suggests a modest policy agenda that would help secure the unraveling family ties.

ACKNOWLEDGMENTS

Richard Belous, who coauthored the first edition of this book, has long left the Center for different pursuits. Preoccupied with his new duties, he could not participate in the revision. Without the resourceful help of Frank Gallo, research associate at the Center, the new edition might never have seen the light of day. Elizabeth Conway, also a research associate at the Center, and David Grinnell offered valuable critical comments. I am indebted to Annabell Lee for keeping score of the changes through several revisions. The illustrations by Al Lediard that enlivened the prose in the first edition are reproduced in the present volume, and Michael Landini converted numbers into figures. Numbers change, but art has a longer life.

The initial study and the present revised edition were prepared under an ongoing grant from the Ford Foundation to The George Washington University's Center for Social Policy Studies. In accordance with the Foundation's practice, responsibility for the content is mine.

Sar A. Levitan
Center for Social Policy Studies
The George Washington University

Part One

FAMILY ALBUMS

Chapter One

FAMILY MATTERS

> *Torvald:* What a horrible awakening! All these eight years—she who was my joy and pride—a hypocrite. . . . Before all else, you are a wife and a mother.
> *Nora:* I don't believe that any longer. I believe before all else I am a reasonable human being just as you are. . . . I must think over things for myself and get to understand them. . . . I am going away from here. . . . Goodby, Torvald.
>
> Ibsen, *A Doll's House*

HARD TIMES

It was bad enough when Ibsen exposed theatergoers to the world of syphilis and drugs, but having Nora walk out on her family was even more shocking to Victorian society. True, other writers had confronted society with marriage without love, or even love without marriage. An artist could depict a profligate Don Giovanni, just as long as the libertine was dragged down to hell in the last act. An Anna Karenina or a Madame Bovary might seek sexual bliss outside the home, but these iconoclasts always seemed to meet the same tragic fate by the end of the story.

Yet here was Ibsen showing the world a woman leaving her husband—not because he was an adulterer, a wife beater, a drunkard, a financial wreck, or even impotent. Nora was leaving because her marriage and family life lacked an almost ineffable quality. Far from plunging his heroine into some inferno, the playwright held out a new hope and vision for Nora. She had a chance—the first real chance in her life—to find her own identity outside the home. No longer would she view herself as the "good" daughter, wife, or mother. To the contrary, a domestic hell was what she was leaving behind. No wonder Ibsen's play was a traumatic experience for many viewers.

But times, tastes, and mores have undergone dramatic changes since Ibsen's day. Today, such subject matter is deemed fit for broadcast even during the "prime time" family television hours. Far from being a rare tragedy, divorce and infidelity, although still not universally accepted, are seen as ripe material for TV situation comedies. The silver screen and the tube constantly bombard us with intimate scenes from a marriage headed for the rocks. Unmarried women procreate to find new meaning in their lives; divorced men take a stab at starting over; and a world of Woody Allen characters find it impossible to determine who their lovers will be the next night. Charlie Chaplin's revolving door sketch still has the power to bring us to laughter and tears, but now it is played with different lovers waiting on either side of the doorpost. Whether the fear of AIDS will change their behavior is still a matter of conjecture.

On the Rocks?

Marriage and the family appear to have fallen on hard times. Assuming that where there is smoke, there is fire, ample evidence exists to support a pessimistic view of the family's future, displayed in continuing high divorce rates. Fewer married couples are willing to remain married "until death do us part." Backing up the divorce statistics are powerful anecdotal stories. With divorce much more common, numerous individuals have witnessed the separation experience, either firsthand or through a relative or friend. Their reports of recrimination, anger, and often guilt, mixed with wrangling over child custody issues and messy property settlements, are enough to leave a sharp impression even on stoics. When the divorce involves children, the separation may remain a lingering ordeal instead of a temporary crisis. No less disturbing is the increasing proportion of children born out of wedlock.

Besides divorce and out-of-wedlock births, other evidence purportedly pointing to a family malaise includes demographic statistics and data on female labor force participation rates. Contrary to the projected population explosion predicted by demographers a mere generation ago, the U.S. fertility rate recently has fallen to a historic nadir. Meanwhile, women in fewer numbers are devoting their lives solely to raising children and maintaining a clean house;

rather, they are seeking paid employment outside the home. The decline in the number of children, coupled with more time spent by women at work, is often cited as further proof that the family is withering. Shifts in sexual mores, social attitudes, religious beliefs, and laws affecting marriage and divorce are also buffeting the family.

Beyond these forces, the expanding welfare system has encroached on many traditional services once exclusively provided by the family. This trend started with compulsory education; schools not only have replaced the family in educating the young, but they also have become custodians of the children while both parents are at work. When hard times hit, people now have other sources to turn to for aid besides kith and kin. Social security makes provisions for orphaned children, and it also has sharply reduced the need for the elderly to depend on their children for financial support. Some analysts and politicians have blamed government income support programs as the culprit behind higher divorce rates and the growing number of unmarried mothers. The grip of the family on the individual's life has been relaxed, and its economic role has been radically altered.

Added to all this is a highly mobile society in which the young are less inclined to follow in their parents' footsteps regarding how to live, where to live, what occupation to pursue, or even what to think and believe. Traditionally, a family has been an organization from which a person is hardly ever blackballed, and a home has been a place where a person is not refused shelter and food. But recently there has been less need to avail oneself of these family resources, and a growing number of individuals are finding alternatives to these traditional havens from a heartless world.

Nagging Fears

While some view the changing role of the family as an inevitable development of the affluent welfare system, others see it as another nail in the coffin of age-old virtues and values that are being discarded by modern society. Some raise the specter that the weakening, if not the dissolution, of the family repeats the fatal mistakes of former great civilizations. Ancient Rome is said to have become decadent as the traditional family systems fell apart and individuals sought sexual gratifications where they could find them. One prominent historian speculated that the Roman Empire's civilization disintegrated when "the privileged classes . . .

came to find their ideals in pleasure. . . . Men grew selfish and fixed their hearts on idleness and amusements."[1] Established morality became bastardized and was replaced by pursuit of pleasure sanctioned by Roman law and blessed by Roman gods. Giving free rein to hedonistic instincts devastated a great culture and its military power.

The nagging fears of repeating history are pervasive and shared by analysts representing widely divergent points on the political spectrum—and not just conservatives. For example, Robert L. Heilbroner, a left-of-center analyst, in sensing "the invisible approach of a distant storm," places domestic fears ahead of even war and the state of the economy as a prime source of our current anguish. He points to "the failure of the present middle-aged generation to pass its values along to its children" and views "extreme sexual relaxation" as adding to the disquieting "mood of our times."[2]

At the heart of the matter are deep forebodings about the future. If the family is not a viable institution, then what will sustain society? Who will raise the next generation and socialize it? How will basic values and norms be passed down and inculcated in children? Whether the concerns are justified or not, they exist. A decreased commitment to preserve a marriage through a lifetime, the anxious observers argue, is bound to affect the quality of life much more profoundly than a whole host of political, social, and technological changes.

The hypothesis is that the children of broken homes may undermine the stability of a society that condones such developments. It is a rare psychologist, educator, sociologist, or other student of childrearing who would question that parents play a decisive role in personality development. Some have even argued that the increasing numbers of unstable individuals who are denied a stable home life threaten the stability of our society. Depriving children during their crucial formative years of love, guidance, and role models provided by natural parents will not only thwart their development but will also have dire consequences for society. The products of broken homes will carry their scars first to the school system and then on to other social institutions, presenting a difficult if not impossible challenge for educators, social workers, police, the judicial system, and employers. Proxy institutions will not be able to provide the care or make up the deficiencies, since they are, at best, poor substitutes for the family. A troubled family background augurs trouble when these children marry and form families of their own. At the root of this anxiety is the belief that if the family is headed for disruption, society as we know it cannot resist a similar fate.

At the other extreme is a minority that welcomes the dissolution of the family as a blessing that will free society from age-old shackles. Distorting his real views, they say amen to Bertrand Russell's assertion, "In its fullest development, [the family] was never very suitable either to urban populations or to seafaring people."[3] The bourgeois family, according to the pronouncements of the institution's detractors, is neither the only structure nor necessarily the best or most efficient one that the human mind could create to produce true social harmony for rearing the young. For many individuals, it is argued, the traditional family experience leaves a sense of alienation just as strong and scars just as deep as a broken home. The vast increase in the divorce rate testifies to the obsolescence of the family and manifests its fragility in modern society. All the efforts to preserve the institution cannot hide the inherent discontent that it breeds. Men and women in Henry David Thoreau's state of quiet desperation are, at long last, being liberated. Increasingly, they do not feel chained down for life. Many of our grandparents and parents, if they had had our new-found freedoms and opportunities, would have used them to better their situation. Indeed, a broken home may provide a far healthier environment for a child than one where the parents are engaged in incessant squabbling.

Whatever conclusions one reaches about the merits of the argument, it is an uncontrovertible fact that the structure and role of the family in the second half of the twentieth century have undergone major transformations, and the changes have not come easily. Those who choose to throw off family shackles are subject, in the words of Eric Hoffer, to a wrenching "ordeal of change." As we enter the uncharted waters of what some analysts call the information age, fundamental institutions inevitably will change, and some will be swept away. Long ago De Tocqueville observed: "What we call necessary institutions are often no more than institutions to which we have grown accustomed." Disregarding the personal and societal problems that are the product of the eroding family structure, this argument asserts glibly that new alternatives are forming to replace the family and traditional marriage. The emerging economic order will require dramatic changes in the current social structure. Some analysts envision a scenario where "paternal authority gives way to the collective authority . . . and postindustrial leisure society then appears to offer, according to age or taste, multiple channels of socialization which used to be the prerogative of the family unit."[4]

Statistics show that the so-called normal family—a working husband, a full-time housewife, and one or more children—now accounts for only 10 percent of all U.S. families. In 1987, divorced, separated, widowed, and never-married persons headed 13 million families, or one of every five in the United States. Four of five of these families were headed by women. Six percent of all women expect never to have children, while about 5 to 10 percent of the American population will never marry, and about 12 percent of all adults live alone. Thus, the living arrangements of more than 90 percent of all households differ from the so-called normal family of the 1950s, and these arrangements are becoming increasingly accepted.

The Economist's Perspective

It may come as a surprise that economists—who often have shed more confusion than light on matters in their own sphere—should venture onto a turf well trod by practitioners of other disciplines, including anthropology, sociology, and psychology. Ironically, the institution of the family and related problems were the first issues tackled by ancient economic thinkers. In fact, the word economics is derived from the Greek word *oikonomia*, which means household management.

Economists have expanded their traditional turf by attempting to illuminate decisionmaking processes for allocating resources not only in the marketplace but also in other human endeavors. Racial discrimination, fertility, politics, crime, education, uses of leisure time, and even marriage decisions in a sense all deal with choices concerning the allocation of scarce resources. As one noted economist put it, in a burst of unbecoming enthusiasm, "Economic theory may well be on its way to providing a unified framework for all behavior involving scarce resources, nonmarket as well as market, nonmonetary as well as monetary, small group as well as competitive."[5]

He is not the first, nor is he likely to be the last, to place high hopes on the future of his discipline, even though the profession's recent record does not hold much promise for such euphoria. Whatever economic theory can contribute to the study of the family, it is clear that the family's evolution will profoundly influence the future of the economy. Many economic, political, and social issues are tied up with the family. The household is the prime unit of consumption. The composition of the family largely determines the type and quantity of goods and services Americans demand from the economy. Family decisions influence the number and types of workers seeking employment, and economic models that do not consider family-related variables tend to do a poor job in predicting labor force participation rates.

In our welfare system, massive government transfer payments, or income support, provide roughly one of every six dollars of disposable personal income, and about one-third of the population receives these payments. The system of income support required to meet basic needs depends largely on the condition and role of the family. So does the prescription for welfare reform. Indisputably, the type of society and economy we shall have hinges in many ways on the conditions and fate of the family.

A STRAINED INSTITUTION

At the close of the 1970s, the outlook for the family appeared bleak indeed. After two decades of declining marriage and birth rates, rising divorce rates, increasing female labor force participation rates, an unprecedented number of out-of-wedlock births and rapid growth in the proportion of nonfamily households, it appeared that the importance of marriage and the family had diminished. Alarmed by these developments, some predicted the disappearance of the family as we know it. They warned that the continuation of these trends would have dire consequences for the family: the share of children residing in broken homes would rise, while women increasingly would abandon the roles of wife and mother for the workplace.

Wrenching Changes

Many of these conclusions were flawed because they were based on cursory and selective data. Human behavior is subject to change, and human decisions rarely follow straight-line extrapolations. Numerous reasons back up the conclusion that marriage and the family are not headed for the rocks, but careful analysis shows some very real and wrenching changes that will impoverish millions of children, stunting the possibilities of many for life. Granted, as Margaret Mead noted, the family is "the toughest institution we have," but the cracks that have appeared in its structure during the past generation cannot be easily filled.[6]

On the more optimistic side, a sanguine scenario assumes that recent divorce rates, rising out-of-wedlock births, and the proportion of children in broken homes will be reversed. But this will not just happen; shoring up the family structure will require significant changes and a resumption of government policies that would buttress the family. The increased participation of women in the labor force may delay marriage, contribute to its dissolution, or reduce birth rates, but other developments will not necessarily weaken the family and probably will not increase the rejection of marriage and motherhood. In fact, a multiple-paycheck household can lead to a far stronger and more stable family. With its heightened reliance on part-time employment, a service economy could be more amenable to the dual aspirations of women.[7] And advances in birth control, enabling better spacing of children, allow women to combine motherhood with careers, although achieving both requires struggle and sacrifice.

While closer inspection of these trends may be painful to traditionalists, there is every indication that the family remains for the majority a central social and economic institution capable of diversity, resiliency, and the ability to adapt and evolve over time. However, the travails experienced by a significant proportion of families and the spillover that their developments have had on the rest of society should not be ignored.

The family has meant many different things to different societies. Polygamous and extended families at one time were the social norm, and these structures continue in some cultures. The federal department most closely associated with the family defined the institution to include any "group of persons who share physical and emotional resources over a long period of time, and whose adult members have, had or will have, as one central purpose the rearing of children."[8] In the Western world during the last few centuries, common usage has implied two adults of opposite sexes who are living together with their offspring and other blood or adopted relatives and whose relationship has been sanctioned by either the state, the established religious authorities, or both. This contract carries with it the presumption of responsibility for the offspring of the union, but the failure of two-thirds of separated, divorced, or never-married fathers to pay child support indicates that this burden is often cast off.

fam·i·ly (fam′ə lē, fam′lē), *n., pl.* **-lies,** *adj.* —*n.*
1. parents and their children, whether dwelling together
or not. **2.** the children of one person or one couple
collectively: *My wife and I want a large family.* **3.** the
spouse and children of one person: *I'm taking my family
on vacation next week.* **4.** any group of persons closely
related by blood, as parents, children, uncles, aunts,
and cousins: *She married into a socially prominent
family.* **5.** all those persons considered as descendants
of a common progenitor: *The Tudor family reigned long.*
6. *Chiefly Brit.* approved lineage, esp. noble, titled,
famous, or wealthy ancestry: *young men of family.*
7. a group of persons who form a household under one
head, including parents, children, servants, etc. **8.** the
staff, or body of assistants, of an official: *the office
family.* **9.** a group of related things or people: *the
family of romantic poets; the halogen family of elements.*

The Random House Dictionary of the English Language,
The Unabridged Edition. Copyright © 1981 . . . 1966 by
Random House, Inc.

This definition of the family excludes the over two million unmarried couples who reported to government enumerators that
they are keeping house together, almost a third of whom were raising children. The arbitrary definition used here is not designed to
convey any normative value judgments, but to avoid the fallacy of
circular reasoning. If the family is defined to include any possible
system of relationships, then, of course, the family is here to stay—
short of a nuclear holocaust. The analysis of today's family and its
future can take on real meaning only when the notion of the family
is given specific form.

Evolution, Not Dissolution

While there is ample basis for concern about the
impact of family deterioration, public opinion surveys have reported consistently that family life and marriage are still considered central to personal happiness and fulfillment. The prepon-
derance of Americans continue to marry, and a Roper poll
concluded, "The most important elements of success are not material in nature, but rather those related to the family—being a good
parent and having a happy marriage are at the top of the list, both
cited by over nine of ten Americans."[9] Such attitudes are held by
teenagers as well as their elders.

The marriage rate (per 1,000 unmarried women over age 14) rose
sharply after World War II as millions of veterans returned to civil-

ian life, then fell almost as precipitously during the late 1940s and continued to decline during the following decade. Although marriage rates rose steadily in the subsequent decade, they remained below the rates of the late 1940s and early 1950s. Since 1972, the marriage rate has declined to its lowest point since the depths of the Great Depression. Yet, this does not indicate a wholesale rejection of marriage and the family. Both men and women are getting married at later ages, which partly explains lower marriage rates.

Similarly, increased women's participation in the workforce does not indicate a rejection of family life. While a woman's economic independence may lead to divorce, her "gainful" employment often keeps a family together. As more women enter the labor force, more husbands and children will have to take on greater housework responsibilities, and working women will probably demand a greater voice in how the family's money is spent. All this indicates continuing basic shifts in sex roles, but the family has accommodated similarly fundamental changes during its history.

Few married couples wish to remain childless, although they are having fewer children than couples of the past. Many younger couples have postponed having children, as both spouses pursue their occupational careers. This situation could contain many benefits for individual families and society; striving for quality instead of quantity will allow families to allocate greater per capita resources to children.

A major source of upheaval in the American family is divorce. Divorce rates rose more or less steadily from the Civil War until the late 1970s before leveling off near record heights. Current projections indicate that 54 percent of first marriages by women aged 25 to 29 will end in divorce; of the 70 percent who remarry, about half will divorce again.[10] The divorce rate remains high, not only by U.S. historical standards; it is at least double the rate among most other industrialized democratic nations.

The number of children involved in a divorce has more than tripled since 1954. Estimates indicate that about half of all children born in the late 1970s will experience a family breakup at some time prior to their sixteenth birthday. For most children, at least five years will elapse before their mother remarries, while 40 percent of these children will reside for 10 years or more in homes where the mother remains unmarried. Furthermore, about half the children who go through divorce and remarriage will experience the breakup of the second family as well. This experience is especially prevalent among blacks: nearly 9 of 10 black children will experience a family breakup at least once, and the length of time spent in a single-parent home will tend to be longer. Black children whose mothers remarry also are more likely to see their new family dissolve.[11]

Recent developments point to continued stability—and even a possible decline—in the divorce rate. The trend toward delaying marriage bodes well for marital stability. Research indicates that individuals who first marry after age 30 are the least likely to divorce, while those who first marry in their teens face the highest probability of marital breakup.

Largely due to rising divorce rates and out-of-wedlock births, the number of families headed by a woman and the number of children living with only one parent also have increased. Yet over 7 of 10 children live with two parents, and nearly all children live with at least one parent. One parent may not be as satisfactory an arrangement as two, but at least children today have a much higher chance of being with either a mother or a father than those in previous generations, when adults were more likely to die before their progeny reached age 18 or were unable to support their children and gave them up to an orphanage.

Granted all the family's visible warts and blemishes, no society has yet created a better and more enduring method of raising its young and passing on basic societal values. History is rife with attempts to form alternatives. The kibbutz movement in Israel is frequently cited, but only 3 percent of Israelis live in kibbutzim. Communist governments, after first downgrading families, subsequently revived "profamily" policies. In brief, alternative arrangements have failed to provide viable substitutes and realistic options to families that are acceptable to the majority of the population. Yet the prevalence of divorce and single-parent families indicates cracks in the traditional family structure.

Most American youngsters now learn to read, write, and do arithmetic in schools outside the home, but still depend upon their families for nurturing and development. Constraints of cost effectiveness and resources limit the delegation of functions usually performed by the family to alternative institutions. Our welfare system can handle cases of dire emergency, but if these exceptions became the norm, we would all be driven to the poorhouse.

Only rarely does our society remove children from their homes and place them in either public or private institutions. Instead, it has chosen—through income transfers; in-kind subsidies, such as food stamps and housing allowances; and other human resource policies—to provide the wherewithal to bolster the family and help it rear the young. It has been charged that these social welfare efforts have sometimes split up families so that they may receive these benefits. Recent proposals and reforms have tried to mitigate these unfortunate outcomes. Yet it would be rash to assume that the bulk of public policy efforts have harmed family life. In many cases, public aid is required to maintain a family as a viable unit.

Prophets of the "Brave New World" may foresee, or even advocate, that alternative institutions should take over the functions of the family. However, the creation of such a utopia, or dystopia, would require a yearning to follow these options. More importantly, it would require a far more radical change in basic human desires and aspirations. Most of us need to achieve our niche as creative members of society. But, as few of us have the ability to fulfill these desires as philosophers and poets, satisfying the need must take a far more mundane, but positive, form. Most of us need, to paraphrase Sigmund Freud, work and love, which can be achieved only through sustained commitments instead of fly-by-night arrangements. Are marriage and children a necessary part of this commitment? Obviously not in all cases, but they are in the vast majority—whether now, in the past, or in the future.

The bleak scenario for the family advocated by "advanced thinkers" is a prescription for social instability. Fortunately, a critical analysis of the evidence does not paint such a dire picture. The family is much more than a fiction of bourgeois society or a product of the industrial revolution. Indeed, it may be as old as humanity itself; according to the Bible, once Adam established some order in his environment, God gave him woman from his loin. The study of our early ancestors shows that men and women have sought stable households since time immemorial. As Richard Leakey and Roger Lewin put it, families "are not just inventions of anthropologists anxious to analyze the lives of technologically primitive people by carving up their social structure into objective but somewhat artificial units."[12] Whether a tribe, an extended family, or a nuclear unit, these institutions have provided an important foundation for identity and a stable outlet for the expression of basic human needs.

Even with a historic perspective and an eye on the new order favored by some, recent shifts in American families demand that public and private policymakers and the concerned public show greater interest in how other social institutions interact with families. For example, family background can have a major impact on the types of remedial employment, training, and welfare policies required and the outcomes of specific programs. Some corporations have found that the provision of family support programs can enhance recruitment of professional personnel and employee productivity. Facing up to these interrelationships is difficult and often costly but necessary.

The attitudes of teenagers reinforce the conclusion that families and parenthood are hardly out of fashion. This is equally true for professional women, who risk the greatest income loss from motherhood. There is every indication that a growing number of young adults are trying to achieve a workable compromise that includes both aspirations.

The changing family structure that American society has experienced during the past quarter-century has caused serious maladjustments. Reliance on a laissez-faire policy to alleviate the consequences of the deteriorating family structure is fraught with danger. Society is likely to muddle through, but a large and growing proportion of families will not have the personal resources to cope with the consequences of family breakdowns. Appropriate human investments are necessary to bolster the weakened family structure.

These are neither the worst of times nor the best of times for the family. Therein lie challenges and opportunities. While we sing hosannas to the family, this need not be to the Ozzie and Harriet model. The goal is to allow pluralism to flourish, but the challenge is to assure that parents assume responsibility for supporting and nurturing their children. The government should play an active role in helping families that lack the resources to adequately rear their young.

Part Two

THE FAMILY IN ACTION: THE KNOT LOOSENS

Chapter Two

LOVE AND MARRIAGE

It's an experiment frequently tried.
W. S. Gilbert, *The Gondoliers*

BASIC VALUES

What may have appeared an amusing one-liner a century ago, when W. S. Gilbert wrote *The Gondoliers*, is now a reality for more than a million American couples annually. Pundits and social scientists have pointed to trends in marriage, divorce, childbearing, and household living arrangements as evidence of eroding family values during the past two decades. According to sociologist Amitai Etzioni, "If we continue to dismantle our American family at the accelerating pace we have been doing so since 1965, there will not be a single American family left by the year 2008."[1] Yet public attitudes as reflected in surveys overwhelmingly affirm the desirability, importance, and rewards of family life. Over 9 of 10 persons polled by the Roper Organization for the *Wall Street Journal* cited being a good parent and having a happy marriage as "very important" elements of success.[2] A report commissioned by Ethan Allen, Inc., "The Status and Future of the American Family," found that 9 of 10 respondents describe their family as the most or one of the most important elements in their lives; 52 percent called their families the most important element in their lives.[3] A Gallup poll conducted in 1986 found that 93 percent of those surveyed were "very" or "mostly" satisfied with their family life, about the same as in 1980. The Ethan Allen survey found that 4 of 5 respondents considered time spent with their families to be "very important," while the same proportion viewed their families as "very close."

19

In addition, Americans appear to value relationships with family members who live outside their household. Two-thirds reported that they visit or phone their parents once a week or more, and one of five communicate with their parents daily. Nearly two-thirds stated that they attend family gatherings because they enjoy doing so; only a small percentage attend out of a sense of obligation or because they do not want to offend family members. The importance of the extended family even encompasses the raising of children: 68 percent of those surveyed agreed that grandparents should have an important role in raising their grandchildren.[4]

Young adults and students also place a high value on family life. Two-thirds of college freshmen polled in 1986 considered raising a family to be essential or very important, an increase compared to the 1970s.[5] Among women aged 18–29, 93 percent ranked marriage as the most satisfying and rewarding lifestyle—more or less the same response as older cohorts. However, age differences in the preferred type of marriage were evident: younger women favored a marriage in which career, housekeeping, and child care responsibilities are shared equally, while older women preferred more traditional marital roles.[6]

Marriage

Marriage, in fact, is experienced by almost all Americans at some time. Some may delay it or terminate it, but very few do not try it. When it comes to marriage, women are apparently more precocious than men (fig. 1). Half of all men who marry enter their first marriage by age 26, and the same proportion of women do so two years earlier. Before they meet their Maker, about 95 percent of men and women have said "I do" at least once. This figure is slightly higher than that in the nineteenth century, which sometimes was only 90 percent. During colonial times, the marriage rate might have been as low as 84 percent in certain areas.[7] Some analysts have predicted that the proportion of men and women who marry may drop a little below the current historically high levels—probably to about 90 percent.

While virtually all Americans take the marriage vows, recently they have been postponing this event.[8] In 1960, only one of four men and one of ten women had never been married by age 26. By 1987, the comparable rates had increased to half the men and more than 4 of 10 women. A trend toward later marriages is also evident in Western Europe.

FIGURE 1.

Nineteen of 20 Americans marry
before they reach middle age (1987).

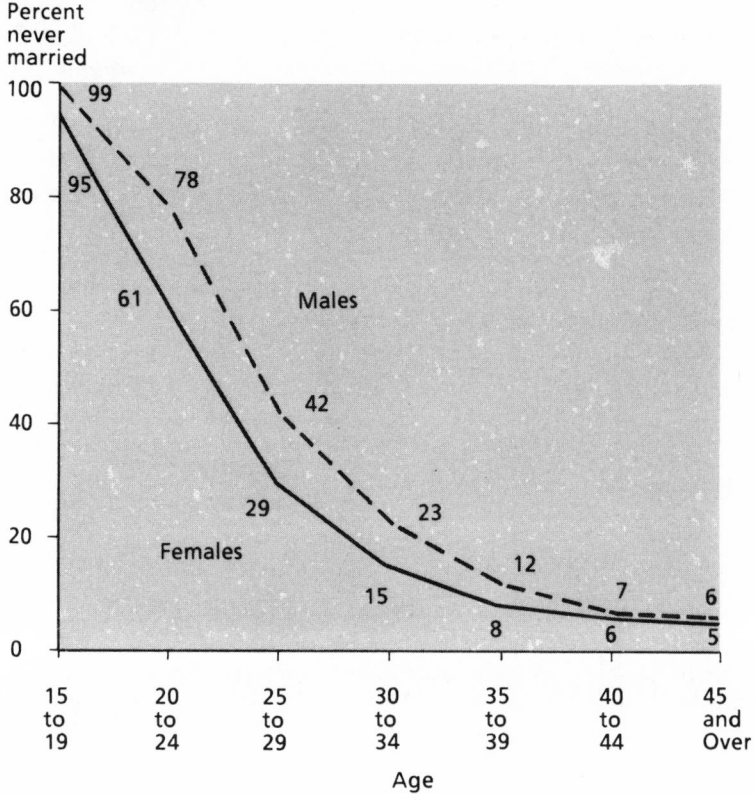

Source: U.S. Department of Commerce, Bureau of the Census

The postponement of marriage is not a new phenomenon. In
1890, the median age of the first marriage for men was 26.1 years
and 22 years for women. Thereafter the age at first marriage steadily
dropped until 1955 to 22.6 for men and 20.2 for women before rising to its current heights. Another change is that the average age

difference between bride and groom at first marriage has declined from four years at the turn of the century to two years today.

The tendency to postpone saying the magical words "I do" need not necessarily dishearten even traditionalists. In fact, many positive social consequences could result from the trend to delay marriage. More young people have decided to opt for longer education and to seek other experiences or establish a career before marriage, rather than move from their parents' home directly into one where a spouse and children wait in the wings. Thus, the bride and groom are more likely to be financially and emotionally prepared for marriage.

Complications arising from the post–World War II baby boom and slow economic growth, compounded by the decline in real average earnings of young adults since the early 1970s, have also played a role in delaying marriage. Women reaching the usual ages when a majority of them first marry experienced a "marriage squeeze" during the late 1960s and early 1970s. Because they were born during an era of rising birth rates, women in this age group (18–24) outnumbered men aged 20 to 26—the normal age when men first married.[9] Also, the economy did not generate enough jobs for the products of the baby boom when they entered the labor market. Two deep economic recessions in 1973–74 and 1981–82 made the going even harder for young workers than for the more mature. The 26 percent drop in real earnings for young males aged 20 to 24 (not attending school) during the 1973–86 period diminished their financial resources for starting a family.

Changes in attitudes toward premarital sex have also had an impact on postponing marriage. Both the pronounced increase in premarital sexuality and the broader acceptance of this behavior have been thoroughly documented. The proportion of adults who found premarital sex unobjectionable rose from one-fifth in the early 1960s to more than one-half in 1985. Three-fourths of those under 30 approve of premarital sex. According to recent surveys, only about one of every five blushing brides was a virgin upon entering marriage. While premarital coitus has been high among lower-income and minority groups, a major factor behind this upward trend has been the increased sexual activity among young college-educated adults from families with relatively high incomes. More recently, the fear of contracting AIDS (and to a lesser extent, herpes) has probably promoted a change in lifestyles among single men and women. A recent poll found that 43 percent of all adults (55 percent of those aged 18 to 29) had altered their sexual practices to avoid exposure to AIDS. While one result could be a reemphasis on traditional, monogamous relationships, the long-term implications are unclear.[10]

The standard "Dutch uncle advice" to young men used to be not to rush into marriage: first, go out and live a bit, or even "sow wild oats," and then ground yourself firmly before taking a wife and raising a family. The image created by Charles Dickens of poverty—a landlord beating at the door, a half-dozen crying, hungry, and sniffling children, an unhappy and nagging spouse, and poor prospects for economic advancement—was enough to make a young man think twice before being tied down too early. In 1890, the median age for men to marry—a relatively ripe 26—was seen as a healthy sign for the future of family stability.

While few Dutch uncles are reported to have told their nieces to go live it up before marriage, there are reasons for believing that delaying marriage is a healthy sign. Marriages at a very young age have a far higher probability of ending in divorce than those at a more mature age.[11] The time spent during a person's early twenties garnering education and credentials, labor market experience, financial resources, and even sexual experience can help to build up "human capital," in economic terminology, and thus foster a stable and productive life.

A Marriage Calculus?

Marital patterns over the life cycle, including the timing and incidence of marriage and divorce, have changed, but the vast majority of Americans still marry at least once.[12] Focusing an economist's lens on marriage may prove fruitful in understanding its almost universal appeal. Using a technique that may seem arcane to some, economists have applied benefit-cost analysis to marriage. Marriage, one can assume, is a free exchange, which, like other commodity trading, increases the level of utility, or well-being, of marriage partners compared to single individuals. As men and women seek out mates, a marriage market is presumed to exist. Economists do not claim that two can always live as cheaply as one, but they can certainly live more cheaply together than apart. The list of gains from marriage often includes improved quality and/or lower prices for health care, food, shelter, recreation, sex, companionship, and even children.[13]

The era of building economic models to predict marriage conditions is still in its very early formative years, and skeptics may properly doubt whether the models will ever reach maturity. Even if the current state of the analysis is superficial and simplistic, the approach suggests that very powerful economic and social forces lie behind the continued pattern of marriage.

The economic gains from marriage are the sum of the value of household production and money income received from employment outside the household. To use a very simple example, suppose the value of household production and money income for two single people were:

	Value of household production	Money income	Value of total output
Male	$2,000	$10,000	$12,000
Female	2,000	6,000	8,000
		Total	$20,000

If these two individuals were married and concentrated their efforts on that production area where they showed a comparative advantage, then the value of production could be as follows:

	Value of household production	Money income	Value of total output
Male	0	$14,000	$14,000
Female	$8,000	0	8,000
		Total	$22,000

Based on this illustration, the overall economic gains produced by marriage are not apparent. All that the above example suggests is that two single people can often live better as one household. It does not require that the people be married. With the rapid growth in the number of unmarried couples in the United States, many individuals are finding it possible to enjoy the benefits of cohabitation without the sanction of either church or state. As long as the model builders overlook such "details," they have a long way to go before they illuminate the institution of marriage.

Because married individuals, especially men, enjoy much better mental and physical health than singles, some analysts speculated that marriage itself was responsible for these benefits. However, these conclusions may have tended to put the cart before the horse because healthier and more stable individuals are more likely to marry in the first place. The overall singles population fares worse because it contains a relatively greater share of individuals with congenital or childhood health problems, widows and widowers, and individuals who are incarcerated or institutionalized. Non-

institutionalized persons who have never been married actually tend to be healthier than married individuals.[14]

Social scientists are still a long way from producing statistical models, or a calculus of marriage, that can accurately explain and predict marriage decisions by men and women in the real world. Any predictions about the future of the family must, therefore, rely upon past and current data as well as some value judgments. An institution that persists despite vast social, political, and economic upheavals is not likely to be abandoned in the foreseeable future, although its role may continue to undergo changes.

UNTIL DEATH?

If Americans have not given up on the institution of marriage, it does not follow that men and women are still willing to remain tied down with the same marriage partner until they meet their Maker. The statistics are conclusive that Americans are displaying a strong propensity to accept divorce and remarriage rather than one official partner for a lifetime. However, a scrutiny of divorce and remarriage data does not show a society that has replaced the family with a random, never-ending game of musical chairs (or beds). Instead, they indicate that while more people end their marriages in divorce, most of these individuals are prone to tie the knot again. Repeating the cycle of divorce and remarriage for a third time is confined to a relatively small portion of the population. Mickey Rooney and Elizabeth Taylor are not representative of the American family. However, second marriages are just as likely to end in divorce as the first.

Divorce

Divorce is one of the most important factors affecting the changing structure of the American family (fig. 2). Divorce rates per thousand married couples show a clearly rising trend since the mid-nineteenth century. While divorce rates in the early twentieth century were low by today's standards, they caused considerable alarm at the time and were much higher than corresponding rates in Western Europe. By the end of the century's first decade, religious leaders and traditionalists had successfully lobbied to tighten divorce laws in many states, but divorce rates continued to increase. Following a pattern established after both the Civil War and World War I, divorce rates skyrocketed after World War II, to a record of 17.9 per 1,000 married couples, as "quickie" marriages were dissolved after the war. While the divorce rates quickly subsided, they did not return to the prewar level. For over a decade the pattern of divorce remained fairly stable, but then began to climb in the turbulent 1960s. By 1973 the divorce rate had surpassed the highs recorded following World War II and peaked at 22.8 divorces per 1,000 married couples in 1979. Since then the divorce rate has dropped slightly and has apparently stabilized. In 1987, nearly 1.2 million divorces and annulments were granted, for a rate of 21 per 1,000 married couples. The U.S. divorce rate is more than triple the Japanese rate and at least double the divorce rates in the other major industrial democracies except England.[15] International comparisons are based on the divorce rate per 1,000 persons rather than the rate per 1,000 married couples.

Country	Divorce rate per 1,000 persons	
	1965	1985 or 1986
United States	2.5	4.8
England	0.8	3.0
Canada	0.5	2.4
Sweden	1.2	2.3
West Germany	1.0	2.1
France	0.7	2.0
Japan	0.8	1.4
Italy	not legal	0.3

FIGURE 2.

The divorce rate has stabilized in the 1980s, but at close to historical peak levels.

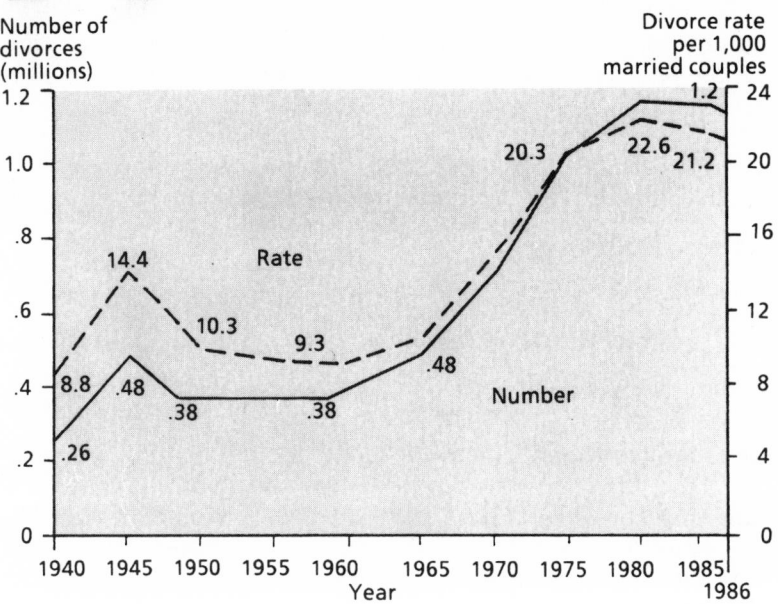

Source: U.S. Department of Health and Human Services, National Center for Health Statistics

In order to examine differences in divorce by race, it is necessary to use data from the U.S. Census Bureau, which measures divorce somewhat differently than the U.S. National Center for Health Statistics. The Census Bureau collects information on the number of divorced (but not remarried) persons as a proportion of all married persons. The Census Bureau figures are much higher than those of the National Center for Health Statistics because they include all divorced individuals, not just those who divorced in a given year. The divorce ratio for blacks has quadrupled during the 1960–87 period, and increased nearly as much for whites:

	Divorced persons per 1,000 married persons with spouse present		
Year	Total	White	Black
1987	130	122	250
1980	100	92	203
1970	47	44	83
1960	35	33	62

The rise in the ratio of divorced to married persons applies to all age groups, but has been highest for people 35–44 years old. During the past generation, the proportion of divorced persons more than doubled, even for persons 65 years and over. The increase for

	Divorced persons per 1,000 married persons with spouse present				
Year	Under 30 years	30 to 34 years	35 to 44 years	45 to 64 years	65 years and over
1987	110	144	170	129	80
1980	96	131	122	91	64
1970	38	45	48	53	47
1960	23	30	35	46	32

the elderly is largely due to the fact that older persons are much less likely than younger individuals to remarry. Annual divorce rates have consistently been highest for those under 30, dropping precipitously with increasing age. In 1984, the most recent year for which data are available, the divorce rate for those under age 20 was 53 per 1,000 married couples, but only 2 per 1,000 for those aged 65 and older.[16]

These data on divorce, disturbing as they may be for the stability of the family, tell only part of the story. Data on the growth of nontraditional family structures place the picture of the American household even more out of focus. While the number of single-parent families has grown significantly since 1970, the most drastic change in the family over the past half-century has been the increased proportion of nonfamily households, primarily individuals living alone. In 1940 families constituted 9 of 10 households, but declined to 7 of 10 by 1987. Interestingly, the allegedly quiescent 1950s witnessed a rapid growth of nonfamily households. The rate of change in family and household structure has slowed considerably in the 1980s.

	1940	1950	1960	1970	1980	1987
	Household structure					
Households (millions)	34.9	43.6	52.8	63.4	80.8	89.5
Families	90.1%	89.2%	85.0%	81.2%	73.7%	72.1%
Married couple	76.0	78.2	74.3	70.5	60.8	57.6
Single head	14.1	10.9	10.7	10.6	12.9	14.5
Nonfamily household	9.9	10.8	15.0	18.8	26.3	27.9
Living alone	7.7	9.1	13.1	17.1	22.7	23.6

Persons living alone account for almost all of the nonfamily households, and numbered over 21 million in 1987. Over half of those living alone are over 54 years old, double their proportion in the adult population. Nearly two of five are widowed, almost a third have never been married, 22 percent are divorced, and the remaining 8 percent are married but not living with their spouse.

High divorce rates and a rising proportion of individuals living outside the family indicate radical changes in family structure that pose difficulties for the individuals involved as well as for society, but the problems should not be exaggerated. Divorce can represent a constructive alternative to a failed marriage. Despite readjustment difficulties, most divorced persons believe that ending their marriage was the best decision. Over 9 of 10 divorced women, and 62 percent of the men, considered themselves happier outside their marriage.[17] The increased proportion of individuals who live outside the family structure is largely a reflection of increasing affluence and a preference for independence; a similar trend has occurred in many other industrialized democracies.[18] Grandparents almost invariably prefer to live on their own, and rising Social Security benefits, bolstered by the expansion of private pensions and savings, have increasingly enabled them to do so.

Divorce is only one factor resulting in marital disruption, and focusing only on divorce rates leaves the impression that family breakdown is a relatively new phenomenon. Research by sociologist Mary Jo Bane indicates that marital disruption was also a problem in the "good old days," even though its causes have shifted. With vast improvements in health, plunging death rates for all ages counterbalanced increases in the divorce rate during this century to such a degree that the rate of marital disruption for women 45 and over was fairly stable until 1970. Bane found that the percentage of "ever-married" women living with their first husbands had changed very little during the twentieth century:[19]

	Age of women		
Year	45–49 years	50–54 years	55–64 years
1910	70.2	64.7	55.0
1940	68.4	64.0	54.9
1970	69.9	65.7	56.6

The offset of the growing divorce rate by the falling death rate, however, did not continue. By the mid-1970s, divorce replaced death as the most important factor accounting for marital dissolution.[20] The divorce rate continued to rise before dropping very slightly in the 1980s (fig. 3). However, it shows no sign as yet of significantly declining.

Divorce and marital separation are not uniform throughout the country but vary by demographic, social, and economic characteristics. Religion and geographic location are also factors. For example, one study found divorce and separation among ever-married white males to be twice as common among those expressing no religious preference as among Catholics. Also, divorce rates in the western states tend to be far higher than those in the East.[21]

Individuals with low incomes experience more than their share of marital disruptions. This may account in part for the much higher divorce rates among nonwhites than among whites. Lower educational attainment also strongly increases the probability that marriage will wind up in divorce. It is difficult to give a specific weight to each of these various factors. However, some researchers have concluded that income levels have a much stronger impact on marriage stability than educational attainment and occupational factors. But there are indications that stability of income and employment, even more than the amount of earned income, plays a major role in the divorce decision.

Family analysts' views of the role of children in preserving a marriage have undergone some radical changes in recent years. The debate persists as to whether couples have children because they intend to stay together or whether having children keeps them from seeking a divorce. The traditional view has been that the birth of a child often stabilizes a shaky marriage. As one analyst in the 1930s put it, "Clearly, children hold their parents together."[22] However, recent research using longitudinal data indicates that the impact of children on divorce is far more complex. On average, couples having serious marital problems tend to postpone bringing children into the world. One study found that marital separation is much less likely among couples with preschool children. But such

FIGURE 3.

The divorce rate has stabilized during the 1980s.

Percent change in the divorce rate from the previous five years

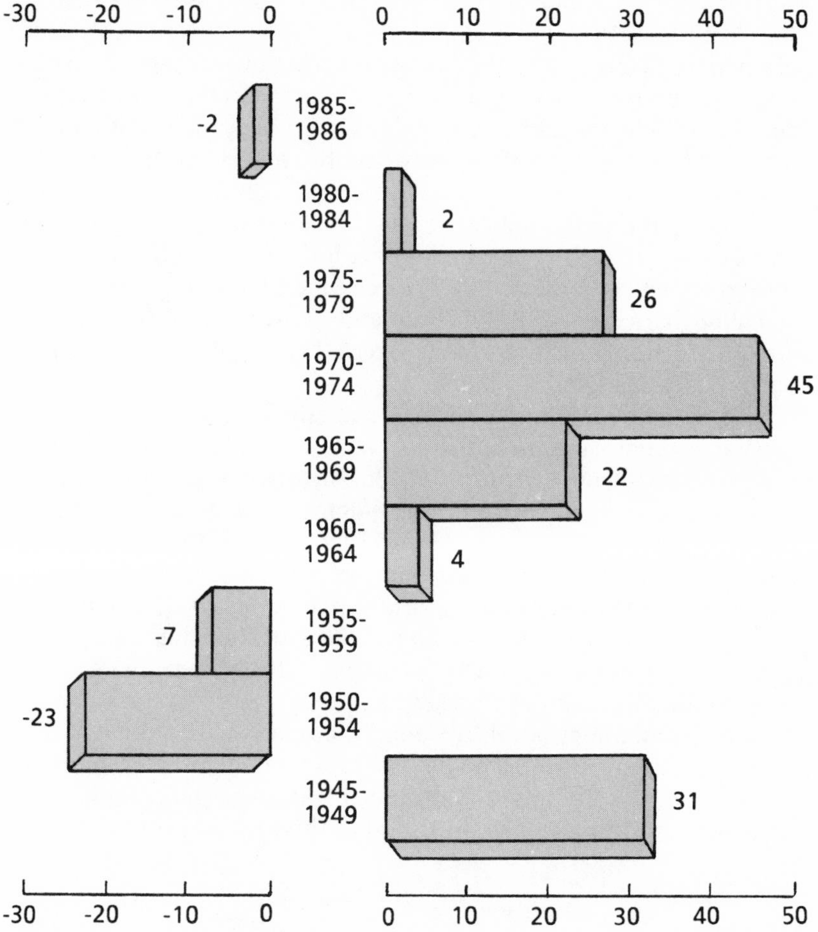

| | | | | | | | | |
|-30|-20|-10|0|0|10|20|30|40|50|

-2   1985-1986

1980-1984   2

1975-1979   26

1970-1974   45

1965-1969   22

1960-1964   4

-7   1955-1959

-23   1950-1954

1945-1949   31

-30 -20 -10 0   0 10 20 30 40 50

Source: U.S. Department of Health and Human Services, National Center for Health Statistics

couples often merely postpone separation until the youngsters reach school age.

It has been argued that laws that make it easier to untie the marriage knot, including "no-fault" divorce laws, have encouraged people to end their marriages. Some studies of state data have shown a high correlation between the ease of obtaining a divorce and the probability that couples will seek to end their marriage. However, a study of conditions before and after the institution of no-fault divorce laws in various states indicates that the legislation did not affect divorce trends.[23] Easier divorce laws may be as much a governmental response to shifts in social mores as their cause.

It is difficult to forecast the future of divorce rates. Roughly half of divorces occur during the first seven years of marriage. There is roughly a four- to six-year lag between the rise in marriage and divorce rates. The recent trend to delay the first marriage, with fewer teenagers and people in their early twenties entering into marriage, might contribute to greater marriage stability in the 1990s.

Some of the most intriguing variables and factors in marriage and divorce decisions are the hardest for social scientists to capture in statistical models. Analysts can feed their computers only so-called hard data—like income and educational attainment—and must ignore nonquantifiable forces that might be the most important factors affecting change.

Having gained acceptance as a socially approved solution to marital conflicts, and as religious constraints play a diminishing role, divorce seems to feed on itself. Also, when considering divorce, a husband and wife might weigh the chances of finding a replacement for the about-to-be discarded mate. With a low divorce rate, the pool of eligible new partners would tend to be small, whereas a higher divorce rate would expand the pool. Labor market conditions should also be considered. As married women achieve a greater degree of financial independence from men, fewer may wish to remain with their present husbands, and those who work with other men may want to extend the relationship from a work bench or office desk to the home. The rapid growth of women in the labor force may therefore continue to influence family dissolutions, undermining any stabilization in the divorce rate.

Remarriage

Divorce does not mean a permanent withdrawal from the marriage arena. Approximately a third of marriages contracted each year involves a previously married bride, while a similar proportion involves grooms who are repeaters. The proportion who remarry drops with age. Three of four women whose first marriage ends in divorce before the age of 30 wind up remarried. The comparable rates are almost three out of five for women aged 30 to 39 years and one out of four for women 40 years of age or older.

Having children delays but does not prevent women's remarriage. For women under age 30 who remarry, the median number of years between marriages is 2.9 if they have no children; 3.1 if they have one or two children; and 4 if they have three to five children. Similarly, divorced women under age 30 have an 80 percent chance of being remarried if they have no children, but their chance is still above 70 percent if they have three to five children.

Most divorced men cannot long endure their return to bachelorhood. In fact, divorced men are over twice as likely to remarry than never-married men are to enter their first marriage. The same social, cultural, and economic factors that play a significant role in first-marriage decisions seem to also influence remarriages. For example, divorced men who have higher incomes and more stable employment patterns are more likely to remarry. Remarriage rates have paralleled trends in first marriages. Both show an increase after 1930 and a subsequent decrease from World War II until 1960. However, in contrast to the slight decline in first marriage rates since 1960, remarriage rates climbed rapidly until the mid 1960s before resuming their decline. One result of a decrease in the remarriage rate has been an increasing number of households headed by women. Since 1940, the number of American families has doubled, but during the same time the number of households headed by women has more than tripled.

Divorce reflects more the rejection of a specific partner than of the institution of marriage. However, sifting through the data indicates that a second marriage has less chance of lasting than a first marriage. While two of three first marriages may be expected to last until death, more than three of seven second marriages are likely to expire before one of the partners.

Unmarried Couples

Since 1960, there has been a significant increase in the number of couples reporting that they are living together without being married. Such "living in sin" is not a recent phenomenon, as the Bible and other ancient sources attest. But being willing to admit it to government enumerators is a relatively new phenomenon. In 1960 the Census Bureau reported that 439,000 households were made up of unmarried couples. By 1987 the number of unmarried couples had more than quadrupled to over 2.3 million, accounting for 2.6 percent of all households. The share of unmarried couple households containing children rose from 21 percent in 1977 to 31 percent in 1987.

Most cohabitation arrangements do not last long, and many of the partners apparently do not view them as permanent. For example, in 1977 about 63 percent of unmarried couples had been living together for less than two years. In earlier years admission of cohabitation before marriage was adequate cause for dismissal from a job and banishment from respectable society. Since then courts have stepped in to protect the rights of unmarried persons living together, and social disapproval has vastly diminished. Before the rules changed, there were good reasons for "sinners" to hide their living arrangements. In the 1980s, despite conservative dominance of the political scene, the reasons for such secrecy have weakened.

WEIGHING THE EVIDENCE

Continued high divorce rates pose one of the greatest threats to the American family. Yet most divorced persons seek a new stable relationship, and very few people marry more than twice. Marriage and the family are still viewed by an overwhelming majority of Americans as a proper and apparently preferred living arrangement.

However, all this does not minimize the problems created by family disruptions. By 1987, the traditional American family composed of a working husband, housewife, and one or more children accounted for only 10 percent of all households, while, single-parent families accounted for 15 percent of the total. If marriage vows were dictated by recorded facts, about half of marrying couples would change the promise "until death" to "until we change partners." Still, living as part of a family seems to be the preference of most adult Americans—and they like to play for keeps and to make it "legal." The increase in the number of unmarried couples seems to be more of a way station than a final refuge in life. Despite a permissive society's toleration of experimentation, most individuals seem to prefer the traditional contractual relationship with all its obligations and restraints.

"We were married in 1964, 1974 and 1980."

It is hard to judge whether society is better or worse off under these relaxed conditions than it presumably was in an earlier, puritanical era. The buffeting to which the family has been subjected has generated tensions and scars that have led many to psychiatrists' couches, and probably more victims did not have the resources to tell their woes to the would-be mental healers. It may be argued that being forced to live in an unhappy and bickering marriage is a worse evil than a divorce. But as long as society condones that solution, individuals are in a position to make a free choice. The challenge is whether Americans will use their new-found freedoms wisely.

For now, it appears that the family is withstanding the changes produced by the new social freedoms. However, the surviving institution exhibits many basic differences from previous and more traditional patterns, at considerable costs to the families involved and to society at large.

Chapter Three

BE FRUITFUL AND MULTIPLY

> And God blessed them; and God said unto them: "Be
> fruitful and multiply. . . ." And they were both naked,
> the man and his wife, and they were not ashamed.
> Genesis 1:28, 2:25

> Every man must marry a wife in order to beget
> children, and he who fails of this duty is as one who
> sheds blood, diminishes the image of God, and causes
> the Divine Presence to depart from Israel.
> *Shulchan Aruch*

NEW CONCEPTIONS

Religions have played a major role in shaping the
family, although the approaches dictated by the same faiths over
time have varied widely, reflecting changing mores and practices.
For example, in the *Shulchan Aruch,* the basic legal text used by
Orthodox Jews in guiding their behavior, the biblical admonition to
"be fruitful and multiply" was interpreted to mean not only that
couples must marry *before* they produce progeny, but also as a
commandment to marry in *order* "to multiply." Failure to obey this
commandment is considered a serious offense not only to God but
also to the entire community.

Similar exhortations and commandments concerning fertility
and children can be found in the doctrinal core of most of the
world's leading religions. Christianity has placed a strong emphasis on marriage and the resulting offspring. The epistles of the
New Testament contain numerous exhortations concerning procreation and proper family life. While husbands and wives are
urged to strive for the world to come, they are repeatedly reminded

of their earthly duties. In the Mormon church marriage combined with parenthood is considered the best assurance of eternal exaltation, which is not available to man or woman in a single state. The Koran not only tells Muslims of Allah's great delight in children but also reveals strict commandments concerning parental responsibilities toward a child's upbringing. Buddhism recognizes many different roads to enlightenment. Some people are called upon to give up having families and devote their full time to a spiritual awakening. However, the Buddha noted that for others, being parents would become an integral part of their spiritual growth. For Confucius, the way toward obtaining goodness was centrally linked with family relationships and responsibilities.

One of the main functions of a family has been to produce, nurture, and socialize the next generation. While the family does not have to be child oriented, the needs of the young have played a primary role in the evolution of this institution. An old nursery rhyme summed up the traditional mores quite succinctly: "First comes love; then comes marriage; then come children in a baby carriage."

However, in a growing number of cases this conventional order has not been followed. Love often results in just living together without marriage. Even if marriage does follow love, the need for the proverbial baby carriage may be long postponed—the result of more effective birth control practices. And since the 1973 Supreme

Court ruling which struck down restrictive state laws regarding abortion—especially during the first three months of pregnancy—legal abortions have become widely available as a means of fertility control. In some cases, the baby carriage is never needed. For many adults, the word *crib* more often is associated with cheating on tests than with a child's bed. With a rise in out-of-wedlock births, the baby carriage—if it can be afforded—has often preceded marriage. In too many cases, nuptial vows have not followed the birth.

As more women receive longer education and enter the labor force, motherhood increasingly must vie with their other options or aspirations. Following the post–World War II baby boom, fertility rates have plummeted to historic lows. All Western European countries except Ireland have fertility rates too low to maintain their current population size, and several have already experienced a decline in population. This trend has been viewed with dire alarm by some, a view forcefully articulated by Ben Wattenberg. He and other observers speculate that declining population will inevitably lead to the loss of political, military, and cultural influence by Western democratic countries. They further argue that falling population will result in reduced domestic demand for goods and services, which in turn will lead to fewer jobs, a diminution of economies of scale, and, thus, lower productivity and living standards. Also, they note that declining fertility rates mean that proportionately fewer working-age adults will be supporting a burgeoning elderly population.[1]

Not all observers share these concerns, noting that long-term population projections are seldom accurate. Even if these forecasts prove correct, it does not necessarily follow that the U.S. would forfeit its political and economic leadership to more populous nations. There is little correlation between population and world influence, as England demonstrated in the nineteenth century and as Japan does today. During the late nineteenth and early twentieth centuries many warned of the "Yellow Peril" posed by the multitudinous Chinese, but the Chinese masses had so little power they could not even prevent foreigners from carving up their own country into European "spheres of influence." Fears of overpopulation in the United States and other Western democracies, much in vogue a decade ago, have quieted, although they remain a real concern in many developing countries.

However, not all observers are dismayed by the decline in birth rates. Some view the development with equanimity, and even welcome it. Current living conditions are far less spacious than in the

Garden of Eden, and manna from heaven has been scarce. Fertility declines, they argue, might prove socially beneficial.

Beyond decisions on whether to bring children into this world, there remains the problem of who will provide for, and socialize, them once they are born. Under traditional social mores and legal sanctions, the answer to these questions was the family. However, as the number of separations, divorces, and out-of-wedlock births has increased, the answers have been changing. These changes have had a dramatic impact, not only on the structure of the family, but also on the role of the state in modern society. The ways in which American society and families cope with these changes could well determine the future viability of the family and the direction of the modern welfare state. Shoring up the family will continue to require changes in a range of institutions: the modern welfare system, private corporations, and, more importantly, the family itself.

Fertility Patterns

Demographers have developed several different ways to measure annual fertility rates. The *crude birth rate* records the number of births per 1,000 population, while the *general fertility rate* considers only the childbearing portion of the population by counting the number of births per 1,000 women between 15 and 44 years old. Finally, the *total fertility rate* measures the number of lifetime births per woman. In order to maintain zero population growth, females must sustain a total fertility rate of 2.1—rather than 2—because not all their daughters survive to reproductive age and because not all of their sons and daughters are fertile.

In its early years, the United States had a higher total fertility rate than many European nations.[2] While early data are fragmentary, the crude birth rate in the United States appears to have been about 50 per 1,000 population in 1800.[3] Thereafter, the American birth rate declined fairly steadily until World War II. The postwar "baby boom" lasted until the early 1960s, when the birth rate resumed its decline, plummeting to 14 per 1,000 by the mid-1970s before rising slightly. The rate for 1987 was 15.7 per 1,000 persons. The total fertility rate has dropped from about 7 children per woman in 1800 to 1.8 today.

Not only have women tended to postpone marriage, but they have also reduced the number of years available for the old-fashioned way of becoming mothers after marriage. The most recent in-

FIGURE 4.

Following the post–World War II baby boom, the American birth rate stabilized after two decades of decline.

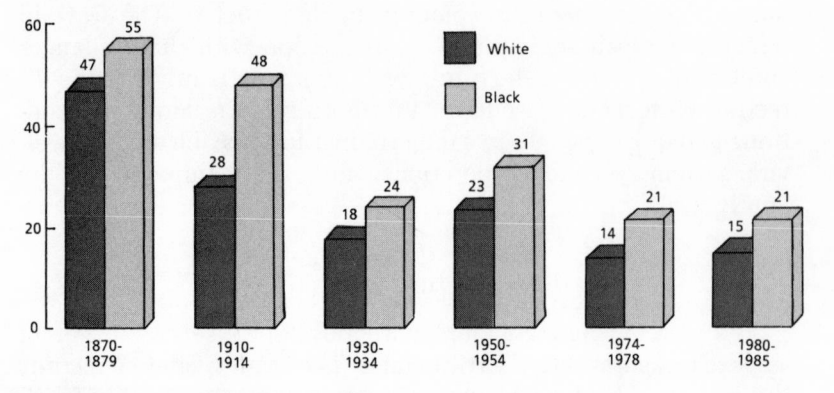

Birthrate per 1,000 population

Source: U.S. Department of Health and Human Services, National Center for Health Statistics

formation available indicates that the median interval between a first marriage and the birth of the first child rose from 15 months in the early 1960s to about 2 years during the late 1970s. By the third year of marriage, only about 18 percent of all women in their first marriage were still childless during the early 1960s, compared with 36 percent by the end of the succeeding decade.

As analysts tend to based their predictions of fertility rates on historic trends, it is important to consider both the long-run and short-term fluctuations of these statistics (fig. 4). Current fertility rates take on more meaning when they are placed in historical perspective.

Baby Booms and Busts

The Great Depression of the 1930s brought a major reduction in American fertility levels. With the nation in dire economic circumstances, many adults put off marriage; if they did marry, they decided that they could not afford to feed as many mouths as their parents did. Given these conditions, the birth rate plummeted to about 18 per 1,000 for women age 15 to 44 by 1933, and it remained under 23 per 1,000 during World War II.

At the end of the war, Americans decided to make up for lost time, and the baby boom was on at full speed. From a low of 2.4 million births in the depths of the Depression and 2.9 million in the final year of World War II, births in the United States rose to a peak of 4.3 million in 1957 but declined thereafter to a low of 3.1 million in 1973 and 1975. Since then, the number of births has risen more or less steadily, reaching 3.8 million in 1987.

All three measures of fertility have plummeted since the peak of the baby boom in 1957. The crude birth rate has fallen by almost 40 percent since 1957. During the same period, the total fertility rate, which considers the age characteristics of the population, and the general fertility rate were halved; the latter rate is now at the lowest level since the government began collecting these data in 1940. However, the decline has slowed considerably in the 1980s and may have been arrested (fig. 5). Women in the older childbearing years have recently shown a slight increase in their fertility rate, probably indicating that many females who postponed mother-hood are deciding that it is either now or never.

Although the U.S. total fertility rate was 1.84 in 1985—well below the 2.1 zero population growth level—the size of the total American population will not decline in the twentieth century. Despite birth rate declines, the number of births has been rising since 1975 due to the large number of women of childbearing age. Births still outnumbered deaths by about 1.7 million during 1987. Also, the United States continues to serve as a haven for immigrants either fleeing persecution in their native countries or seeking to partake in the abundance of economic opportunity. Most of these immigrants have been young adults.

Population bulges, such as the post–World War II baby boom, are like a boa constrictor digesting its prey. The age-cohort bulges can be tracked as their ramifications are evolving. The postwar baby boom resulted in a surfeit of women whose childbearing years span the period from about 1960 to about 2000—long enough to sustain a growth in the native American population for several decades. It will take about 65 years for the American population to stabilize at zero population growth, even if current rates hold firm. The Census Bureau projected in 1984 that if the total fertility rate

FIGURE 5.

During the 1980s, fertility rates have apparently stabilized.

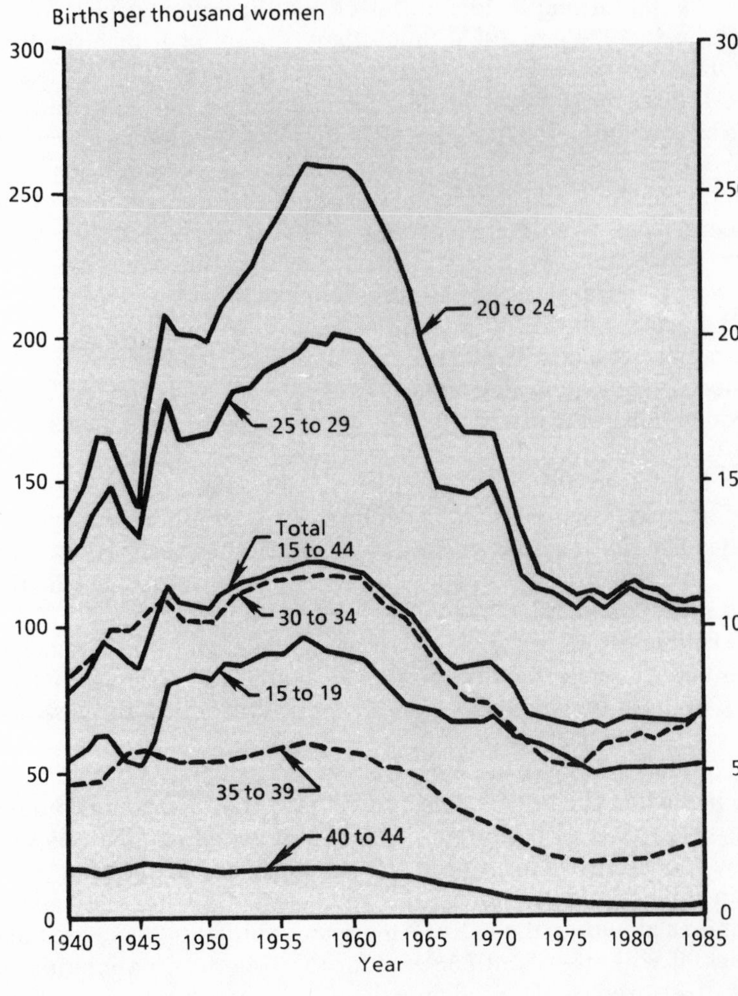
Births per thousand women
300
250
200
150
100
50
0
1940
1945
1950
1955
1960
1965
1970
1975
1980
1985
Year
20 to 24
25 to 29
Total
15 to 44
30 to 34
15 to 19
35 to 39
40 to 44

Source: U.S. Department of Health and Human Services, National Center for Health Statistics

FIGURE 6.

U.S. fertility exceeds that of other major democratic industrial countries (1985).

Comparative total fertility rates (U.S. = 100)

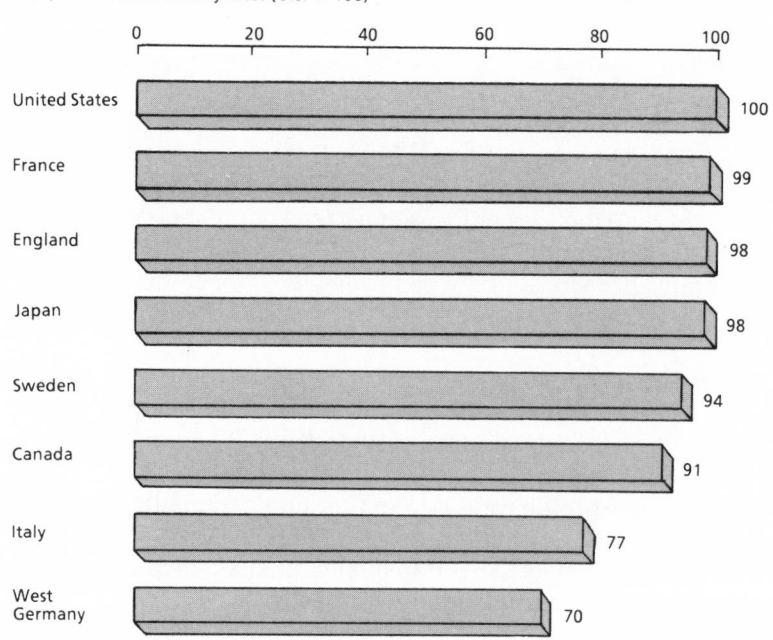

Source: *Population Bulletin*, March 1987

nudged down to 1.6, the American population would still not stop growing until about the year 2025, when it would reach approximately 276 million people—an increase of nearly 15 percent over 1986. If the total fertility rate had jumped back to 2.3, the American population would be about 273 million in the year 2000. Both levels are well below the 300 million population prediction for the year 2000, which until recently was the ballpark estimate given by many reputable demographers.[4]

The United States is far from unique in these fertility trends, and falling birth rates seem to be the rule in most industrialized nations regardless of their political or economic regimes. Thus far the United States continues to experience a higher birth rate than all other major Western democracies (fig. 6).

Lower birth rates have caused far more public concern in European countries than in the United States, because population size has already begun to drop in West Germany, Austria, Denmark, and Hungary. West Germany's native population has been falling steadily since 1972, with annual deaths exceeding births. Given the present course, the German native population will fall to 55 million by the year 2012, a 10 percent decline in less than one generation. Similar to Western Europe, all Eastern European nations except Poland and the Soviet Union have fertility rates below zero population growth.

The uneven swings in the U.S. birth rate since the 1930s have already affected the age distribution of the American population (fig. 7). In 1920 the age configuration of the population looked very much like a pyramid. The largest group of the population was children under 10 years of age, who formed the base of the population pyramid. At that time, each successive age group was smaller than the one preceding it.

However, with steep fertility declines during the 1930s— followed by continued low birth rates during World War II—the percentage of children under age 10 declined. Then came the baby boom, which was succeeded by declining birth rates. By the mid-1980s, the profile was far from the simple triangular shape depicted half a century earlier. Several large birth cohorts are now sandwiched in between much smaller groups, so the profile resembles a tiered cake put together by an amateur. If current fertility trends continue—coupled with a longer life expectancy—the American population profile could look more like an inverted pyramid. Smaller and younger cohorts would be supporting a far larger and increasing number of older Americans. The changing relative composition of the age cohorts has created wide variations and imbalances between the demands of successive birth cohorts for educational facilities, health care, and provisions for the aged. It also has placed uneven strains on American labor markets as birth cohorts reach successive stages in their work lives.

IS PAST PROLOGUE?

Based on the assumption that the past is prologue, social scientists have long attempted to predict fertility rates and population trends. They have used a wide range of different models, which incorporate numerous demographic, social, and eco-

FIGURE 7. Wide variations in the birth rate have changed the age
profile of the American population.

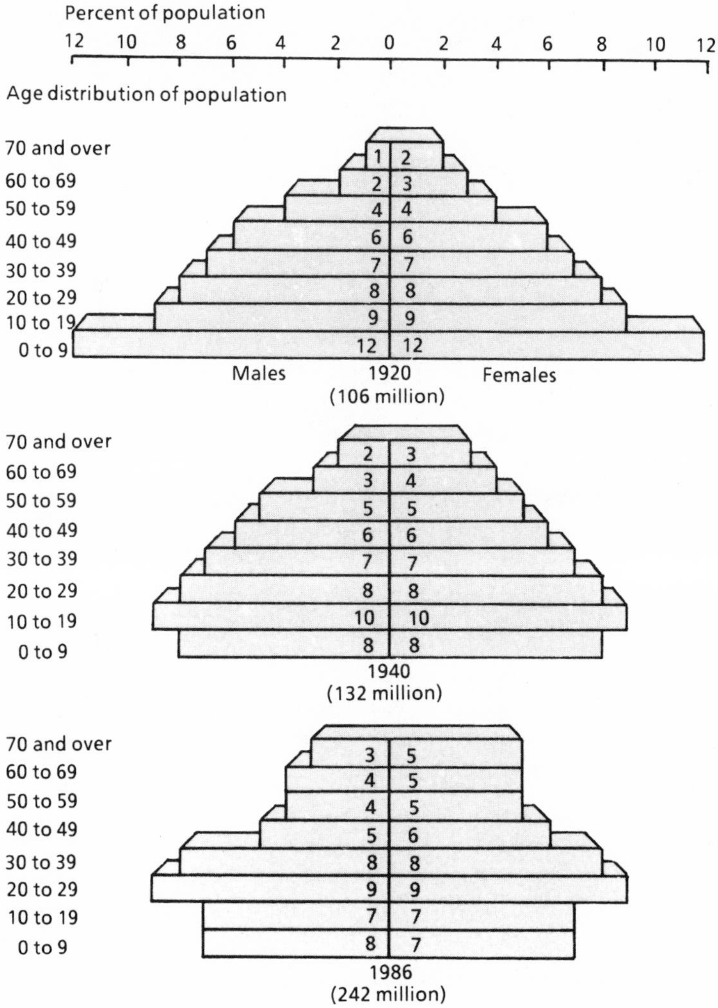

Percent of population

12   10   8   6   4   2   0   2   4   6   8   10   12

Age distribution of population

Age	Males	Females
70 and over	1	2
60 to 69	2	3
50 to 59	4	4
40 to 49	6	6
30 to 39	7	7
20 to 29	8	8
10 to 19	9	9
0 to 9	12	12

Males   1920   Females
(106 million)

Age	Males	Females
70 and over	2	3
60 to 69	3	4
50 to 59	5	5
40 to 49	6	6
30 to 39	7	7
20 to 29	8	8
10 to 19	10	10
0 to 9	8	8

1940
(132 million)

Age	Males	Females
70 and over	3	5
60 to 69	4	5
50 to 59	4	5
40 to 49	5	6
30 to 39	8	8
20 to 29	9	9
10 to 19	7	7
0 to 9	8	7

1986
(242 million)

Source: U.S. Department of Commerce, Bureau of the Census

45

nomic assumptions. Not surprisingly, the predictions of fertility rates have not converged on any one path.

The track record of fertility predictions leaves much to be desired. Many analysts predicted continued low birth rates—and even close to zero population growth—following World War II. Actually, fertility levels skyrocketed. The best-known miscalculation of population trends was made in the early 1800s by Thomas Malthus. In his famous essay on population, Malthus predicted that human reproduction would increase at a geometric pace while food supplies would lag way behind, since they could only grow in a much slower arithmetic progression.[5] Events in the leading industrialized nations—including fertility patterns, major productivity increases, and family planning—did not follow the course envisioned by Malthus. In fact, for the United States, agricultural productivity has outstripped human fertility.

A New Boom?

Their poor batting averages have not discouraged analysts from projecting fertility rates, although the tools keep changing. In recent years advanced statistical research methods and computers have replaced gut feelings and crystal balls. One current school of thought does not view the recent dearth of births as a lasting phenomenon, anticipating a significant upswing in the birth rate starting in the 1990s.

Three economists—Richard Easterlin, Michael Wachter, and Susan Wachter—have championed this view. Their hypothesis is that the birth rate is a function of the size of the birth cohort currently within the childbearing years. As individuals of a small birth cohort mature, they tend to face relatively little competition from their peers, compared with the intense struggle faced by members of a large birth cohort. Because their numbers are low, they have an easier time gaining admittance to a desired college or vocational training program. When they enter the labor force, members of the small birth cohort experience little difficulty in finding ample entry-level positions and opportunities for rapid advancement. As a result, they will be in a better financial position, and they will be able to afford an early marriage and more children. The net impact of all these advantages is an increase in the birth rate relative to that of the previous cohort.[6]

Members of a large birth cohort will face opposite conditions; it will be harder for them to receive the desired education and training, and the competition for entry-level positions will be intensified. Because they will take much more time to establish themselves, they will postpone marriage, and the birth rate will tend to fall.

Backers of this analysis believe that it explains both the 1946–57 rise in fertility rates and the subsequent baby bust. A small birth cohort hit the labor market following the Great Depression and World War II, and its members found a strong demand for their services in the labor market. Their economic prospects were so much brighter than they had expected as children of the Great Depression that they tended to marry early and raise large families. However, the experiences of the next birth cohort were very different, as the products of the baby boom faced tough competition from early childhood. As the supply of qualified workers vastly expanded, individuals who lacked advanced training or skills faced bleak employment prospects. Because this birth cohort's prospects were far less rosy than their parents', its members tended to postpone marriage and vastly reduce the number of children per family. Hence, the baby boom bubble burst.

If the latter hypothesis is correct, the cycle is about to repeat itself with another fertility upswing, though in all probability it will be smaller than the original postwar baby boom. Assuming that the next generation will be able to support more children, the question is: will they want them? The initial cohort born after the end of the baby boom started to enter the labor market during the 1980s. By the end of this century, we will know whether the fertility patterns of the baby bust generation will duplicate those of their grandparents. A major obstacle to such a repetition is that the average earnings of adults aged 20–29 have dropped since 1973. In contrast, the earnings of young men in the post–World War II period kept on rising. Young couples today therefore have to depend to a much larger extent on the earnings of wives than did their grandparents. These gender shifts in earnings may present a serious obstacle to rising fertility, even for a declining age cohort.

Charles Westoff is a leading representative of analysts who believe that in the near future birth rates below the zero population growth level may prove to be irreversible. It appears that women who entered the labor force are there to stay. The diffusion of sophisticated bedroom and household technology, combined with changing female aspirations and attitudes, has eased the transition into the labor force for many women. This factor will hold down the fertility rate. Coupled with these conditions are a record num-

ber of divorced women who head their households. A sharp decline in real wages followed by sluggish growth during the past 15
years has meant that a growing number of families require two
paychecks to maintain the standard of living to which they are accustomed and to do a little better. One net result is that the proportion of all American women in the prime childbearing years who
work outside the home rose from less than two of five in 1960 to
over 70 percent by 1987. In fact, according to this school, instead of
rising, the American fertility rate may even decline from the already low level of about 1.8. Analysts who predict a new baby boom
counter these arguments by noting that despite the flocking of
women into the workplace and the taste they gained for financial
independence, fertility rates increased following the war.

The increase in female labor force participation rates already
may be having an impact on fertility as it responds to cyclical economic fluctuations. Fertility rates have tended to move in the same
direction as swings in the business cycle, rising during economic
booms and declining during economic recessions. Now, however,
as female labor force participation rises, fertility rates may be moving in a countercyclical fashion. Several factors contribute to this
behavioral change. Employment opportunities for women have increased despite continued high unemployment in the first half of
the 1980s, and with rising educational attainment women would
have foregone much more income by not working than they previously would have. Women in the labor market tend to have fewer
children. In 1987 working women 18 to 34 years old expected to
have 2 children, compared to 2.3 for those not in the job market.
This analysis suggests that as long as women's real wages continue
to rise and their labor force participation continues to increase, fertility rates could remain low.[7] The Bureau of Labor Statistics projects that by the year 2000, 83 percent of women aged 25 to 44 will
be working or looking for work, 10 percentage points higher than in
1987.[8]

In view of the rapid pace of change the family has undergone in
the past few decades, what explanations best account for declining
fertility? Of course, given the historical and persistent trend of decreasing fertility in industrializing nations, it is the baby boom
rather than the baby bust that was unusual. But the influx of
women into the job market, divorce, more effective contraceptive
techniques, a desire for fewer children, and abortion all contributed to lower fertility rates.

Almost all of the decline in fertility occurred between 1960 and

TABLE 1. Women's expectations, their influx into the labor market, and a rising divorce rate contributed to the drop in fertility.

	Births per woman (total fertility rate)	Expected lifetime births of wives (18–34)	Wives in the labor force	Divorce rate per 1,000 married couples
1955	3.6	NA	29%	9.3
1960	3.6	3.2	32	9.2
1965	2.9	3.1	35	10.6
1970	2.5	2.6	41	14.9
1975	1.8	2.3	44	20.3
1980	1.8	2.2	50	22.6
1985	1.8	2.2	54	21.7

Sources: U.S. National Center for Health Statistics, U.S. Census Bureau, and U.S. Bureau of Labor Statistics

1975 (table 1). Working wives are not only likely to have fewer children, but they tend to delay marriage. Sociologist Andrew Cherlin estimated that 16 percent of the drop in fertility was attributable to the postponement of marriage by women.[9] However, while the influx of women into the job market undoubtedly played some part in declining fertility, the rise in women's labor force participation predated the decline and has continued at a rapid rate since 1975 when fertility behavior stabilized.

The number of abortions occurring until January 1973 when the Supreme Court legalized the practice nationally (in Roe v. Wade) is not known. Abortions increased from 750,000 in 1973 to 1.5 million 6 years later, but increased only to 1.6 million by 1985. Thirty percent of pregnancies not ending in miscarriages or stillbirths are aborted, but the number is concentrated among unmarried women, who obtain four of five abortions. Three of five pregnancies by unmarried women are aborted, compared with 9 percent by wives.[10]

Rising divorce rates, decreases in the number of children women expected or desired to have, and more effective contraceptive techniques most closely coincide with and probably best explain fertility reductions. Almost all of the rise in the divorce rate occurred between 1965 and 1975. Divorce reduces time spent in marriage, when births are of course most likely. Until 1976 the U.S. Census Bureau considered it improper to question single women about the number of births they expected to have during their childbearing years. The number of lifetime births expected by wives dropped from over 3 in 1960 to 2.3 in 1975, but dipped only slightly to 2.2 a decade later, a pattern closely paralleling the changes in the fertility rate.

The rise of more effective contraceptive techniques may have been the most important factor in fertility declines, reducing the average number of births per woman from about seven in the early years of the Republic to a little over two during the Great Depression. However, until birth control pills were first marketed in 1960, most contraceptive techniques had relatively high failure rates. Married women questioned in 1965 said that 21 percent of their births in the previous 5 years had been unwanted, compared with only 7 percent for wives questioned in 1982. The reduction in unwanted births accounts for nearly 40 percent of the fertility drop from 1961 to 1982.[11] In 1960 probably at least 9 of 10 married couples employing contraceptives were using techniques with relatively high failure rates. However, improvements in bedroom technology have been dramatic, with most of the change occurring between 1960 and 1973. By the latter year, less than a third of married couples using contraceptives employed techniques with relatively high failure rates, a proportion that has remained the same since that time. The following methods were most commonly used by married couples:[12]

	1965	1973	1982
Sterilization (wife or husband)	12%	24%	41%
Pill or IUD	25	46	27
Other methods	63	31	32

The major factors that contributed to the decline in fertility are interrelated, and it is impossible to disentangle their relative effects. Given the Western European experience, it is possible that American fertility rates could drop further. Another breakthrough in contraceptive technology could significantly reduce out-of-wedlock births and have a smaller but still important effect on the fertility behavior of married couples. Improved contraceptive techniques could ironically also help to increase fertility. The most common contraceptive method among couples is now sterilization, which is practically irreversible. According to one survey, about 10 percent of couples who were surgically sterilized would like to undo the procedure, presumably because they want another child.[13]

While the crystal ball does not indicate a further drop in fertility, neither does it provide any signs of an impending increase. There is virtually no difference in the number of lifetime births expected by younger and older women of childbearing years.

FAMILY STRUCTURE

Whatever the future of the fertility rate, the important questions center on its impact on the structure of the family. The assumption that a low birth rate reflects either a rejection of children or a weakening of the family does not stand up under close scrutiny. A smaller number of children per household can improve the quality of family life, and it may enable parents to provide better child care.

Smaller Families

Average family size has steadily declined from 3.8 in 1940 to 3.2 in 1987. The decrease in total fertility rates has not been due to any statistically significant increase in childlessness, but rather to a sharp decline in the number of women who have experienced four or more births. Of the women born in 1870 and who married at some point in their lives, nearly half had four or more children and about a fifth had none. By comparison, a third of the women born in 1925 had four or more children and only a tenth remained childless. The cohort of current young women who are potential mothers, of course, has not finished its production of children. In the meantime, statistics on birth expectations can be used as a rough estimate of the fertility distribution for women born during the baby boom. If these expectations prove to be in the ballpark, the current crop of young women will continue this smaller family trend. In 1987, half of all married women aged 25–29 years expected to have two children, 9 percent to have four or more, and only 5 percent to remain childless. About 10 percent of the women in the 1870 birth cohort, and 25 percent of those in the 1925 birth cohort, had two children. Of course, declining infant and childhood mortality rates have made it possible to have far fewer births in order to attain a given family size as well as to alleviate the heartbreak families once commonly experienced due to the death of their young. The death rate per 1,000 children in every age group has dropped dramatically since the turn of the century, as follows:

Age	1900	1986
Under 1 year	162.4	10.4
1–4	19.8	0.5
5–14	3.9	0.3

The major trend does not appear to be toward childlessness. Instead, couples are using birth control to limit the number of children they have.

Medical advances may yet alleviate infertility, but despite great publicity the new prenatal technologies have so far had little impact. About one of six married couples trying to conceive a child are unable to do so. Since 1965, infertility among both young and childless couples has actually increased. The causes are not known, but may be partly attributable to a rise in sexually transmitted diseases. Of the over 3.5 million annual births, only 10,000–20,000 result from artificial inseminations, and in vitro fertilization and surrogate mothers accounted for fewer than 600 births in 1986. While artificial insemination is inexpensive, the other two methods are costly and not affordable by most couples.[14] Religious, legal, and economic factors remain serious obstacles to mass adoption of these new technologies. In the foreseeable future, they are not likely to offer much competition to the old-fashioned method of conception.

Some women who enter the labor force may decide not to have any children. The mixing of work outside the home with childbearing is becoming increasingly the norm, although labor force participation tends to defer motherhood. The proportion of mothers with children under 18 working full time rose from 29 percent in 1975 to 41 percent by 1986. Between 1955 and 1987, the proportion of ever-married women between the ages of 20 and 24 who were childless rose from 33 to 40 percent, and for those between 25 and 29 the proportion without children increased from 20 to 26 percent. Added education tends to discourage or to postpone motherhood.

Predicting size of families on the basis of expectations is no less hazardous than most projections. There is many a slip between expectations and the actual number of births. Moreover, until the mid-1970s, the Census Bureau gathered data only from married women about their future family plans. Given the growing number of births outside of marriage, the birth expectations and actual fertility rates of unmarried women could have a strong impact on the size of the average American household.

Quality, Not Quantity

The reduction in the size of the average American family can provide positive benefits that could improve the quality

"We have a small family . . . just Bob, me and the hamster."

of life for both children and parents. While participation in the labor force is not inherently incompatible with motherhood for a growing number of women, it does seem to reduce family size. The women's liberation movement has made some inroads in the allocation of family chores, yet child care in a majority of families is still mostly the mother's responsibility—and it seems that many working mothers still do not get significant help with these chores from other family members. In order to enter the labor force, a growing number of women seem to have opted for having fewer children.

Because it is a highly subjective concept, the impact of the number of children on the quality of family life is difficult to measure. Furthermore, the data on family life are very meager, so analysts are forced to use proxies and simulations.

One fairly obvious impact of the number of children on the quality of family life is that the median earnings of full-time year-round workers are barely adequate to support a family of seven above the poverty threshold. An annual income of $20,000 represents a per capita income of $10,000 for a family of two, but only $4,000 for a family of five, and even one child can push a low-income family into poverty.

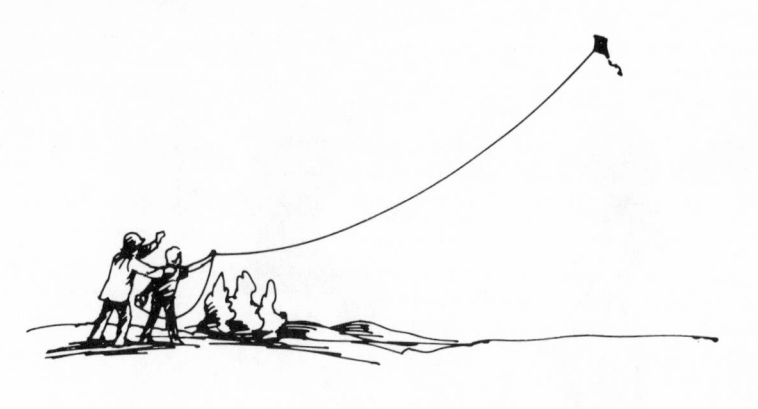

One proxy that analysts at the University of Michigan's Survey Research Center used to measure the subjective notion of quality was educational attainment. Education affects an individual's future occupational opportunities, earnings, and ability to land a job that also provides a high degree of personal satisfaction. Educational attainment might, therefore, be one rough measure of the quality and quantity of resources received by each child within a family. One hypothesis that was tested predicted that sharing family time and money with siblings would reduce a child's achievement level; all other factors being equal, as the family size increases, the schooling expected for each sibling would be reduced. The model employed in this study emphasized that a larger family size tends to strain the parents' ability to devote time, energy, and money to each child. Family size had a stronger negative impact on educational attainment for females than for males, but for either gender the most important influence on educational attainment was the size of parental income. As expected, the higher the parental income, the more education a child tended to receive. But the data also suggested that a larger number of siblings can adversely affect their test scores.[15] Other studies on intrafamily sibling differences in educational attainment have reached similar conclusions. In fact, it appears that family size is an even more important determinant of the schooling received per child than the birth order and spacing of siblings.[16]

There is little consensus among demographers and other social scientists on this issue. Some have suggested that the impact of added children may be exaggerated and that economies of scale apply to the quality of family life. Running the washer to clean several children's clothes instead of one child's probably adds little marginal cost. A story can be read to two children as well as to one. Cooking and shopping burdens might not grow proportionately as the number of children increases. Analysts at the University of Michigan Survey Research Center used the economy of scale hypothesis to explore the allocation of resources and the time inputs devoted to childrearing by its sample of families. They concluded that the time devoted to preschool children did not diminish significantly as their number of siblings increased, but in low-status families (defined by income and the occupation of the household head) the quality level (as measured in the study) given to each child suffered.[17]

Other data reinforce the finding that the added burden of additional children is not entirely offset by economies of scale. It might be argued that as a family becomes more affluent, it can afford to purchase more services outside of the household to help reduce the burden of childrearing. Because other people would be paid to take on some of the chores of childrearing, parents with high incomes would not have to invest so much of their own time in having larger families. While affluent parents might be able to afford this method of childrearing, apparently many of them have not chosen this route; in fact, they devote to each preschool child about twice as many total housework hours as do low-status families. Of course, part of this difference reflects a tendency for affluent families to have fewer children than low-income families. Because wealthier parents appear to be very concerned about the quality of care received by their children, raising larger families demands a major investment of their time.[18] Also, given the high cost of domestic and child-care services, even many affluent families find it difficult to finance such services.

Part of the economic burden for larger households would be mitigated if employers considered family size in determining compensation or if the state provided income transfers or tax credits on the same basis. Most industrial countries provide family allowances to ease the burden of childrearing (and also to increase the population). But in most countries these allowances are inadequate to significantly affect childrearing. However, except for dependents' deductions allowed by the tax system, the United States compensation system fails to take into consideration the number of dependents for whom a worker may be responsible. Even the earned income tax credit for low earners ignores the number of dependents a worker has to feed.

Using the tools of their trade, economists have applied a theoretical twist to the debate. They suggest that the concept of marginal utility can help explain the phenomenon of smaller families. The first automobile or other commodity purchased by a family tends to have a higher marginal utility—or value—as far as the family is concerned than a second or third. The smaller the number of children, the more each child will be treasured and the greater the resources that can be allocated to each offspring.

Higher-income families may find it easier to provide quality resources to more children compared to lower-income families, but on the average the former have brought fewer children into the world compared to the latter. In recent years, women in the middle-income groups have recorded the lowest fertility rates. All other factors being equal, families in which both spouses work tend to have fewer children than those in which only the husband works.

Family Life Cycles

Shifting fertility and mortality rates, coupled with changes in birth spacing intervals, have had a strong impact on family life cycle patterns. The interval between marriage and the first birth conceived after marriage has lengthened, but because more births involve premarital conception or because out-of-wedlock births are followed by wedding bells, the stork bringing the first child remains almost as efficient today as in past decades. However, the intervals between succeeding births have lengthened, and an increasing proportion of women never give birth to a third child.

With increased life expectancy and barring divorce, a husband and wife can expect to spend many more years together before one of them dies. And most of the added years would occur after their children had left the home. For couples married in 1900, one partner (more often the husband) was likely to meet his or her Maker almost at the same time the last child left home. Increased life expectancy has added more than 11 "empty nest," or child-free, years at the end of the typical parenting cycle since 1900. At the same time, couples, on average, have postponed having their first child. Adding these child-free years into the total, the couple now can expect to spend about 14 or 15 years together without any children. Given an average of 47 years of married life for couples who carry out the vows of "until death," it appears that couples now entering

marriage can expect to spend about 30 percent of their time together without any children in their home.

In short, changes in the fertility and mortality rates have had a
radical impact on the nature as well as the length of family life cy-
cles. The adult family life cycle now has been been almost divided
into two separate periods: the first period is the one in which children are born and raised to adulthood; the second period is one in
which parents live apart from their children. Even couples who do
experience the joys of parenthood also can expect many child-free
years together.

BEING FRUITFUL

Adults today are not following the first commandment God gave to Adam and Eve with the same zeal manifested by
past generations. The fertility rate has fallen to a historic low in
America, and a similar trend has been experienced in every other
advanced industrialized nation. In the United States, the decline in
fertility does not reflect a significant increase in childlessness.
Rather, a decreasing proportion of women are spending their prime
childbearing years exclusively as baby producers, instead adding
work outside the home to the responsibilities of motherhood. A
household with four or more children has become a rarity.

As the number of children per family diminishes, parents can
boost the resources devoted per child, and even low-income families may be able to improve (with government help) the quality of
childrearing. Though fewer in numbers, children may become
even more cherished within families and by society at large.

Family planning and solutions to medical problems that once
blocked fertility are providing adults with many more options for
being fruitful and multiplying. Multiplying, however, is a blessing
only if the children produced are wanted by their parents. Being
fruitful now seems to include greater consideration for opportunities offered to the parents as well as to their children—including for many women the rewards received from employment as
well as motherhood. As more women seek employment outside the
home, a growing number of men and children will have to assume
greater responsibility in the daily chores of family life, although
traditional roles of husband and wife are changing very slowly.
This breakdown in stereotyped gender roles would have a very
positive influence on improving life within American households.

A declining population growth rate requires diverse social and economic adjustments. Shifting American fertility rates have altered the age profile of the nation's population, and, combined with changes in mortality rates, the average family life cycle now shows a different pattern from the past. The size of the U.S. population continues to grow, albeit at a slower rate than in the past. This trend is likely to continue into the next century before the annual number of deaths exceeds the yearly number of births and gains from immigration, if in fact this ever occurs.

Chapter Four

THE CARE AND FEEDING OF CHILDREN

> My dear, sweet Billy:
> Mommy has gone away. Sometimes in the world,
> daddys go away and the mommys bring up their little
> boys. But sometimes a mommy can go away, too, and
> you have your daddy to bring you up. . . . Listen to
> your daddy. He will be like your wise Teddy.
> Love, Mommy . . .
>
> "Mommy went away?"
> "Yes, Billy."
> "Forever, Daddy?"
> Avery Corman, Kramer versus Kramer

A HOUSE DIVIDED

An unhappy family life and a broken home are often assumed to create even more trauma and lasting scars for the children involved than for their parents. This is not to minimize the suffering experienced by a rejected spouse, because the anger, fear, recrimination, and self-doubt can be destructive. For children, however, the problem may be exacerbated if their family disintegrates when they are in the vulnerable periods of their early development.

The traditional family model pictures a child as being raised by both natural mother and father, who provide guidance, protection, and socialization. Even in stable families, growing up with two loving parents is not devoid of conflicts and occasional tensions. As the annual crop of divorces has increased, relatively more children are being raised by only one of their natural parents. And with remarriages, even many children who have two adults in the house are not living with both their natural mother and father. Added to divorces and broken homes, out-of-wedlock births are an increasingly disturbing phenomenon; they now account for over one of every five births in the United States. Clearly, the family with only one parent in the house has become an all too frequent and vexing occurrence on the American scene.

Whether a married couple should remain together or seek a divorce is a private matter between two adults. However, the massive number of children involved raises a whole host of sensitive and troublesome problems that can have a major impact upon the rest of society. Family breakup and the absence of one or both parents raises numerous deep-seated concerns: who will raise the next generation and socialize it, and what role and responsibilities should society—either through the public or the private sector—undertake? Will the products of broken homes create massive problems for educational, judicial, and social welfare institutions?

A chief concern is what will happen when children raised in single-parent households come of age to form their own families. Will the lack in childhood of a stable two-parent family prove to be an insurmountable roadblock for many individuals in the next generation's efforts to form such lasting ties? Will their parents' difficulties present a negative role model that impairs their ability to establish a satisfactory and stable family structure? The problems of broken homes may be visited upon generations to come.

Care and Custody

Social pressures to keep a marriage going if children are involved have diminished. Most adults now believe that it is socially permissible for a married couple to get a divorce when they cannot get along—even if they have children. At the same time, the vast majority of American adults also believe that a child raised by one parent in a broken home will face many added difficulties. Less than a fourth of adults believe that parents should remain in an unhappy marriage for the children's sake. Only 12 percent of divorced persons feel that incompatible parents should remain married, even though 70 percent of divorced parents feel that their own children suffered as a result of the break-up.[1] The Hobson's choice is between a marriage that has turned into a battlefield—with the children caught between the trenches—and being raised by a single parent, more often the mother.

Often it is not at all clear who will raise and provide for the children under current conditions. As so aptly depicted in the film *Kramer versus Kramer*, the established legal provisions regulating child custody are being challenged. Under English Common Law, the father had almost absolute rights over his children. Legal divorce was rare, shotgun marriages legitimized premarital conceptions, and the vast majority of single-parent households arose from the death of a spouse. As divorce became more frequent, the law shifted to give mothers preference in child custody cases. In America, by the early part of the twentieth century, this preference in favor of the mother had become almost absolute. In most states, the only way a father could win child custody rights over the mother was by proving to the court that his former spouse was seriously delinquent in her behavior as a mother. Although this legal doctrine has been undergoing significant changes in recent years, few children are currently raised by only their male parent. In some states, courts have awarded joint custody to both divorced parents, but in almost all joint custody cases the children reside with one parent. This area of family law remains unsettled and in a sharp state of flux.

But even if child custody has been determined, there still remains the thorny issue of who will provide the financial support to raise the children. Bringing up a child, as any parent will testify, involves a major capital investment. Estimated expenditures for rearing children until age 18 vary from $70,000–170,000 per child depending upon family income, size, and the wife's work schedule. For a middle-income family with two children, the estimated outlays (in February 1988 dollars) were $210,000 if the mother worked part time and $239,000 if both parents worked full time. The cost of providing a college education, which has greatly outpaced inflation in the 1980s, would add another $30,000 for each offspring. Families tend to commit roughly the same proportion of their expenditures to childrearing regardless of total income: about 30 percent for one child, 40 to 45 percent for two children, and nearly 50 percent for three children. However, since low-income families spend almost all—and in many cases more than all—of their income, they devote a much higher proportion of family income to rearing children than do more affluent households.[2]

Even if a mother receives child support payments, amounts too often tend to be very small. Many fathers fail to provide any child support, and enforcement of their legal obligations has proven to be difficult. While Congress has made some efforts to prod states and irresponsible fathers, inadequate child support payments remain a serious problem.

Broken Homes

As the divorce rate has increased, the number of children affected by a marital separation also has grown annually (fig. 8). Divorces involve each year more than 1 million children under 18 years of age. In 1985, nearly half of all divorcing couples did not have any children under the age of 18, while 8 percent of the divorces involved three or more children. This compares with the mid-1960s, when 37 percent of divorcing couples had no children under 18 years of age, and 20 percent of divorces involved three or more children. As a result, the average number of children per divorce decree has declined from a high of 1.34 in 1968 to the current level of less than one child per decree. The average number of children per divorce, as well as the decline over the past two decades, is almost identical to the trend for all families.

Fertility declines have helped mitigate the number of children affected by divorce, but the number has more than tripled since the mid-1950s. Hence, while 6.5 per 1,000 children under 18 years of age were involved annually in a divorce in the mid-1950s, the comparable proportion rose to a high of 18.7 per 1,000 in 1981. Since then, this rate declined slightly to 17.3 four years later.

Consequently, the proportion of children who live with two parents has declined significantly. Back in 1960, roughly seven of eight children lived with two parents; now this proportion is down to under six of eight. However, nearly all children under 18 years of age still live with one or both of their parents. About 2 percent live with a grandparent or other close relative.

However, statistics on children who live with two parents mask the changes in family structure. Just because a child has two parents in the house, it does not follow that they are the child's natural parents. Divorce and remarriage patterns have greatly complicated the picture (fig. 9). About 9 percent of all children under 18 are living with one natural parent and one stepparent, and 64 percent of children under 18 years of age are living with their natural fathers and mothers.[3]

Child custody laws are undergoing some changes, but about nine of ten children who live with only one parent reside in a household headed by their mother. The proportion of all children

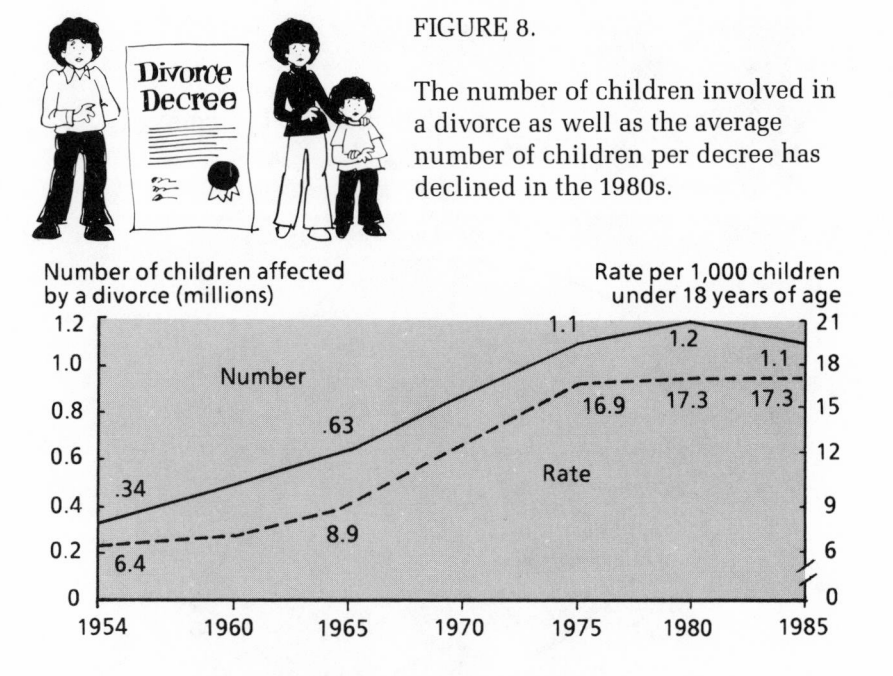

FIGURE 8.

The number of children involved in a divorce as well as the average number of children per decree has declined in the 1980s.

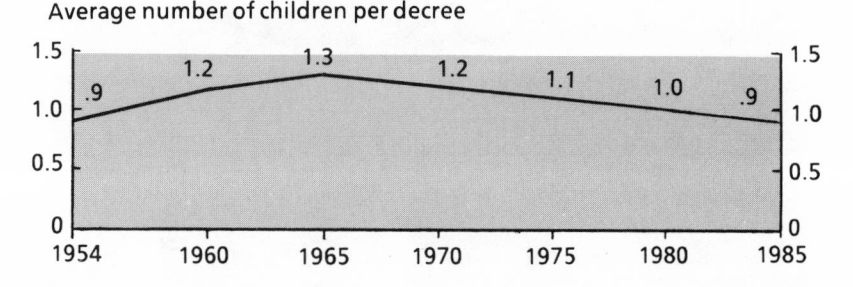

Average number of children per decree

Source: U.S. Department of Health and Human Services, National Center for Health Statistics

living with only their mother is about one in five, two and a half times the rate 25 years earlier. The fathers' liberation movement notwithstanding, fewer than 3 percent of all children currently live with only their father. Divorce and marital separation are the prime reasons behind children living with only their mother in almost two-thirds of the cases, while 6 percent of the children in a female-

FIGURE 9.

Nearly two of three children are
living with their natural parents
(1987).

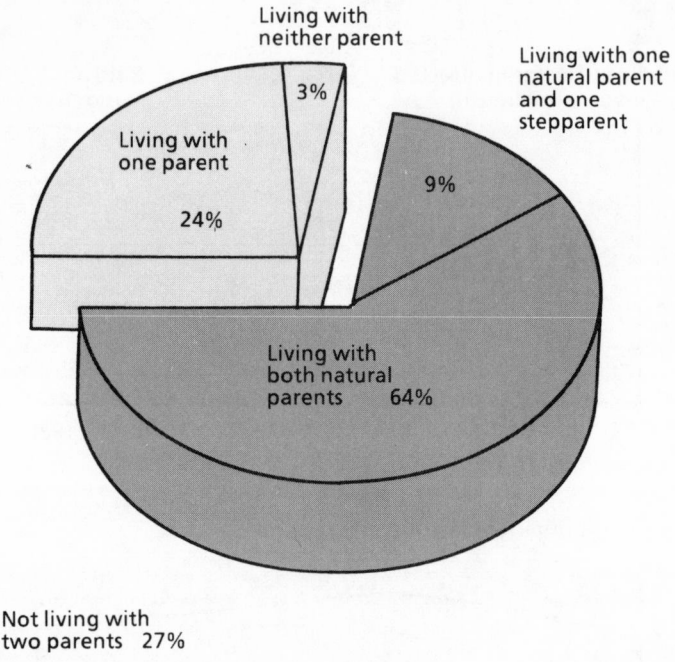

Source: U.S. Department of Commerce, Bureau of the Census

headed household are orphans and another 30 percent live with
their unmarried mothers.

The vast increase in the proportion of children being raised by
only one parent may be jolting. However, before one longs for the
"good old days" when separations and divorces were rare, related
variables should be considered. At the turn of the century, the
chances that a child was not living with any parent were greater
than today because many children then were orphans. Children
born between 1911 and 1920 had a 22 percent chance that one of

their parents would die before they reached 18 years of age, and another 5 percent were affected by divorce. Because of improved health conditions, children born in the 1940s faced only a 20 percent chance of losing a parent through either death or divorce. Not until the 1960s did rising divorce rates outweigh the effects of falling death rates on a child's chances of growing up with both parents. As a result, the percentage of children who live with at least one natural parent—instead of in institutions, with foster parents, or with other relatives—has been increasing. In 1940, about 1 of 10 children did not live with either parent, compared with 1 in about 37 today. Living with one parent instead of with two may not be the best of all possible worlds, but this condition is preferable to being raised in institutions or by other relatives. A greater number of black youngsters, compared with white children, live with no parents (7 percent and 2 percent, respectively).

This historical review is not to mitigate current conditions, because the decline in the relative number of two-parent families has been at the root of many grave societal problems involving millions of children. However, it is necessary to have a realistic picture of past conditions for perspective on the present reality. Previous generations had their share of disrupted families, although the reasons accounting for the breakups were different than today. While most of the growth of single-parent families is due to increasing trends in marital instability and out-of-wedlock births, a significant proportion of this growth has been offset by the rapid decline in the number of children who are housed in orphanages or with relatives.

THE IMPACT ON CHILDREN

The substantial number of single-parent families and the decline in the percentage of children now living with both natural parents are matters of deep concern to American society. The task of evaluating these changes, however, has proven elusive; frequently the most important issues are the hardest to analyze. The social and behavioral sciences have yet to develop a calculus that can even capture—let alone weigh and measure—all of the numerous complex variables.

While the increase in divorces, broken homes, and children born out of wedlock may have many indirect and undetected consequences for the entire population, the consequences for youngsters undergoing family disintegration are major and direct. The

proportion of children who live in broken homes has been viewed as an index of social disorganization by the nineteenth-century sociologist Emile Durkheim, as well as by more recent observers.

The conventional view is that a child who experiences a broken home, or who never has known what it is like to live in a two-parent family, will be at a serious disadvantage compared with children raised in more stable and traditional environments. The child from a broken home will face a far greater risk of stunted personality growth and development. A disrupted family life may also cause serious problems in the future.

Several investigators recently have challenged this view, claiming that statistical evidence does not fully coincide with these notions, but the data they have marshaled is of dubious persuasion. In part, their arguments are based on the assertion that the generally held view about the burden carried by children of divorced parents reflects traditional morals and mores more than empirical evidence.

While the total impact of parental separation upon childhood development remains uncertain, the economic burdens are subject to verification. Even if a child experiences no psychological problems in adjusting to a disrupted household environment, in most cases the family's financial support for the children is radically diminished. Child support of youngsters in broken homes has proven to be a difficult problem, and the economic prospects of living in a female-headed household are, on average, much bleaker than those in a husband-wife family.

Child Development

Prior to the recent advances in statistical and computer-aided research, studies of the impact of broken homes on children relied heavily on the case study approach. Using this methodology in the 1920s, one analyst found a common pattern in many separated families. The initial intellectual acceptance of separation by family members was followed by an emotional or "gut level" period of shock, which hit the children even more seriously than their parents. When normal patterns and habits were disrupted, an increasing sense of bitterness and pain followed, accompanied by prolonged frustration, which frequently hindered adjustment to the new living arrangements.[4]

This view that divorce itself and living in a one-parent family hinder child development became the predominant judgment and was accorded the status of conventional wisdom. However, as data sources expanded and research technology improved, analysts employed newly designed statistical survey methods to examine much larger samples than could be studied under the case study approach. Using these newer—and presumably better—research methods, analysts tested whether significant statistical differences existed between children from stable two-parent households and those raised in broken homes.

Of course, these computer studies in turn are subject to serious flaws. One major problem has to do with data samples. Even sound findings based on properly selected variables may have limited applicability if the data come from only one city or area, which cannot represent the entire American population. The validity of using cross-sectional data—information collected at a single point in time—to predict what will happen during the course of several years may be highly fallible. Even the most advanced research models usually contain untested key assumptions reflecting unstated value judgments, which produce misleading findings.

Measuring personality characteristics and social relationships involves a high degree of subjectivity, compounding the difficulties faced by the investigator. Moreover, it is hard to model the path of causation and to control for the various factors, even if subjective opinions can be held to a minimum. The net results of being raised in a broken home are often difficult to disentangle and separate from economic and social status variables. In fact, all these various forces may be highly interrelated in many cases. Also, a good portion of the data fed into computers for these studies come from individual self-assessments of doubtful accuracy. For example, depending upon the circumstances, a child's responses about his or her ability to make and hold onto friends are not only subjective, they may also be intentionally misleading. For similar reasons, a female head of a household might find it very difficult to acknowledge that she believes her children have been damaged because of her divorce, or she may attribute her children's deficiencies to the divorce even if their difficulties are not related to that event. In many of the studies, researchers have tried to create controls that will reveal some of these self-assessment difficulties.

In brief, finding hard evidence is elusive. The proper mode of statistical comparison requires that children from broken homes should be compared with children from intact families burdened with parental conflicts. Such a comparison assumes not only that the investigator can find families with deep-seated problems and can distinguish their difficulties from those of "happy" families, but also that he or she can persuade them to air their dirty laundry to a sociologist.

These reservations about the attitudinal and child development studies notwithstanding, the findings of this statistical research should not be rejected outright. On the whole, the studies tend to paint a picture that is somewhat different from the standard notion. If the results of these investigations are within the ball park, the net result of a broken home for child development is not as harsh, or necessarily as detrimental, as is often assumed.

Arguing that in the vast majority of cases the causes of a divorce can be found in deep-seated problems such as alcoholism, drug abuse, violence, nonsupport, adultery, and desertion, one study questioned whether these parents, had they remained married, could have provided a better environment for their children than a single-parent household. Though only about one of ten single mothers reported that her children were harder to handle after the divorce, mothers who experienced a high degree of trauma during the divorce process also reported that their children were the least happy. About half of the divorced women sampled in the study remarried by the 26th month after their divorce. Hence, many children lived only a short time in a one-parent family. Of the remarried mothers, about three-quarters believed that the lives of their children were better in the second marriage than in the first, while more than 80 percent of the divorced mothers indicated that prior to the divorce they seriously feared the separation would harm their children.[5]

Another study found a positive relationship between juvenile delinquency and broken homes, even when the economic status of families was considered. The study suggested a strong relationship between juvenile delinquency and broken homes if the single-parent household resulted from the death of a parent rather than a divorce.[6]

Other studies have tried to compare selected personality characteristics, as measured by standardized tests and interviews, of children raised in broken homes and youngsters living in two-parent families. This body of research has tended to find that several personality characteristics, including health and mental problems, appear to be more related to family social and economic status than to divorce. Researchers have found no evidence of a clear-cut superiority of adolescents raised in two-parent families compared with children who live in broken homes. Some studies have found no statistically significant differences in school grades, attitudes toward school, and participation in school activities. In fact, some researchers have even contended that the "inimical effects" often associated with children from broken homes compared with those from intact families are almost uniformly absent.[7] Investigators have also compared children from broken homes with youngsters raised in unhappy, but intact, families. The results indicate only very small differences in personality measures between the two. Also, children from broken homes have a lower chance of experiencing psychosomatic illnesses than youngsters in unbroken, but unhappy, families.[8] Other researchers claim that parents' divorce does slightly increase the likelihood that their children also will experience a divorce.[9]

A good portion of the impact of a broken home may be related to how a child viewed family life prior to the divorce. One study of college-age youths found that children subjected to constant parental bickering before a divorce adjust more easily to a broken home than do youngsters who are taken by surprise.[10]

While the majority of studies concerning the impact of broken homes on children have concluded that divorce may not be as detrimental to child development as is often assumed, not all investigations agree with this finding. For example, based on a sample of 18,000 youngsters, a study commissioned by the National Association of Elementary School Principals found that children from broken homes are late to school or miss more days of class more often and are more likely to drop out or be expelled than children residing with both parents. Of all the elementary and secondary school children sampled, 40 percent of those living with one parent were low achievers, compared with 24 percent of those living with a father and mother. At the other end of the scale, 30 percent of the two-parent children were ranked as high achievers compared with 17 percent of single-parent youths.[11] However, it is not clear from this study how much of these differences can be traced to divorce and how much to economic and other social conditions.

Labor economists have examined the impact of family disruptions on youths' ability to remain in school and/or their prospects in the labor market. As might be expected, teenagers living with one parent are more likely to seek and hold a job than classmates living with two parents, regardless of race, family income, the educational attainment of the family head, or family size.[12] A related hypothesis, which was tested, is that having an adult male in the house helps a youth in landing a job. The findings indicated that a youth who lives in a household headed by a female has slightly less chance of finding gainful employment than a youngster who lives in a male-headed household.[13]

The body of research concerning the impact on child development of being raised in a broken home suggests that the patterns are highly complex, and the results defy simple conclusions. Nevertheless, Alvin Schorr concluded that most children from single-parent families are just as able to cope with life problems as children raised in two-parent families.[14] However, having noted this, analysts who deny the debilitating impact of divorce upon children, like the captain of the *Titanic*, may fail to perceive the approach of an iceberg. One clear conclusion emerges from the multifaceted investigations attempting to fathom the impact of family breakdown upon the children involved. The computer will oblige with results to support any argument, depending upon the data the programmer feeds it, which in turn depends upon the assumptions made by the investigator and the available data. It is very difficult to capture the psychological impact of a broken home. Even a child who grows up to be a success in the eyes of the world can be stunted inside.

Child Support

Besides facing difficult psychological adjustments, most children who experience a family disruption are also forced into reduced economic circumstances, and that is clearly quantifiable. The median family income of households headed by an unmarried female is only about half that for all families. Divorce is a significant predictor of shifts in the economic status of women, and the direction is almost always downward in the cases of divorce and separation. This does not hold for men.

A profile of single family heads shows that they are mostly female; the chances are greater that they are members of a minority group; they are less educated; far less regularly employed; and much more likely to be poor. Roughly a fifth of all single-parent families have preschool children, and almost one of four female-headed households receives some income from a public assistance program.

Only about one in three divorced, separated, never married, or remarried mothers with children receives child support payments from the father (fig. 10). Child support payments, when they exist, tend to be meager. In 1985, the mean amount paid by fathers not living with their children but contributing to child support was $2,200, and payments have fallen far behind the pace of inflation since the Census Bureau began collecting information on child support payments in 1978. In contrast, the typical two-parent family with two children (with a 1985 median income of $32,600) would spend roughly $11,000–12,000 annually on their kids—a level of spending which exceeds the total income of the average single mother with two children ($10,500). Child support accounts for only 15 percent of the total money income of the average single mother. Divorced mothers are most likely to be awarded and to receive child support. If they remarry, however, their chances for receiving such payments decline. Separated mothers are about half as likely as divorced mothers to receive any payments, while never-married mothers face by far the lowest probability of getting any payments.

There is also a clear pattern between child support payments and the personal characteristics of the unmarried mother. Black and Hispanic women are much less likely to receive child support payments than white mothers. The average payment to a white mother is 30 percent greater than the amount a black mother receives. Also, older women and women with more education tend to receive larger payments. Women who get child support payments also are more likely to be employed than those who do not.

The father's ability to pay—measured by his earnings the year before the divorce or separation—is a key factor in determining both the chances that payments will be made and their magnitude. The length of the marriage has little influence on whether a father

FIGURE 10.

The chances that a divorced, separated, never-married, or remarried mother will receive child support payments are slim.

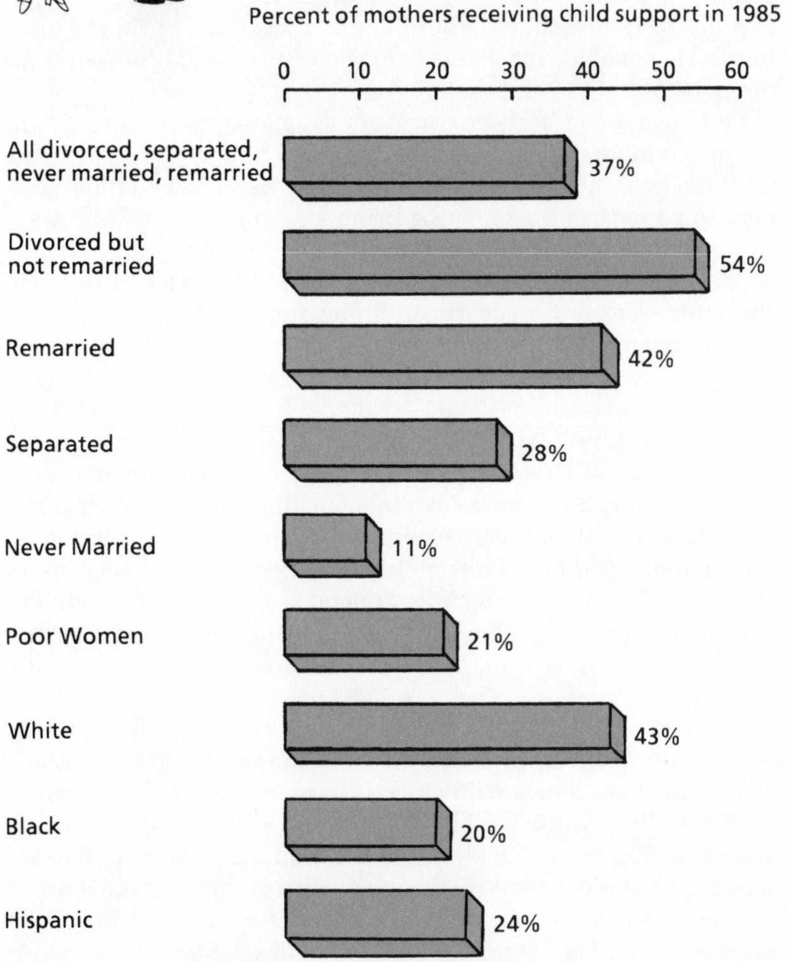

Percent of mothers receiving child support in 1985

```
0    10    20    30    40    50    60
```

All divorced, separated, never married, remarried	37%
Divorced but not remarried	54%
Remarried	42%
Separated	28%
Never Married	11%
Poor Women	21%
White	43%
Black	20%
Hispanic	24%

Source: U.S. Department of Commerce, Bureau of the Census

will support his children, but if he does the mothers who were married longer tend to get higher payments. As time passes after the separation or divorce, men are less likely to make regular contributions or to pay at all.[15]

Enforcement of child support has been lax, although the responsibility to provide support for children exists by statute or common law in all American jurisdictions. At the time of a divorce or separation a court determines the amount of support; the awards vary widely between—and even within—jurisdictions. However, the court order is only the first hurdle in what can prove to be a very long and ultimately unsuccessful process. Often payments are not made, or they are irregular or less than the awarded amount. The parent with custody of the children can take legal action, but this has been an expensive and futile experience in many cases.

Recognizing the grave problems of the rising number of children in female-headed families, and stimulated by high budget deficits, the federal government has prodded and encouraged the states to force delinquent fathers to meet their paternal obligations. Limited state action resulted in tougher federal child support laws in 1975 and 1984. The 1984 amendments gave the federal Office of Child Support Enforcement broad authority to establish the standards necessary to ensure that state child support collection programs would be effective. The law requires that states take some of the following measures when the noncustodial parent fails to provide support in a timely manner: garnish part of wages; impose liens on property; withhold state tax refunds (a similar federal income tax provision was enacted in 1981); require the delinquent parent to post a bond to guarantee payment; and provide credit bureaus with information on delinquent spouses.

While the states have made some progress in collecting overdue child support money—collections grew from $2.4 to $3.9 billion in the three years after 1984—the improvements have been disappointingly slow. The proportion of mothers who were awarded child support grew only from 58 to 61 percent from 1984 to 1986—but the proportion who actually received payment declined slightly. Only half the states had implemented the enforcement procedures required by Congress two and a half years after the 1984 amendments were enacted.[16] Consequently Congress is considering requiring automatic wage withholding in cases where child support is ordered by a court.

Family disruption has induced many women to enter the labor force. Given the low educational attainment of many single female parents, and racial and sex discrimination in the labor market, it should come as no surprise that their earnings often are inadequate to lift their families out of destitution. For many female-headed families, the income garnered from work has proven to be less than a godsend and in many cases less than welfare payments. Over half of single mothers with minor children live in poverty.

The private decisions of two parents splitting up a home have spilled over to affect the rest of society because of inadequate child support payments. Reduced economic circumstances are likely to be one of the most immediate and direct impacts a child from a broken home will experience. Besides emotional trauma, the fact that a father is no longer living in the house can be a major economic blow to a child.

PARENTS AND CHILDREN

Currently the majority of American children are still raised by two parents and do not experience family disintegration. Yet the traditional picture of childrearing is far less valid now than it has been in the past. The single-parent family appears to be a permanent and pronounced fixture on the American scene. Nearly half of all American children now growing up are expected to experience a family breakup at some point, many of them twice. Part of the growth in single-parent families reflects a new determination by unmarried mothers to raise their own children. By contrast, in the past many single parents tended to turn their children over to relatives or orphanages, and the children would be raised by neither parent.

The impact of these new forces is hard to quantify or evaluate. Reduced economic circumstances alone tend to affect the child's probability of continuing in school, and consequently the child's labor market prospects. It is more difficult to form any hard and fast conclusions about the effect of family breakup on children's personality development and their ability to form social relationships. Though some studies indicate that most of the children from broken homes are just as able to cope with the problems of life as children from two-parent families, their findings and conclusions must be regarded as highly tentative because of serious methodological problems.

One major impact of broken homes has been to shift a greater proportion of financial support for children onto public sources. Only a very small minority of single mothers receives any child support payments, and most often these payments must be supplemented by earnings and government income transfer programs.

These developments pose serious challenges to the family's traditional role and structure. The family as an institution has proven to be highly resilient in the past, and new arrangements are evolving, albeit too slowly, to meet contemporary challenges. Meanwhile the toll in human grief for the individuals involved and its ensuing effects in eroding social stability are not abating.

Chapter Five

THE FAMILY AND WORK GO TOGETHER

> When a girl leaves her home at eighteen, she does one
> of two things. Either she falls into saving hands and
> becomes better, or she rapidly assumes the
> cosmopolitan standard of virtue and becomes worse.
>
> Theodore Dreiser, *Sister Carrie*

FAMILY WORK ROLES

When Caroline Meeber boarded the train for Chicago in 1889, with her cheap imitation alligator-skin satchel and purse containing a grand total of $4, Dreiser tells us that she was "full of the illusions of ignorance and youth." No husband would be waiting to love, provide for, and protect her. She would have to make her own way in a cold city, and she would have to enter the rough and tumble world of the wage earner. Her opportunities in the labor market would be far inferior to those for most men. She would be relegated to "women's work," which consisted mostly of positions on the bottom rungs of the job ladder. The wages would be less than those earned by men, and the chances for advancement would be slim. This harsh reality facing her would soon enough obliterate all of her youthful illusions.

If she had a choice between falling into saving masculine hands accompanied by a hearth and home or becoming a working girl, it was assumed that she would pick the former option, as would any reasonable and properly brought up young woman. The presumption was that if a woman had chosen gainful employment it was because the matrimonial option had failed to materialize or because the unfortunate woman had married a man who was not a good provider.

These views concerning a woman's place in the industrial society were taken as self-evident and were shared by women and men alike. The nuclear family was supposed to symbolize a successful refuge from a rough world, and within the family there was to be rigid division of labor along sexual lines. The husband was the breadwinner, while the woman was the good wife, mother, cook, and housekeeper. If a woman could afford to stay home and not work, then her place was to remain in the house. Whether or not women had been brainwashed into believing this ethos, a vast majority of them espoused these norms in the not too distant past.

The tables have turned almost completely. With more than half of the female population, including mothers of toddlers, in the labor force, there have been tremendous shifts in societal norms. Between the early 1950s and the present, the gap between male and female labor force participation rates narrowed from 50 to 20 percentage points. In fact, wives have accounted for the bulk of new female workers who now labor outside the home. Eli Ginzberg has called this dramatic growth of women seeking gainful employment in the paid labor force "the single most outstanding phenomenon of our century."[1] At one time it was the working woman who was led to believe—through novels, magazines, movies, and a whole host of cultural devices—that she was the oddity. Something was lacking in her life that would only be filled by being a full-time wife and mother. Now these perceptions have been reversed, and the woman who does not have a career outside the home is often depicted as the individual whose life lacks fulfillment.

Laboring in the workforce and being a wife and mother are not, of course, mutually exclusive. Over sixty percent of married mothers are trying to live both roles. Sixty-one percent of all women and 54 percent of men polled in 1985 indicated that marriage would be most satisfying to them if both the husband and wife worked and shared the child care and housework. These attitudinal findings indicate vast shifts in social roles, but women still face, in part, a double standard. While 72 percent of women state that a wife should quit her job for the sake of her husband's career, only 22 percent of women thought that husbands should do the same. Men responded in a similar manner, with 62 percent stating that the wife should quit her job, while only 22 percent stated that husbands should return the favor.

On the subject of who stays home to care for children, nearly three-quarters of those polled in another survey agreed with the statement that "mothers with young children should go to work only if the money is really needed." Still, working mothers with young children and their husbands take a different view. Over 80 percent of these parents state that their children are "just as well off" as if the mother did not work.[2]

Adding Underpaid to Unpaid Work

An old nursery rhyme may have been true in the past:

Clap hands, clap hands, until Daddy comes home
Because Daddy's got money and Mommy's got none.

But this is currently far from an accurate picture of many American households. Motherhood has become far less of a roadblock to paid employment outside of the home. There is a high probability that the child will have to clap hands alone, with another relative, or in a day care facility, until both daddy *and* mommy come home. And once both parents are home, daddy is not the only person who has money. This fact raises questions not only about the role of the woman outside the household, but it also challenges her traditional subordinate status within the home, even if the wife does not match the husband's earnings. Indeed, while emphasis is placed on the impact of female employment on the workforce, a far more subtle transformation may be taking place inside of the family. Instead of liberation, some women may find that they have become part of the "secretarial proletariat." As one feminist writer put it: "Many working women are married (I was married during my last job; since my husband was sick at the time, I was the sole support of the household, on a salary that was half of what my husband could make with the same qualifications). Then we have two full-time jobs instead of just one—underpaid clerical worker and unpaid housekeeper."[3]

Regardless of equity, the old patterns of stereotyped sexual work roles within the family were clear and largely unchallenged. For better or for worse, these traditional arrangements are being replaced by varied life styles. It cannot be expected that family structures will come away untouched as new patterns of work life emerge. Some fear that these complex forces will weaken the family institution and could be one more nail in its coffin.

When a girl now reaches her eighteenth birthday, she usually has far wider choices than those faced by Dreiser's heroine. The opportunity for additional formal education is now open to more women than in previous generations. Today more women are enrolled in college than men, and other women enroll in vocational training and other institutions that prepare them for occupational careers. The rewards of work have attracted a growing number of young women, and their resulting economic independence permits postponement or even rejection of marriage, although the latter is an infrequent occurrence.

By contrast, in the past the job was more of a way station than a permanent decision—an experience to be had before falling into saving hands. Women's labor force participation reached a peak in their early twenties, and then fell as they withdrew from paid employment to get married and have children, while depending on the husband for support. As the children grew up, some women reentered the labor force. All in all, this female labor force pattern was quite different from the one displayed by men, most of whom continued to work well past midlife.

Women's work life patterns are changing, moving closer to men's (fig. 11). This could have a major impact on the family. As more young women have sought the challenges and opportunities of the labor market, they have tended to postpone marriage. While women have a long way to go before they achieve equality with men in the workforce, a growing number of women, aided by Uncle Sam's pressures, have found employment on higher rungs of the job ladder.

Women who achieve economic self-sufficiency and higher job status may tend to reject marriage because they will not need a man to provide for them. This speculation has obvious flaws. By developing their own careers women might opt for different lifestyles. But rejection of vicarious living through a husband's career and children should not be equated with repudiating marriage. Men have been economically independent for years, yet they have clung to the institution of marriage and have been willing to support it.

Indeed, 93 percent of women under 30 indicated that marriage would give them the greatest satisfaction and happiness as a lifestyle.[4] This does not negate the possibility that the entry of married women into the workforce could affect the family if it increases the divorce rate. In the past a wife may have stayed in a bad marriage because opportunities for entering the labor force and making it on her own were limited. Financial insecurity and dependence on the part of the woman, not love, may have been the glue that held many a marriage together. As a woman experiences or believes that she can earn her own way in the world, shifting work roles could prove

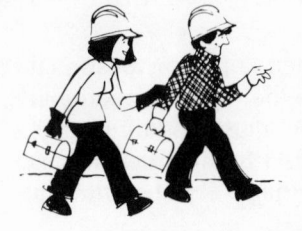

FIGURE 11.

While differences persist, the behavior patterns of women in the labor force are moving closer to those of men.

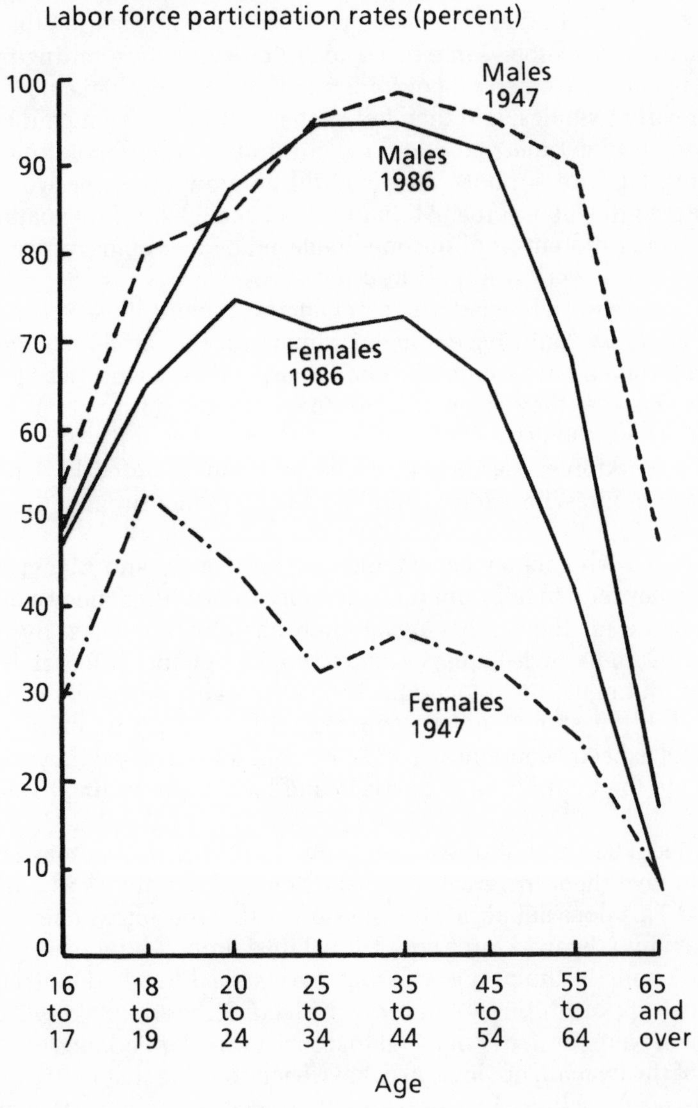

Labor force participation rates (percent)
100
90
80
70
60
50
40
30
20
10
0
Males 1947
Males 1986
Females 1986
Females 1947
16 to 17
18 to 19
20 to 24
25 to 34
35 to 44
45 to 54
55 to 64
65 and over
Age

Source: U.S. Department of Labor, Bureau of Labor Statistics

to be an added incentive to break up a family or not enter the bonds of matrimony in the first place.

The massive entry of mothers into the workforce has intensified concerns whether a working mother can be as good a parent to her children as a full-time housewife. If the mother is not at home for a good portion of the day, the availability of suitable child care becomes a major problem. Aside from the emotional concerns over adjustments to new child care arrangements, the economic costs cannot be ignored. Good institutional child care is costly, and society is moving slowly in funding such facilities. As the number of children in public schools declined, part of the government's "savings" were allocated to the care and education of younger children. "Free" schooling for 5-year-olds is becoming universal, and facilities for 4-year-olds and even younger children are expanding. Still, provision of child care is an economic as well as a highly emotional issue, and it will remain a controversial public policy issue for many years to come.

A second problem faced by wives who are wage earners is the reallocation of work roles within the family. As women behave more like men in the labor force, men and women will have to adapt to new roles in the home, an adjustment that could have many positive effects on family life. More than a reallocation of cooking, cleaning, shopping, and childrearing responsibilities is involved; there is a need to reexamine traditional power relationships within the family. Some mistakenly confuse sexually stereotyped work roles with the real essence of what it means to be part of a family. Shifting work responsibilities have a good deal of evolutionary potential for the family, and they can have many positive impacts on home life. When matters concerning the household exchequer are dealt with, a mother is much less likely just to shrug her shoulders and lament that "father knows best" if she has had a major role in filling the family's coffers. A family with two wage earners may be expected to have a far different pattern of sharing responsibilities than the traditional one-earner household.

Ethos and Reality

The old ethos concerning a woman's place in the home is more a creation of Victorian ideology than a description of historic reality. Any future predictions about women in the labor force should consider the various economic, social, and political factors that have led to the major upsurge in female labor force participation rates. While the vast numbers of women entering the workforce may have transformed the home and the workplace, it is still a long way from being a glorious revolution for most females. Job discrimination, occupational segregation, lower wages, and limited room for advancement still face all too many female workers.

To assert that a woman's place was in the home while the man's natural habitat was the workplace made some sense in a society of farmers. When agriculture was the prime source of employment for the vast majority of the population, the man's workplace was not that far removed from the home, and the wife was beside him sharing in homestead chores. In addition to cooking, cleaning, and caring for children, wives also provided the needed labor for spinning, weaving, and making soap, shoes, candles, and many of the other essentials consumed by the household. While many jobs were allocated on the basis of sex, there was no question that women worked very hard—often right along with the men—in this agrarian economy.[5] Under these conditions, women's work was vital to the survival of the family. Very few women have ever belonged to a leisure class that had no work responsibilities, toil, or obligations in the production process.

What has changed is not the fact of women's work, but the institutional arrangements, occupations, and settings in which they labor. Under current labor force definitions, a person is counted in the workforce if the individual works without pay for 15 hours or more a week for a family business. If one were to extend the definition of a family business to include raising children and maintaining a home, then virtually all homemakers would be counted as part of the labor force.

The industrial revolution separated the workplace from the home. During the colonial period, spinning and weaving were household chores done by women and children. Most of this country's early factories produced textiles, and instead of spinning and weaving in the home many women did these jobs in factories. Because of a rapidly growing economy and frequent shortages of labor, employers sought women for certain types of jobs and favored them because they constituted a cheaper source of labor than men. A good number of the hands that performed the work on the new machines belonged to women.[6] In fact, using women as a source of labor was in some ways encouraged by the government. Alexander Hamilton insisted that one of the chief benefits of promoting industrialization was that it would raise the living standards of the masses. He noted: "It is worthy of particular remark, that in general, women . . . are rendered more useful by manufacturing establishments than they would otherwise be. . . . The rise of manufacturers has elevated the females belonging to the families of the cultivators of the soil from a state of penury . . . to competence and industry."[7]

Lacking historical perspective, one could easily believe that conflict over a woman's place in society is a recent phenomenon. But even a cursory examination of social history discloses that past generations and families were racked by the same tensions. It took a concerted effort from the pulpit and other social agencies—reinforced by novelists and newspaper scribes—to persuade women that their prime function was to play the role of supporting helpmate to their husbands, and to create a haven for them from the outside world. Unmarried women were regarded as pitiable encumbrances, as females had a biological destiny that they were forbidden to fulfill without marriage vows. A long list of nineteenth-century educators, theologians, and political leaders who espoused these views could be cited. Even in the 1930s, anthropologist Margaret Mead asserted that a woman had the choice either of becoming an achieving individual and less of a woman or of being a woman and "therefore less of an achieving individual." As recently as 1955, Adlai Stevenson told the Smith College graduating class that their primary task was to "influence man and boy" through the "humble role of housewife."[8]

Yet until well into the nineteenth century the economy often required the labor of women to meet the needs of expanding manufacturing industries, and a minority of women desired to establish careers outside the home. In 1833, a textile mill owner wrote the secretary of the treasury, "our greatest difficulty at present is a want of females, women and children; [I] have my fears we shall not be able to operate all our machinery another year." However, by the mid-nineteenth century employers had turned to a cheaper and more plentiful supply of labor—immigrant men. By 1870 only about 15 percent of females age 16 or older were working outside the home, and one woman author advocated taxing men who displaced women from occupations.[9] Concern over the specter of male unemployment also was used as an argument to discourage women from entering the labor market. These economic and demographic changes contributed to the intensification of the notion during the height of the Victorian era that a woman should confine her work to the home.

The Work Ethic

Other observers stressed fertility factors. Theodore Roosevelt saw ominous warnings in the fertility trends at the turn of the century. The upper crust of society, or, as he put it, "the highest races," were vastly reducing the number of children they brought into the world, while the lower orders continued multiplying. Roosevelt and others felt that the "better people" ought to have more children and that a woman in this category who was so "selfish" that she should not reduce her activities outside the home was nothing more than "a criminal against the race."[10] Recently, social commentator Ben Wattenberg has revived this thesis in a different context, warning that an increased proportion of Americans who are not of "white European stock" will "yield . . . social turbulence," and that low American fertility rates will "make it difficult to promote and defend liberty in the Western nations."[11]

Researchers have tried to place this change in attitudes toward working women in a larger social context. As romantic love or infatuation replaced arranged marriages, the goals of marriage and the family were elevated. Domesticity was expected to provide spiritual bliss. Victorians saw the family, to use Ruskin's words, as "a sacred place; a temple of the hearth."[12] Also, notions concerning childhood changed. Focusing on the highly structured bourgeois family system, Christopher Lasch has suggested that industrialization of the production process required an "industrialization in reproduction." Children were recognized as persons with distinctive attributes, making childrearing more demanding and expensive as a result. Lasch argued that the "bourgeois family simultaneously degraded and exalted women." Specialization of work roles within the family haven became more detailed and segregated along sexual lines. Childbearing and rearing came to be viewed as a full-time occupation for married women who belonged to the bourgeoisie. Along with private property, the rise of the nuclear family was to provide a refuge from a rough competitive world, and a wife's main role came to be the custodian of this haven. The division of labor that took place in the marketplace was mirrored within the family. According to Lasch, therefore, the zenith of laissez-faire capitalism during the late Victorian era required that society strengthen its mores concerning a woman's place in the home.[13]

Whether any, or all, of these speculations explain female labor force participation patterns toward the end of the 1800s remains a matter of taste, but there is little dispute about the facts. A dual standard for women was in full force by the end of the Victorian era in America. Unmarried women outside the upper circles of society might be encouraged to enter the workforce for a time, but the proper role for them was to marry and bear children.

By 1890, fewer than one of five women age 14 years and over was in the labor force. The vast majority of these workers were single; married women living with their husbands showed a much lower propensity to enter the workforce than single women. More than a third of single women were in the labor force, but only one of 20 married women sought paid employment.[14] Two groups of married women might work outside of the home without societal disapproval—immigrant women (who worked in northeastern industrial centers) and black women (most of whom labored in the South). These women were not expected to adhere to the norms concerning a woman's place. One study conducted during this era found that three of four female workers were immigrants.

A black woman faced far different economic and social conditions from the rest of the female population. Because the chances were far greater that black men could not earn enough to keep their families out of destitution, black wives were obliged to enter the labor force in greater relative numbers than white wives. About 4 percent of white wives sought employment, but about 25 percent of black wives were in the labor force during this period. Black widows faced even harsher economic realities, and more than two-thirds of them became wage earners.[15] Most of the black women who worked were either field hands or domestic servants.

While wives were subordinate to their husbands, an agrarian economy blurred the sharp work distinction between spouses. The realities of farming created an internal labor market within the household where chores were allocated and products were exchanged and consumed. There was no question that both the husband and wife worked to provide the means of household subsistence. As the work location was removed from the home, the movement of women into the labor force started to rise ever so slowly initially and accelerated beginning with World War II.

Because paid employment was not a socially acceptable option, middle-class women found respectable alternate exits from home. Various volunteer causes, not all in the genteel tradition—for example, the suffragist movement—attracted the interests and occupied the time of many women. Apart from earnings, there is often not much difference between the work done by volunteers and that done on paid jobs, and many unpaid workers perform tasks that have a direct equivalent in the paid workforce. A national commission concluded in 1979 that distinguishing between work that is paid and work that is not can be "a somewhat arbitrary practice."[16]

Women played a major role in the social and legislative campaigns of the pre-World War I Progressive era. Also, many of the liberal reforms of this period were directed toward improving the working conditions of women. Coming from the "upper crust," reformers Bessie Van Vorst and her sister-in-law, Marie Van Vorst, were prevented by prevailing custom from becoming wage earners, but this did not stop them from dressing as factory girls and exploring the conditions of female employment. The results of their direct observations (published in 1903 as *The Woman Who Toils*) aroused the country to the lot of female factory workers. A minimum wage for women and children, as well as laws covering the maximum number of hours they could work, was high on the agenda of reformers. Middle-class groups, such as the National Consumers League, were often the prime forces fighting for these laws, and married women played a major role in these reform movements.[17]

The concern that the family is being besieged is not new. The ethos and reality displayed a good deal of tension, even when only a few married women dared to become paid workers. Many women were pursuing both leisurely and charitable interests outside the home. During the early part of this century, many male observers were struck by tensions created by the changing status of women. Alarmed by the changes, the popular press, as well as some learned journals, was quick to predict the demise of the family. At one time it may have been the norm to envision a domestic joy created by a wife who labored only in the home. However, even back then there was a realization that it might be "an illusory center, or perhaps not a center at all."[18] An Emma Bovary, or a Joanna Kramer a century later, wanted and reached out for something more than this norm, and they were not alone.

Ours is not the first era that has experienced the anxieties caused by a changing status of women. Family work roles have always had to adapt to and accommodate shifting economic, technological, and social conditions. The world in which the bulk of the labor force was devoted to the production of goods is fading, just as did the world in which agriculture dominated the economic scene. The shift from manufacturing to service and information-processing activities is bound to have an impact on the family. New norms concerning family work roles are evolving. However, as indicated by historical changes in work roles, the family has shown a remarkable ability to survive and adjust to new realities. There are many different patterns of work roles under which the family can flourish, and those who equate the institution with the pattern that reached its ascendancy during the late Victorian era reflect their biases or their ignorance of the past.

WOMEN AT WORK

Between the early part of this century and World War II, the role of women in society may have changed, but women did not rush into the labor force (fig. 12). Sociologists displayed a voracious appetite for investigating the family, carefully centering their attention on social and economic variables that might lead to a stable marriage, safe subjects even for Victorian social scientists. Alternative lifestyles and family work patterns remained, however, outside the pale. The idea that the husband would be the sole provider in a family and the wife would not be in the labor force was usually assumed as a given.

Cultural biases aside, the issues studied by the social scientists, focusing on the tasks performed by women, reflected the stability of family structure during the first four decades of this century. Women's participation in the labor force and the dual standard regarding the demographic characteristics of women who sought employment registered little change during this period, but more occupational opportunities opened to them as a result of changing technology. In 1920 approximately 12 percent of the women at work were in professional jobs, the same percentage as two decades later. Nearly three of four professional women were elementary school teachers or nurses. One notable change was that as typing and stenography expanded, these occupations became women's work, and by 1930 one-third of the female labor force was employed in clerical occupations.

Barriers to female paid employment were in line with social norms, and sometimes these norms became institutionalized in laws. The Social Security Act of 1935—the cornerstone of the welfare system—established what later became aid to families with dependent children (AFDC). Destitute and husbandless mothers were entitled to receive support payments, and these mothers were not expected to work, reflecting not only the dearth of jobs during the 1930s but also the belief that a mother's place was in the home with her children. Some of the problems that have beset AFDC in recent years stem from the fact that mothers from all economic classes have entered the workforce, and the belief that most welfare mothers should work. The structure of other social security payments and the tax system often favors the older family work pattern; for example, social security benefit rules favor families in which only one spouse works. These problems reflect not only gender bias but also the comparative recency of the upsurge of women in the labor force. Often formal institutional arrangements lag behind changes in social and economic conditions.

World War II—A Launching Pad

World War II stands as a major break in female work patterns. The war effort's high demands for labor and patriotic fervor induced many women to join the labor force, boosting the size of the female workforce by 32 percent during the war. Beyond the unprecedented numbers, women entered numerous occupations that were previously the exclusive domain of men. "Rosie the Riveter" became a folk heroine. Gainful employment was sought not only by single and minority women but also by married women. This massive dose of work experience persuaded many women to remain in the labor force after the war. The influx of women into the workforce has continued ever since.

Wives and mothers have played a key role in the changing composition of the labor force in recent decades. The number of married mothers in the labor force has increased fivefold since World

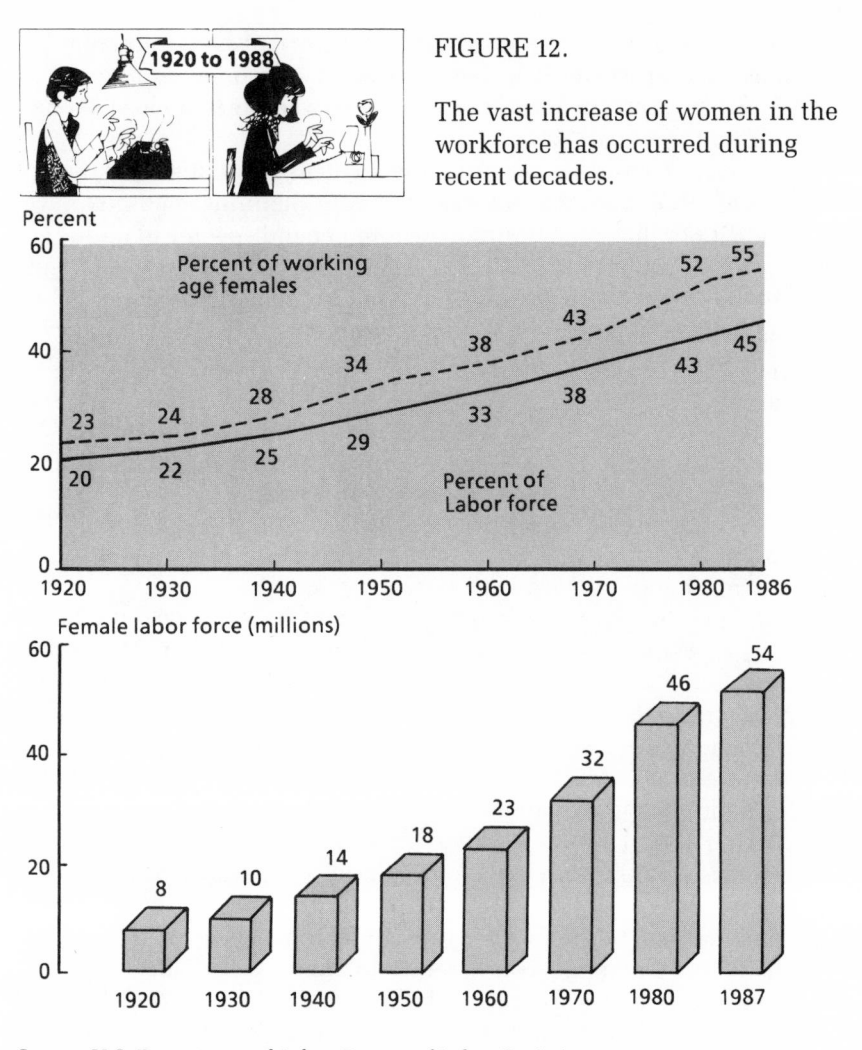

FIGURE 12.

The vast increase of women in the workforce has occurred during recent decades.

Source: U.S. Department of Labor, Bureau of Labor Statistics

War II, while the total number of female workers has more than tripled. By 1987, about 15 million married mothers with children under 18 were working or seeking work, accounting for 64 percent of the mothers with children that age—compared with 30 percent two decades earlier, and less than ten percent in 1940. Since the end of World War II, women, mostly married, have accounted for about three-fifths of the total increase in civilian employment.

American women of all classes and backgrounds have entered the labor market. More than half of all married women are now employed. In 1987, 27 million working wives comprised close to one-fourth of the entire labor force.

Several factors stand out in any analysis explaining the rise in female labor force participation. Family planning methods have made it possible to determine the number and spacing of children, while the friendly neighborhood supermarket and improvements in home technology have facilitated household maintenance. This has reduced the amount of time required to carry out the woman's traditional role of running a household and raising children, and it has given women more time to devote to other activities including employment outside the home. As more women obtained longer doses of education and higher paying jobs, the income foregone by not working rose.[19] Social and cultural factors have also played a role as the stigma once associated with wives' working has vastly diminished, and as attitudes toward fathers' participation in child-rearing change, albeit rather slowly.

Money has also played a role in attracting women to the labor market. While discrimination based on sex remains a powerful force in the workplace, women's groups backed by civil rights laws have prodded employers to open better paying "men's" jobs to women, and employers have changed many time-honored hiring and promotion practices. Opportunities for higher pay and status have induced more women to seek work outside the home.

After World War II, some analysts predicted that family work patterns would return to the older norm. They reasoned that rising productivity and economic growth would continue to boost the income earned by husbands, thus reducing the need for another check and inducing wives to return to their homes. This, of course, did not happen, as economists failed to consider the nonpecuniary attractions of work and the appetite for more income. Not discouraged by one failure to predict women's behavior, economists turned to other models that would explain the labor market behavior of married women.[20]

The newer economic theories focus on the entire household instead of just on the individual. They assume that the decisions to enter the labor force, including the number of hours spent at the workplace, depend on many variables affecting family life. The supply of labor is treated as a joint household or family decision.[21] For example, as a husband's income rises, his family will be able to purchase more timesaving household goods, which will reduce the

number of hours required to keep up a home and give the wife more time to work outside the home.

Since World War II, American households have shown a strong propensity to increase their consumption of goods and services. Many wives joined the workforce to finance these upward consumption patterns. Like the mechanical rabbit leading the greyhounds around the racetrack, families have often required another paycheck in the chase for the "good life" as these aspirations have consistently stayed ahead of productivity. In the inflationary 1970s and early 1980s, another check became necessary just to maintain the standard of living to which the families had become accustomed. By 1987, three of five husband-wife families had at least two household members in the labor force; in most cases these were the husband and wife.

Many working wives make a significant contribution to the income of a household. The average working wife now contributes 28 percent of her family's annual income, and full-time working wives who labor all year supply 40 percent of the household exchequer. The median income for married couples where the wife works is 50 percent higher than in couples where she does not. From 1970 to 1986, the number of children in husband-wife families declined by almost 13 million. Nevertheless, the number of children whose mothers work rose significantly. As a result, two-thirds of children in husband-wife families now have working mothers—up from 38 percent in 1970.

Reductions in family size have also helped women enter the labor force, although the direction of causation is difficult to ascertain. One might say that women first decided to have fewer children, and this decision led them to seek employment outside the home. Conversely, it could be argued that women first decided to enter the labor force, and this decision led them to have fewer children. Obviating the need to enter into a chicken-and-egg controversy, it appears that both forces have symbiotically worked to reinforce these family and labor market trends.

In addition, a growing number of women are heading households. Most of these women must work out of economic necessity. The number of divorced, separated, and widowed women working or seeking work has nearly tripled since 1950, while the total labor force has grown by 90 percent. About three-fourths of divorcees now work, but only one-fourth of widows are in the labor force. The latter are generally older, and many receive public or private pensions.

About 60 percent of female-headed families include minor children. The women heading these households provide for over 13 million minor children and for over 8 million additional household members. Over a quarter of female family heads are widows, over half are divorced or separated, and 18 percent are single women who have never married—although over three-quarters of them have had children. The growth in female-headed households has been a strong force leading to the increase in the number of women who have entered the labor force.

Educational attainment is more highly correlated with labor force participation for women than it is for men, who, once out of school, tend to stay in the labor force regardless of educational attainment. By 1985 the participation rate ranged from 21 percent for women with an elementary education to 71 percent for women with a college education. Also, the job opportunities for college-educated women have increased substantially. Better-educated women are able to take advantage of the rising demand in the expanding professional and technical occupations. Though the number of professional women is still small relative to men, women have made significant gains in these fields. Women who have invested in a college education—and graduate studies—may also be more reluctant to forgo the rewards from work in professional fields because the income forgone by staying at home is greater than for less educated women. Women with four or more years of college and who work full time, year-round have incomes that are more than double those of women with less than a high-school education.

While economic factors are undoubtedly important in explaining the increased proportion of women in the labor force, cultural forces have also played a key role in these changes. The women's liberation movement has had a major impact on heightening the career aspirations of women. Movies, TV, novels, and other media in recent years have often depicted the joys and problems of working women. The net result of these various cultural forces has been to increase the socal acceptability—or even inevitability—of women in the workforce.

Working Conditions

Working outside the home no longer carries a social stigma for women; indeed, it is considered an honorable pursuit, even for mothers with young children. The unprecedented influx of women into labor markets and the working conditions they experience have affected family life. Suppose a wife with a working husband and only a high-school education takes a part-time job as a semiskilled worker. Even if her remuneration is low, her earnings may represent a sorely needed addition to the family's budget.

While women have made some inroads into occupations with higher status and earnings, the majority still hold jobs in traditionally female occupations with low pay and limited career opportunities. Though women now constitute about a fifth of all engineers, mathematicians, computer programmers, scientists, doctors, college professors, lawyers, and judges, most of their employment growth has been concentrated in clerical and service occupations. By 1982, roughly 81 percent of all clerical workers and 59 percent of all service workers except those working in private households were women, compared with 53 percent and 40 percent, respectively, in 1940 (table 2). After 1982 the U.S. Bureau of Labor Statistics altered its method of occupational classifications. More recent data are therefore not comparable with earlier data. However, between 1982 and 1987 the proportion of women workers in managerial jobs continued to grow, and the proportion in blue collar positions declined. In 1987 nearly half of all working women were still employed in administrative support or service occupations. Male employment shows far less concentration, and less than 10 percent of all male workers are in the ten largest occupations for men.

TABLE 2. Despite some gains, women remain highly concentrated in a few occupational groups.

Occupational group	Percentage of female employment		Percentage of total employment	
	1982	1940	1982	1940
Total				
Number (thousands)	43,256	11,920	—	—
Percentage	100	100	43.5	25.9
White-collar workers				
Professional, technical workers	17.7	13.2	45.1	45.4
Managers, officials, proprietors	7.4	3.8	28.0	11.7
Clerical workers	34.4	21.2	80.7	52.6
Salesworkers	6.9	7.0	45.4	27.9
Blue-collar workers				
Craftworkers, foremen	2.0	0.9	7.0	2.1
Operatives	9.6	18.4	29.5	25.7
Nonfarm laborers	1.2	0.8	11.7	3.2
Service workers				
Private household workers	2.3	17.6	96.9	93.8
Service workers (except private household)	17.3	11.3	59.0	40.1
Farm workers	1.1	5.8	17.5	8.0

Source: U.S. Department of Labor, Bureau of Labor Statistics

The concentration of women in a few occupations makes possible a subtle form of discrimination. It reduces the opportunities for advancement, while providing employers with an excess supply of female workers for specific jobs slots. This factor exerts a strong downward pressure on wages for many female occupations. The laws of supply and demand—once the female concentration factor is considered—are the major determinants keeping down wages for "women's work." The unseen hand does the dirty work, and personnel directors can blame low women's wages on the "system." A more overt type of discrimination, although equally difficult to prove, is the presumably objective classification of "women's" occupations under job evaluation systems, which frequently tend to underestimate the true complexity and responsibility of the jobs done by women.

While some analysts argue that these conditions are forced on women by external economic factors, women's occupational choices also are affected greatly by the socialization process as they

*"We have thousands of opportunities for women
with college education. How fast do you type?"*

grow up. When youngsters are asked "What do you want to be when you grow up?" most girls choose far fewer occupations than boys. Through schooling and other cultural forces, young women often are shunted out of certain fields, such as the physical sciences and skilled trades, that are traditionally considered men's work.

Whether or not occupational segregation acts as a discriminatory mechanism, it blocks women from moving up into higher positions. A typical example is classifying positions requiring similar or identical qualifications. While the only requirement for both "claims adjusters" and "claims representatives" in an insurance company may be a college degree, men have been placed as adjusters and women have been hired as representatives. Not only is the starting salary higher for adjusters, but these positions—unlike that of the representatives—are tied into a promotion system leading to better jobs. Government policy has tried to counteract sexual discrimination in the labor force. The Equal Pay Act of 1963 and Title VII of the Civil Rights Act of 1964 prohibit discrimination in employment based on sex as well as on race, color, religion, and national origin. In addition, Executive Order 11246 bans similar discrimination by federal contractors and subcontractors. The 1972 Equal Opportunity Act gave the Equal Employment Opportunity Commission the authority to sue private companies for job discrimination. However, during the 1980s the Reagan administration relaxed the enforcement of these laws.[22]

The gender wage gap proved stubbornly resistant to change until the 1980s. Between 1960 and 1979 women who worked full-time year-round earned only three-fifths of men's salaries. However, by 1986 the ratio increased to 70 percent. These comparisons must be used with caution; factors other than sex may account for the earnings differentials. For example, female full-time workers tend to labor fewer hours than male full-time workers. However, even after standardization, there is a statistically significant difference between the wages paid for men and women in the same occupational groups. The actual ratios and ratios adjusted for differences in hours worked showed the following pattern of female earnings to male earnings in 1985 for full-time, year-round workers:

Occupational group	Actual ratio	Adjusted ratio
Total	64.6	70.4
Executive, administrative, and managerial	61.3	67.2
Professional specialty	66.4	72.8
Technical and related support	69.2	73.0
Sales	49.8	56.4
Administrative, including clerical	65.9	69.9
Precision production, craft, and repair	64.9	68.2
Machine operators, assemblers, and inspectors	58.8	62.4
Transportation and material moving	61.2	67.0
Handlers, equipment cleaners, helpers, and laborers	80.6	82.6
Service workers, excluding private household and security	62.1	64.7

What is true for occupational groups also holds for specific occupations. Based on a national sample, the median hourly earnings for full-time workers in 1986 showed the following gender differentials in these occupations:

Occupation	Women	Men	Female/male earnings ratio
High-school teachers	$6.99	$8.13	86%
Nursing aides, orderlies, and attendants	3.91	4.83	81
Office clerks	5.11	6.47	79
Computer operators	5.49	7.52	73
Janitors and cleaners	3.44	4.99	69
Waiters and waitresses	3.01	4.63	65

These earnings comparisons give some idea of the wage disparity between men and women, but they do not present more than a prima facie case of discrimination. For example, many women do not have as strong an attachment to the labor force as men, and females often demonstrate higher turnover and quit rates than males working at similar types of jobs. Also, because of different expectations about future prospects in the labor force, some women do not make as great an investment in education and skill training as men. Economists have tried to determine whether these various differences in work patterns and human capital investments can explain part of the gap between the earnings of men and women. When the data are adjusted to take into consideration these various factors, the earnings gap between men and women narrows. However, there still exists a statistically significant difference that cannot be explained by any of these forces. Sexual occupational segregation and earnings differentials are not, of course, isolated from each other. The chances are that the forces counteracting occupational segregation along sexual lines will be slow, and a significant earnings differential between men and women will persist for some time.

The Census Bureau and the National Academy of Sciences have recently conducted detailed examinations of gender earnings differences, adjusting for work history, schooling, the concentration of women in certain occupations, the effect of unionization, and many other characteristics of both individuals and companies. Depending upon the education of the woman, gender differences in education and work history account for a fourth to a third of the male-female wage gap, and the concentration of women in certain occupations explains 17 to 30 percent of the difference as follows:

	Woman's educational attainment		
Characteristic	Dropout	High school	College
Occupational concentration of women	30.3%	30.0%	17.4%
Work experience	13.9	22.2	22.6
Schooling or training	12.9	0.8	12.7
Other individual or company characteristics	2.4	7.1	12.8
Proportion unaccounted for	40.5	39.9	34.5

Over a third of the difference could not be accounted for by any measured characteristic of the individual or company. The results provide powerful evidence of the discrimination women face in the labor market.[23]

"Dorothy's a wonderful wife . . . she earns $30,000 a year!"

Some analysts have postulated that the time women spend out of the labor market due to family responsibilities is the major reason for the gender wage gap. The Census Bureau's findings indicate that this factor is important but not dominant in explaining earnings differences. Only 13 percent of 21- to 64-year-old men have been without a job for six months at a time (other than because they were in school) since their 21st birthday, compared to nearly half of the women. The gap is narrower—but still substantial—for men and women in their twenties. Even for young women, most of their prolonged absences from the job market are due to family responsibilities, while these duties play an insignificant role in explaining why men are not working.

Also, while the earnings of wives have made an important contribution to household income, only in a minority of cases has this contribution been close to, or greater than, a husband's earnings. Fewer than one wife in five under age 55 in two-earner couples earns more than her husband.[24]

Women's entry into the workforce outside the home has been described as a revolution, but they have yet to storm the barricades, if their pay and occupations are taken as an index of success. The goals of equality and equity in the job market are still a long way from becoming a reality.

THE EFFECTS ON FAMILIES

Rising divorce rates and the increase of women's participation in the workforce have major effects on the family. Of primary concern is the impact that the economic independence of women will have for rearing children and marriage decisions. Too frequently changing work roles are construed as causing deterioration of family life in America.

Work and Marriage

In their more imaginative or possibly scary predictions, some futurologists have assumed that the vast upsurge of women in the workforce may portend a rejection of marriage. As they are better able to support themselves, according to this hypothesis, women will favor an independent working life rather than marriage. The converse is that women's increased earning power could encourage marriages. It takes a certain amount of financial security before most men and women are willing to tie the knot. Ample data show that economic downturns tend to postpone marriage because the parties cannot afford to establish a family or are concerned about rainy days ahead. As the economy rebounds and prospects improve for employment, financial security, and advancement, the number of marriages also rises. In the past, only the man's earnings and financial prospects counted in this part of the marriage decision. Now, however, a woman's earning ability can make her more attractive as a marriage partner—a modern version of the old-fashioned dowry.

The trick is to quantify these common sense but conflicting hypotheses associated with working women and marriage in order to reach some judgments about their net effect. As usual, the data are inconclusive, and the researchers need to make giant leaps to reach "definite" conclusions on the subject. The above forces often interact and sometimes cancel out each other.[25]

Coinciding with the increase in women working outside the home is a sharp increase in the divorce rate. Yet, it may be wrong to jump to any simple conclusions regarding causality. Just as it may be argued that married women are more prone to seek a divorce if they work, a reversal of this cause-and-effect hypothesis could explain these data. Perhaps more married women believe that their marriages may end and decide to prepare themselves for the prospect of heading a household. Or, foreseeing many more child-free years, they may want to start a career even before their children are ready for school or grow up and leave home. This would induce seeking employment outside the home, even if the marriage stayed intact.

Assuming that women's increased labor force attachment affects decisions regarding marriage and divorce, the net impact of such decisions is unclear. An "independence effect"—the realization that she can be a good provider—may increase the chances that a working wife will choose divorce over an unsatisfactory marriage. But the reverse is equally plausible. A working wife increases household income, which may relieve some of the pressing financial burdens that contribute to marital tension and often play a key role in divorce. By raising a family's standard of living, a working wife may bolster her family's financial and emotional stability.

Psychological factors also should be considered. For example, a wife blocked from a career outside the home may feel caged or shackled to the house—a situation some have dramatically likened to a pressure cooker with no safety valve to release the steam. She may view her only choice as seeking a divorce. On the other hand, if she can find fulfillment through work outside the home, work and marriage can go together to create a stronger and more stable marriage.

Given these conflicting and diverse factors that may have a bearing on divorce, statistical demonstration showing direct positive relationship between the two is unattainable. Often studies have reached the conclusion that families in which the wife is working are no more likely to separate or divorce than households in which only the husband is in the labor force.[26]

The relationship between the expanding female workforce and reduced fertility rates appears to be clearer. With advances in family planning, a majority of wives have managed to combine motherhood with work. The entry of women into the workforce has not led to a vast increase in childlessness among married couples, but, instead, to a lower fertility rate than that among nonworking mothers, when other social and economic factors are taken into consideration. Yet some reservations may be appropriate. In Germany, for example, fertility rates of the native population during the past 15 years declined even more than in the United States, but with little increase in female labor force participation.

The wife's responsibilities outside the home have not led to a major reallocation of responsibilities within the family. With the rising costs of household help, the option to pay another person to do the housework is beyond the means of the vast majority. Also, there are limits to the chores that can be passed on to the neighborhood supermarket clerk or appliance seller. Even more than in the office or factory, too many household chores cannot be mechanized. Although opinion polls show that the vast majority of husbands in two-earner couples espouse an equitable division of domestic responsibility, the working wife continues to shoulder the brunt of this burden. According to a 1987 survey, 27 percent of women continue to perform all household work without the help of the traditional "family head." But the survey suggests that such practices are changing. Younger couples tend to share household chores.[27]

When the number of hours a working wife labors outside the home are added to the time spent on household chores, some studies have concluded that most working wives wind up laboring more hours per week than their husbands. Rough estimates based on data from the late 1960s and early 1970s indicated that a wife may average 65 hours on her combined jobs inside and outside the home (assuming that she holds a full-time job in the labor market). This exceeded the average time husbands spent working on the job and in the home by about eight hours per week. However, a more recent study based on data from the mid-1970s indicates that married women labored about the same total hours in their combined jobs as did men—roughly 60 per week. There was only a very small increase in the hours of housework done by married men (still under three hours per week, or one-sixth the time spent by working wives).[28] No detailed examinations of the time spent by spouses on household chores have been performed since the 1970s. It is difficult to make accurate estimates of time use by men and women, but it appears that there still exists a significant sexual division of labor, even if total hours worked may be becoming equal for many married men and women.

Just as pathologies within labor markets—such as sexual discrimination—have been slow in changing, so will home adjustments to the new realities of both husband and wife working outside. In the absence of social upheavals, the slow evolution is toward family work roles based more on equality and less on sexual stereotypes. Many working wives appear to be assuming a larger role in making major family-related decisions than nonworking wives with no earnings, but again, change has been slow.

Child Care

As the number of working mothers with young children rises, child care facilities become increasingly important. In 1986 there were 52 million children under age 15, over half of whose mothers worked. The types and quality of child care used by working mothers vary widely. Most child care arrangements have remained informal and in the child's or caretaker's home, although formal child care centers now account for a substantial proportion of day care arrangements. Private day care centers currently take care of 14 percent of preschool children with working mothers, while nursery or preschool facilities handle an additional 9 percent of the children in this age group. The proportion of working mothers of preschool children using formal day care arrangements has grown sharply in recent years, from 16 percent in 1982 to 25 percent in 1985.

Proposals to expand child care services should be high on the agenda of all levels of government and private employers. Advocates contend that the lack of child care facilities blocks many women from entering the labor force and that more working mothers would use formal child care institutions if they were subsidized facilities. But costs are an obvious problem in an era of high budget deficits. Although cost estimates for alternative forms of child care are necessarily based on untested assumptions and are therefore questionable, using formal child care facilities is significantly more expensive than having a relative provide child care in one's own home or entrusting the child's care to a relative or a neighbor. Besides cost considerations and preferences for informal as opposed to institutional arrangements, the locations of the facilities and their hours of service are also prime factors in parents' choice whether to place their child in a day care facility or to choose another alternative.

In families with both parents present, fathers care for 19 percent of preschool children while the mother works; mothers simultaneously work and care for 9 percent of these children. This does not necessarily imply a greater willingness by fathers to care for their children; rather, it reflects the fact that all mothers surveyed in this study were employed, while an unknown proportion of fathers were out of work, placing upon them the responsibility for child care.

Mothers working part time care for 16 percent of preschool age children during working hours, while those working full time do so for only 5 percent. In families with a mother working full time, a smaller fraction of fathers care for the children during the wife's working hours. These families rely more heavily on organized day care centers than families in which the mothers work part time: organized day care centers serve 27 percent of the children under age 5 whose mothers work full time, but only 15 percent of those with mothers working part time.

Child care is most critical for separated, divorced, widowed, and never-married women who head families. Most of these women must work—many of them full time—to support their families. Single mothers seldom receive help with child care from the fathers of their children, while their income—on average, less than half that of two-parent couple families—is often insufficient to afford organized day care. Still, 27 percent of preschool children in female-headed families attend organized day care centers. Grandparents care for a much higher proportion of preschoolers in these families (16 percent) than for those in two-parent families (3 percent).[29]

After-school care of children with mothers in the labor force is largely the province of parents. Nearly two-thirds of school-age children in such families stay with a parent after school. About 11 percent of school-age children—the so-called latch-key kids—are without adult supervision after school, while the rest are cared for by adult siblings, other relatives, or nonrelatives. In families where the mother works full time, the proportion of school-age children supervised by a parent falls to 54 percent, while the share of latch-key kids rises slightly to 14 percent. Supervision by adults other than parents also is higher for children in these families.[30]

Many Americans still subscribe to the notion that the well-being of children inevitably suffers when their mothers work outside the home. Three-quarters of respondents to one survey believed that a mother with young children should not work unless the money is really needed.[31] Though feminists may bristle at such views, protesting that society does not ask whether working men make good fathers, the old beliefs still may determine public policy. Possibly the most significant blow to the expansion of child care was delivered by former president Nixon. In vetoing a bill providing for expansion of federal funds for child care, he cited the potential harm of child care to the fabric of family life as one objection.[32] The Reagan administration also endorsed this view, championing the mother's role as housewife.

The evidence does not indicate that children are worse off because they are entrusted to the care of others. However, the increased time at work by parents in recent years has unquestionably reduced the time spent at home. Over the 1973–85 period, men and women reported a one-third decline in leisure time, from 26 to less than 18 hours per week.[33] While the increased income generated from work has made parents better providers, it has certainly also left them less time to spend with their children. The overall effect of this development is still being debated by psychiatrists, psychologists, sociologists, and assorted other experts.

NO GOING BACK

If the survival of the family depends upon women returning to the home to become full-time housewives and mothers, the institution's future existence is indeed fragile. There has been no decline in the career aspirations of women, and continued progress in family planning and household management will let more women become both wives and mothers as well as workers outside of the home. As the potential rewards and work opportunities for women expand, the psychic and economic attractions in the marketplace are likely to exert an even greater pull. The occupational choices and prospects for advancement up the job ladder should be expanding. Coupled with this are the increasing number of positions within service industries. Unlike jobs in the goods producing sector of the economy, service industry jobs tend to be more flexible in meeting the particular needs of many women, including part-time employment and flexible work schedules. The growth of the service sector should make it easier for more women to function as workers both inside and outside the home.

Slow productivity growth, leading to sluggish gains or declines in the real earnings of young people, will induce more families to depend on two wage earners just to make ends meet or to finance their growing consumption expectations. Women in the workforce, including the majority of married women, are in the labor force to stay, and ironically this represents a return to the oldest known traditions. The "virtuous woman" of the Bible worked and labored very hard. This model of virtue "seeketh wool, and flax and worketh willingly with her hands." And she is "like a merchant's ships; she bringeth her food from afar. . . . She considereth a field, and buyeth it; with the fruit of her hand she planteth a vineyard." And what about her husband? The Good Book tells us that he "is known in the gates, when he sitteth among the elders of the land."

It was only with the rise of the industrial revolution—and then only when it was in full swing and immigrants supplied adequate and cheap labor—that wives were viewed as full-time mothers and creators of a haven from a society that creates stresses and strains. The current American family has a long way to go before it fully adjusts to these new and shifting work patterns. The greatest changes will be the reallocation of work responsibilities within households. A decrease of chores allocated along traditional sexist lines coupled with women sharing more effectively in the family decisionmaking process are the primary adjustments that will be made. Barring radical upheavals, both economic realities and social norms are likely to move, albeit ever so slowly, in this direction.

These changes in family work roles—unlike fads that come and go—will probably have some of the deepest and most lasting effects on the institution and upon American society. Instead of dissolution, they offer real opportunities for improved, more stable, and richer lives within families.

Chapter Six

FEMALE-HEADED FAMILIES

> | Mrs. Boyle: | We'll go. Come, Mary, an' we'll never come back. I've got a little room in me sister's where we'll stop till your trouble is over, an' then we'll work together for the sake of the baby. |
> | Mary: | My poor little child that'll have no father! |
> | Mrs. Boyle: | It'll have what's far better—it'll have two mothers. |
>
> Sean O'Casey, *Juno and the Paycock*

MATRIARCHY

At one time the opinion expressed by Mrs. Boyle would not have been fit for respectable society. It still is far from being the majority view. Yet a growing number of American children are being raised in households that do not include their father or any other adult male. The female-headed family has become commonplace on the American scene.

Female-headed families are not a recent invention of the feminist movement. With high death rates in the past, it was not uncommon for a wife and mother to find herself a widow at a relatively young age, forced by this grim reality to take on the responsibilities of heading a household.

In fact, this event was so familiar that society invented a different set of mores for widows than for women who still lived with their husbands. For example, during the American colonial period a wife who ran a business concern was seldom socially acceptable. However, if her husband died, the community accepted her stepping in to run the family business.[1]

No Man at Home

Some social scientists have viewed female-headed families as a prime cause of sustained poverty. A 1965 report by Senator Daniel P. Moynihan (then an assistant secretary in the Department of Labor) is possibly the most publicized study supporting this hypothesis. Moynihan concluded that "at the heart of the deterioration of the fabric of Negro society is the deterioration of the Negro family." A matriarchal structure that is "out of line with the rest of the American society," the report argued, "seriously retards the progress of the group as a whole." Moynihan claimed that being raised in a female-headed family was correlated with academic failure, juvenile delinquency, crime, and being rejected for military service. The report concluded that "Negro children without fathers flounder—and fail."[2] Black children whose fathers were not living at home were shown to be even more seriously disadvantaged than black children being raised in husband-wife families.

Besides a greater chance of destitution, according to the report, children reared in female-headed families were also unable to master basic skills and acquire values necessary to function in American society. Until the black family structure was stabilized and strengthened, many federal social welfare programs would run into serious roadblocks, the report asserted. Moynihan favored programs that would foster stable family patterns.

Needless to say, the Moynihan Report was hardly universally accepted. Ignoring the issues raised by Moynihan, the critics charged that instead of blaming outside cultural and economic factors for conditions within black ghettos, the report indicated that blacks themselves were responsible for their own poverty. Scholarly analysts focused on details, arguing that the report drew inexact conclusions from weak and insufficient data, and that it made the error of linking statistical relationships with causality. The poverty of female-headed families, the detractors claimed, was forced upon blacks by outside forces.[3]

Other analysts charged that pathology is in the eye of the beholder. They argued that what the Moynihan Report viewed with alarm was, in reality, a rational and alternative family system that had developed to meet the unique cultural needs of black society. Arguing that black families displayed numerous strengths, sociologist Robert B. Hill concluded that it was wrong to use a white family system as the measuring rod for black households. Hill's case rested on the following characteristics of the black family.

1. Strong kinship bonds: Black families showed a high propensity to absorb other relatives into their households; for example, few black babies born out of wedlock were put up for formal adoption.

2. A strong work orientation: Despite low wages, poor working conditions, and few chances for advancement, a majority of the females heading black families worked during the year.

3. Adaptability of family roles: Contrary to claims of matriarchy, black families tended to be far more "equalitarian" than other ethnic households.

4. A strong religious and achievement orientation: The church historically has been, and remains, a key institution within the black community, and it has had a major positive impact on black family life. Also, most of the young blacks who enrolled in college came from homes in which the family heads never even finished high school.[4]

However, as the proportion of female-headed black families grew, these arguments became far less prevalent, and they have now largely been discarded. When the Moynihan Report was issued, a quarter of all black children were being raised by their mothers, but by 1987 the proportion had more than doubled. Nearly 90 percent of black children born today are projected to spend at least part of their childhood in a single-parent family.[5] Many prominent blacks have voiced apprehension about the continuing breakdown of the black family. In a panel discussion following a widely watched and influential Bill Moyers CBS TV special, "The Vanishing Family—Crisis in Black America," former U.S. Equal Employment Opportunity Commission chair Eleanor Holmes Norton noted, "I think increasingly that alarm is being sounded from within the black community, and that is the important change." The Reverend Jesse Jackson, urging higher moral standards, declared, "Somebody must say that babies making babies is morally wrong."[6] The Urban League conducted a "male responsibility" campaign with the slogan, "Don't make a baby if you can't be a father." The regrettable aspect of these exhortations is that more than two decades elapsed until it became respectable to address the issues raised by Moynihan.

Not Just the Ghetto

Within the last two decades, single motherhood has become a growing feature of middle-class white society as well.

The sheer increase in the number of female-headed families is significant in itself, but the accompanying attitudinal changes are no less important. More women, and also men, now share the views expressed by Sean O'Casey's Mrs. Boyle concerning the legitimacy of the female-headed family. Having a man in the house is no longer regarded, according to this view, as a prerequisite to raising children, even if he is necessary for initiating the process—at least until test tube babies become more commonplace.

Faced with continued exploitation within the traditional husband-wife family structure, during the 1970s some feminist publicists saw a male-free household as the only way women could improve and enrich their lives. Hence, feminism during that decade often seemed to be antifamily. Some militant liberationists viewed the female-headed household not as an institution to be decried but as a positive affirmation of a new lifestyle. But by the early 1980s such views had nearly disappeared. The "new agenda," Betty Friedan noted in 1979, would be to enable women to live in equality with men under the same roof. Most often this would take the form of a husband-wife family, but living under different arrangements than the gender-stereotyped household of the past. Friedan's views proved prescient, as by 1987 most women's organizations were devoting considerable attention to families and work.[7]

The female-headed family will remain a significant feature on the American scene for many years, more often representing economic hardship than an alternative means of fulfillment. The conditions experienced by women who head families and their children present serious problems covering a range of social issues from welfare to labor market discrimination. Trying to be a family head, mother, and an active member of the labor force has been a difficult challenge for most women. Working females who head households are at an even more serious disadvantage than other women. A large portion of these women have found it impossible to pull their families out of poverty without government help.

A NEW WAVE?

Almost all of the growth in families headed by women has occurred since 1970.

	Proportion of families with single heads		
	Total	Female	Male
1940	15.6%	10.8%	4.8%
1950	12.3	9.3	3.0
1960	12.4	9.8	2.6
1970	13.1	10.7	2.4
1980	17.5	14.6	2.9
1987	20.1	16.2	3.9

The proportion of families headed by women underwent little change between 1940 and 1970, but increasingly the factor responsible for this family structure was divorce rather than the death of a husband. Female-headed families are particularly prevalent among black families, of which 42 percent are headed by women—more than triple the proportion for whites (fig. 13).

Owing to declining marriage and remarriage rates, the length of time that a single mother may expect to remain single increased to about six years in the mid-1980s. Examined from the perspective of the children, nearly a quarter of all children were being raised by a single parent in 1987 (usually the mother)—double the proportion living with one parent a decade and a half earlier. By the time they reach age 18, about half of all children are expected to spend at least part of their childhood in a single-parent family.[8] The increase in single mothers since 1970 is approximately equally attributable to divorce and births to unmarried women, but the overall average masks distinct racial differences. Divorce is the primary cause for the rising number of single white mothers, while out-of-wedlock pregnancies are the principal reason accounting for recent increases of black single mothers. Divorced or separated women raise two-thirds of the minor children being brought up by a single mother, including nearly four of five white children but less than half of the similarly situated black children. The mothers of half of these black children have never been married (fig. 14). However, the incidence of out-of-wedlock births by white mothers has been growing unabatedly in recent years.[9]

In contrast to divorces, out-of-wedlock births have continued to rise rapidly in the 1980s. Teenagers accounted for a third of the 828,000 out-of-wedlock births in 1985, compared to half of similar births a decade earlier. Roughly three of five out-of-wedlock births are first births. Currently more than a fifth of all births, and 60 percent of black births, are to unwed mothers (fig. 15).

Other industrialized democratic nations evince no clear pattern

FIGURE 13.

The proportion of families headed by females is rising.

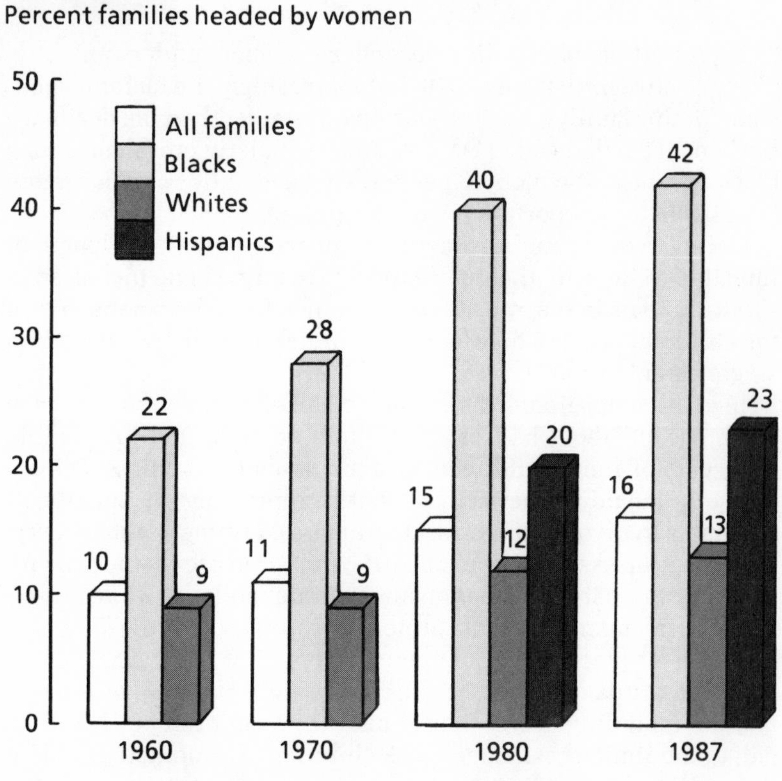

Percent families headed by women

Legend:
- All families
- Blacks
- Whites
- Hispanics

Data by year:

	1960	1970	1980	1987
All families	10	11	15	16
Blacks	22	28	40	42
Whites	9	9	12	13
Hispanics			20	23

Source: U.S. Department of Commerce, Bureau of the Census

in the proportion of births which are out of wedlock, ranging from one percent in Japan to 48 percent in Sweden. In both Sweden and Denmark, out-of-wedlock births may be more a product of cohabitation than of single motherhood. In a number of other countries, the problem of out-of-wedlock births is as grave as it is in the

FIGURE 14.

The mothers of half of black
children in female-headed families
have never been married (1987).

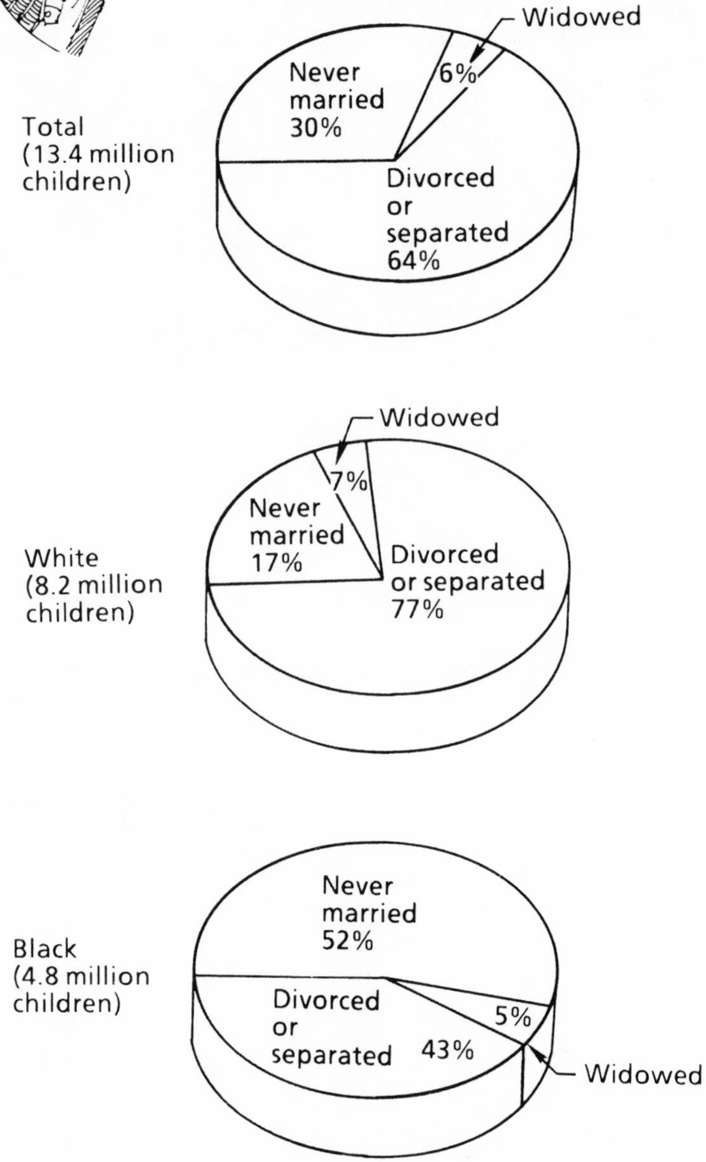

Total
(13.4 million
children)

Never married 30%

Widowed 6%

Divorced or separated 64%

White
(8.2 million
children)

Widowed 7%

Never married 17%

Divorced or separated 77%

Black
(4.8 million
children)

Never married 52%

Divorced or separated 43%

Widowed 5%

Source: U.S. Department of Commerce, Bureau of the Census

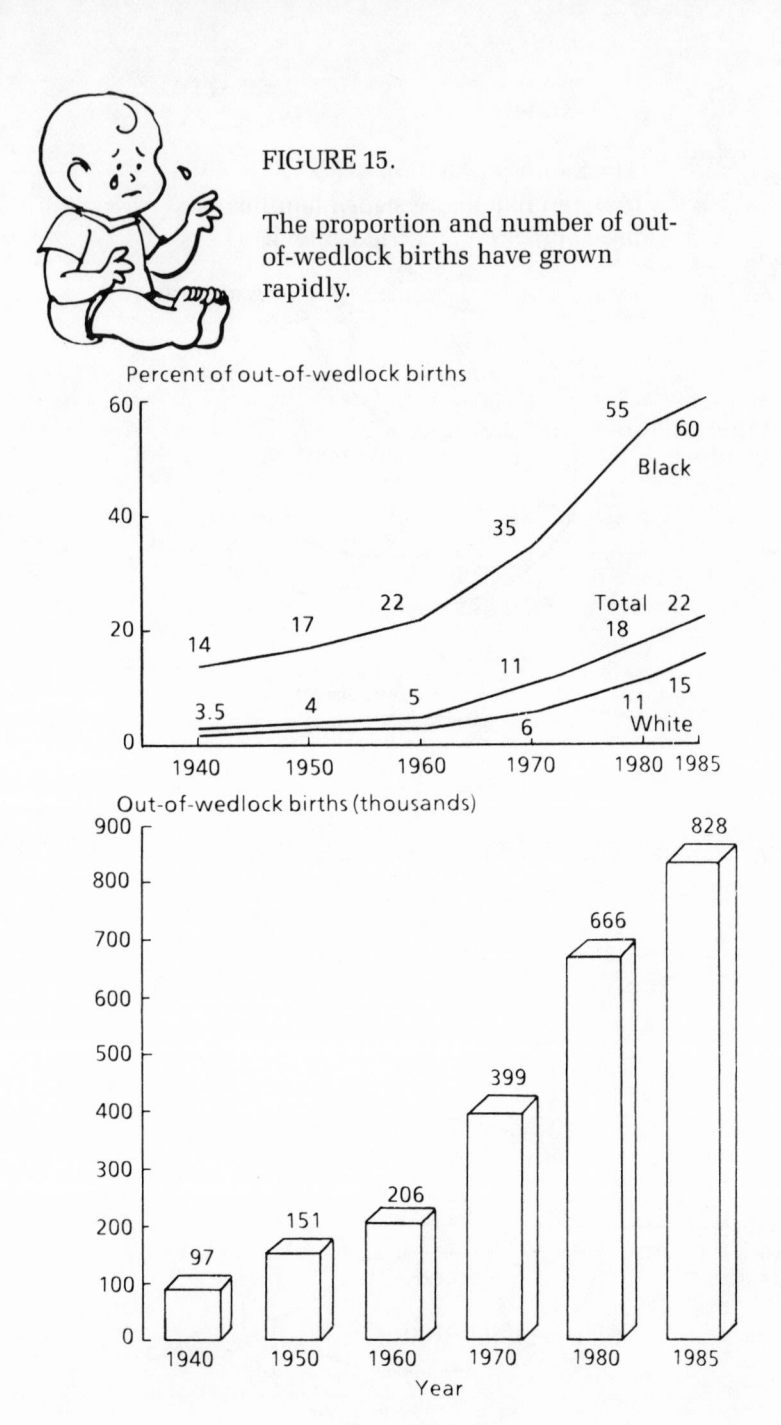

FIGURE 15.

The proportion and number of out-of-wedlock births have grown rapidly.

Percent of out-of-wedlock births

Out-of-wedlock births (thousands)

Source: U.S. Department of Health and Human Services, National Center for Health Statistics

114

FIGURE 16.

Out-of-wedlock births are a rapidly growing problem in many democratic industrial nations.

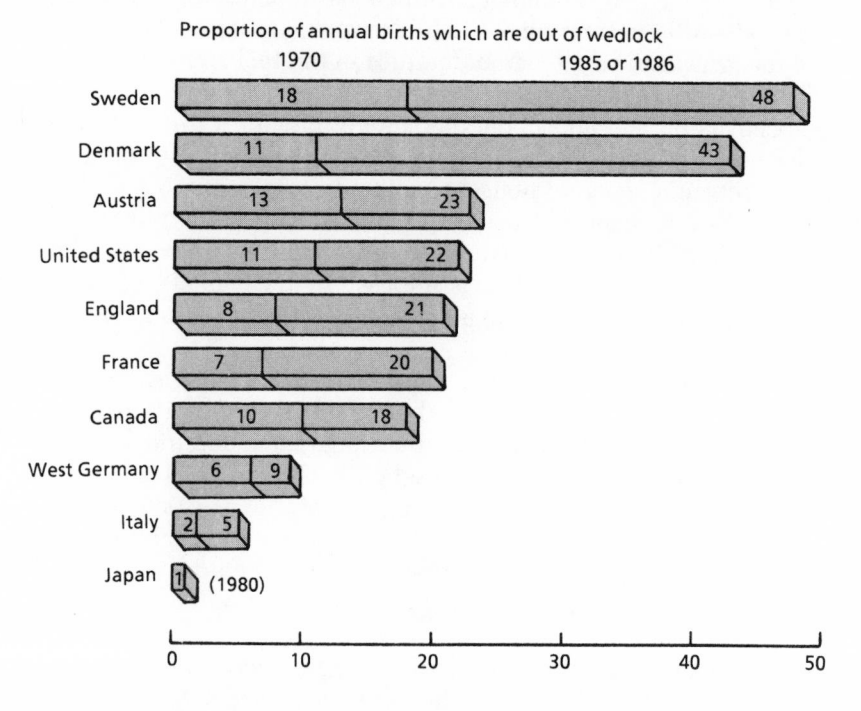

Source: Council of Europe

United States, and as in the United States the proportion has increased rapidly in recent years (fig. 16).[10]

While the U.S. growth in single-headed families is alarming, the problem appears to be stabilizing—but at disturbing levels—among the families with minor children who are of greatest concern:

Families with children under age 18 headed by single mothers

	Total	White	Black
1960	7.4%	6.0%	20.8%
1970	10.2	7.8	30.5
1980	17.6	13.4	46.9
1984	19.0	14.7	48.7
1987	19.7	15.5	48.4

Among whites, the growth of single mothers in the 1980s has returned to the more modest increases of the 1960s, while the proportion of black single mothers has apparently stabilized. Another recent phenomenon is that single fathers have increasingly assumed responsibility for rearing their children, accounting for 30 percent of the growth of single-parent families in the 1980s; these families have fewer income problems than female-headed families.

Census Bureau household data do not provide a full picture of the number of single mothers because they count only mothers who set up a separate household. In addition to the 6.3 million female family heads with minor children, another 1.8 million single mothers live with relatives or friends. Because the earliest comparable data are for 1983, it is impossible to gauge changes over time in the number of single mothers living with relatives or friends.

Single-parent families are far less common in Western Europe. In 1980, the latest year for which data are available, in no other country but Finland (10 percent) did single-parent families account for more than 6 percent of all households. The comparable U.S. figure was 13 percent. However, the rapid increase in out-of-wedlock births in Western Europe in the 1980s may have significantly increased the proportion of female-headed households. In Western Europe, as in America, divorced mothers headed most single-parent families.[11]

Politicians, pundits, and analysts (sometimes indistinguishable) have vigorously debated the factors responsible for the rise in female-headed families. Black single motherhood was once widely attributed to the lingering effects of slavery, but more recent research has indicated that married couple families predominated among blacks in the late nineteenth and early twentieth centuries. Also, according to Census Bureau data, young blacks were just as likely to marry as whites until after World War II. The relatively greater proportion of black single mothers compared to whites may have largely been due to higher rates of mortality among black men, a result of poverty rather than family abandonment.[12]

The rise in welfare benefits has been blamed for providing women with an economic incentive either to terminate their marriage or to bear children out of wedlock. To date this case has rested on anecdotal reports and has little evidentiary support, but AFDC has probably had some effect in increasing the number of single mothers.

In the 1980s, analysts began a long-overdue examination of the obvious missing factor contributing to the rise of female-headed families—men. According to one feminist writer, a male revolt against traditional family values began in the 1950s. Men's desires for both self-fulfillment and independence were mirrored in and stimulated by *Playboy* and other "male" magazines that unabashedly advocated a hedonistic lifestyle unconstrained by the fetters of family ties.[13] This thesis ignores repeated public opinion polls indicating that men prefer matrimony to bachelorhood, which is well reflected in their propensity to marry. In addition, divorced men are more likely than women to say that they are less happy after getting divorced, and more prone to remarry.

The declining earnings of young men over the past decade and a half may have contributed to the rising proportion of unmarried women with children born out of wedlock. If young men can't earn enough to pull their weight in supporting a family, they are less likely to wed. The average earnings of 20- to 24-year-old men who are not full-time students declined, after adjustment for inflation, by 26 percent from 1973 to 1986, from $12,169 to $9,029 (in 1986 dollars). The decline was particularly severe for blacks (46 percent) and high-school dropouts (42 percent), the young men who are most likely to sire children without marrying the mother. In 1986 the average young black man not in school earned 62 percent of the poverty threshold for a three-member family, and the average high-school dropout earned 78 percent of that threshold.[14]

The principal causes accounting for the increasing prevalence of female-headed families are divorces and loosening restraints on premarital sex, combined with ineffective contraceptive practices. In addition, the increased availability of welfare benefits and the declining earnings of young men also have contributed to the rising proportion of female-headed families.

Economic Realities

Of the major differences between female-headed and husband-wife households, those based on income are the easiest to quantify. Poverty haunts only 1 of 16 husband-wife families and 1 of 9 single fathers, but about 1 of 3 female-headed families. Female-headed families account for more than half of all families in poverty, and for more than a third of all poor persons.

The distribution of income among female-headed families is decidedly skewed toward the low end of the scale, in contrast to husband-wife families, and even households headed by men, where

FIGURE 17.

The income distribution of female-headed families is highly skewed toward the low end of the spectrum (1985).

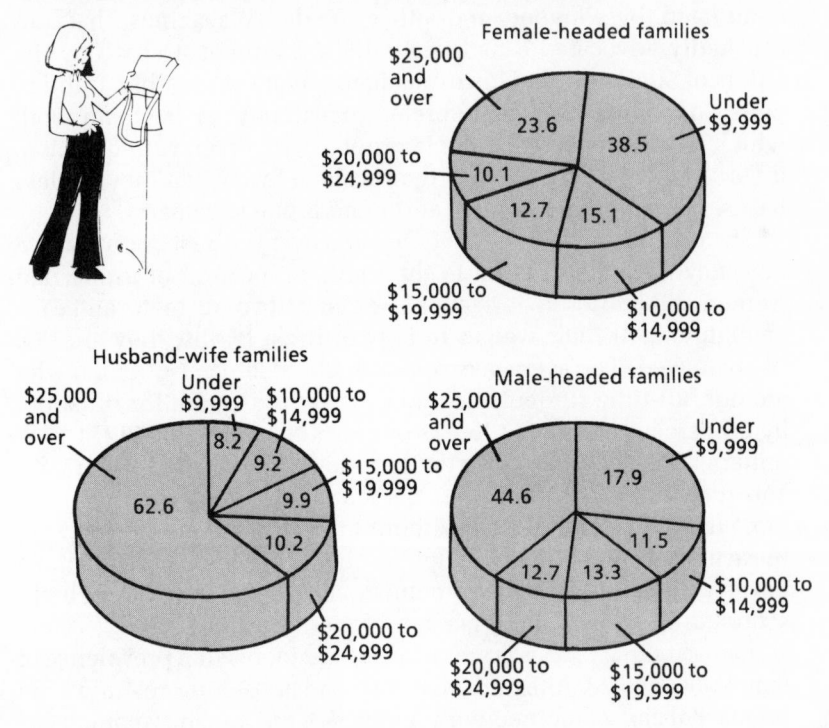

Source: U.S. Department of Commerce, Bureau of the Census

income distribution is skewed toward the upper end. In 1985, a quarter of the families headed by women had incomes as high as $25,000, compared with more than 60 percent of all husband-wife families and 45 percent of families headed by men (fig. 17).

The median income of female-headed families is less than half that of husband-wife households. Where dependent children are involved, the median drops to one-third. Female family heads with children under 6 years old have incomes on average only one-fourth that for female-headed households with no youngsters. Except for 1979, more than half of the families headed by single mothers with minor children have remained poor, and for single black and Hispanic mothers the poverty rate has consistently remained at about two-thirds.

Destitution of female-headed families is highly correlated with the age, education, and employment status of the head. Three of four 15- to 24-year-old women who head families are poor. The poverty rate among high-school dropouts is nearly 50 percent, compared to 16 percent for the women with some college education. Less than 19 percent of working women heading families are impoverished, compared with 55 percent of the women not working.

The females heading families who fall into poverty are extremely poor and likely to remain so for extended periods. In 1986, the income of the average poor family headed by a woman was only about half of the poverty threshold. The deprivation of these families is exacerbated by the fact that their poverty remains chronic. In the late 1970s (the latest period for which data are available), the average duration of poverty was as follows:

	All families	Black families
Single mothers	7 years	12 years
Two-parent families	4.6	6

Female-headed families also face a variety of other problems, many tied to their poverty. Single mothers are likely to complete fewer years of schooling, and because of their limited income they are likely to become overly dependent upon welfare. The children of single mothers incur the most serious consequences. Many exhibit school or behavioral problems. While only 13 percent of the children in two-parent families lack medical coverage, nearly a third of the children being raised by their mothers have no health insurance, and the majority would have no coverage without the federal medicaid program. Finally, the daughters of single mothers are themselves more likely to become single parents. Although many of these difficulties are associated with being poor, poverty only partially explains the increased probability of daughters becoming single mothers.[15]

The absence of a spouse undoubtedly handicaps single mothers in supervising their children, especially those who need greater attention. However, there is no evidence that a single mother's employment deleteriously affects her children. In fact, the income a mother can produce clearly promotes her family's welfare.[16] By 1986, two-thirds of the mothers with minor children, whether single or married, were working, although more single mothers were working full-time year-round. About half of single mothers in any given year are supported by the aid to families with dependent children (AFDC) program. Very few of these women have any other source of income.

Teenage Unwed Mothers: A Threatening Trend

In the past decade, the increasing prevalence of teenage pregnancies has deservedly captured national attention. Almost half of all babies delivered to teenage white mothers are born out of wedlock, and for black teens the proportion is a staggering 90 percent. Nearly a fifth of unmarried pregnant teens report that their pregnancy was intentional. Almost 300,000 babies of unwed teenage mothers were delivered in 1985. Since 1950 the proportion of births to teenage mothers which were out of wedlock has increased more than fourfold.

1950	13.9%
1960	15.4
1970	30.5
1980	48.3
1985	58.0

The proportion of unmarried teenage girls who have remained virgins has dropped from slightly over 60 percent in the late 1950s to less than a third currently. Most of the change occurred in the 1970s, and the proportion may have stabilized in the 1980s, but the most recently available survey data are for 1982.[17] In 1960 half of all married women had first tied the knot by age 20, but less than a tenth of the women now marrying are teenagers. Moreover, "shotgun" marriages seem to be out of fashion. Finally, while contraceptive use has increased significantly among sexually active teens, about a seventh take no precautions and a large but unknown proportion of the others do not use contraceptives either consistently or effectively.

Out-of-wedlock births would be even more prevalent except for the decline in the teenage population and the option of abortion. Following the postwar baby boom, the number of teenagers began to drop after 1976 and will continue to decline until 1990. Nearly three of five unmarried pregnant teens choose abortion, including two-thirds of whites but only 45 percent of minorities.[18]

After giving birth, the unwed teenage mother faces the difficult challenge of raising the child. In more than nine of ten cases, the teenage mother decides to keep the child; the others are put up for adoption or live with relatives.[19] On average, single black teenage mothers show a higher propensity to keep their children than do white teenagers. More than 80 percent of unmarried teen mothers live with their parents or relatives.

Unmarried teenage mothers are much more likely to drop out of school than are teenage girls who are not mothers.[20] Some of these women later manage to obtain a high-school equivalency degree, but a follow-up survey of 20- to 26-year-old women who became parents as teenagers suggests that they never catch up with their peers who remained in school.[21]

Age at first birth	Diploma	High-School Equivalency degree
Less than 15	23%	6%
15	24	21
16	28	21
17	38	15
18	52	10
19	68	9

Even when family background and other variables that attempt to measure motivation and ability are considered, being an unmarried teenage mother cuts short a young woman's educational chances.

As sociologist Arthur Campbell noted, "The girl who has an illegitimate child at the age of 16 suddenly has 90 percent of life's script written for her."[22] In most cases it is a bleak scenario. It will be difficult for her to provide for and raise the child. Her lack of education and other difficulties will make it hard to find and hold a steady job. She may feel compelled to marry a man she might not otherwise have chosen, and the chances are far greater than average that this marriage will not last.

Many of the calamitous consequences of an out-of-wedlock birth are of course borne by the children. Pregnant teenagers frequently do not receive adequate prenatal care, which may adversely affect the fetus. Later in life, the offspring of unwed teen mothers often do poorly in school and exhibit behavioral problems, and the daughters are more likely to follow their mothers in becoming pregnant in their teens. Society also pays a high cost for illegitimate births to teenagers. In 1985 the federal government spent $17 billion on AFDC, medicaid, and food stamps alone to assist poor women who had given birth as teens.[23]

A VEXING DISORDER

Sin is not a recent invention, and premarital conception is not new. Historian Richard Lingeman estimated that a third of the recorded births in Concord, Massachusetts, during the two decades prior to the Revolution were conceived prior to marriage.[24] This is roughly the same proportion as in recent years. Whatever the consequences of premarital conceptions in the past, the problem today is that the young women tend not to marry the fathers of their children, and if the wedding bells sound before the birth of the child, the marriages are far more likely than other marriages to end in separation or divorce.

While there is a high probability that a woman who either conceives or bears a child before marriage will wind up with a husband at some time, the probability is also great that she will again become a single parent. For the child born prior to the marriage, these circumstances may mean a series of traumatic experiences. The child may first face the world of a one-parent family. If the mother marries, the child for a while may live in a two-parent but unstable household that is likely to be shattered, thus returning the youngster to life in a single-parent household.

In the mid-1980s, premarital conceptions and births in the United States have continued to rise at a rapid pace. A decade ago, it was thought that increased availability of contraceptives, wider dissemination of birth control information, and a decline in the number of teenage girls would reduce out-of-wedlock births. Sadly, this has not come to pass. After increasing 29 percent from 1970 to 1977, the growth in extramarital births accelerated to 49 percent during the 1977–84 period, and jumped by another 8 percent in 1985 alone. This was not due primarily to a larger cohort of unmarried women: the birth rate for single women aged 15 to 44, which fell 3 percent from 1970 to 1977, rose 21 percent from 1977 to 1984.

The number of unwanted, terminated pregnancies will depend on the future acceptability and legality of abortions. Roughly three of five pregnancies to unmarried women currently result in legal abortions. For lower-income women, government programs to finance abortions have a major impact on whether a pregnancy is terminated. Federal legislation, sanctioned by the Supreme Court, cut off federal funding for abortions except where the mother's life is endangered. Only 14 states and the District of Columbia use their own funds, paying for 188,000 or 12 percent of all abortions in 1985. Several states have also attempted to make it more difficult for women to obtain abortions, and the Supreme Court has tended to invalidate many such provisions. For example, in *Thornburgh v. American College of Obstetricians and Gynecologists* (1986), the Court struck down parts of a Pennsylvania law requiring that women be warned about the dangers of an abortion. Nearly half the states require minor women to notify both parents or obtain court approval before getting an abortion. A number of these states, including most recently California, require parental permission for abortions performed on minors. In the fall of 1987, a federal appeals court invalidated a similar law, and another such case is scheduled for review during the Supreme Court's 1987–88 term.[25] The Reagan administration strongly supported banning or restricting abortions.

During the past few decades divorce has been the principal factor behind the rise in female-headed families, but births to unwed mothers are fast becoming nearly as important. In 1985, about 600,000 divorces involved children, but the number has apparently peaked. In the same year, roughly 500,000 out-of-wedlock births were first births to women who had never been married, and the total has continued to rise unabatedly in the 1980s.

Not only has the incidence of female-headed families grown in the past half-century, but the reasons for their prevalence have changed radically. First, widowhood is no longer the prime factor causing women to head their own households. As a result, the average age of the female family head has declined, and the chances are far greater that her household also includes children. This phenomenon has become pervasive throughout all sectors of society. Second, a growing number of these households appear to have been formed out of free choice as an increasing number of women have opted for heading their own households.

The word *family* used to evoke a picture of a husband, a wife, and their children living together in one household. Now, a variety of cameos surround the central picture. Rarely do these cameos portray the return of a separated woman to her parents' or grandparents' household, taking her children with her. An increasing percentage of never-married or formerly married mothers are heading their own households instead of living as a subfamily unit in someone else's household, exacerbating the precarious status of female-headed families. In extended families a divorced, separated, or never-married mother could count on the financial and social support of other adult family members to help provide for basic needs and ease such problems as child care. Whatever advantages a woman currently perceives in single parenthood over a bad marriage, most female-headed families find the going very rough economically. Even when they could combine, before the recent federal changes, work with welfare and other transfer payments, many female heads could barely lift their families out of poverty—and a significant number lived below the poverty threshold. Either by choice or by circumstances beyond their control, a large number of households are being run without the full-time presence of a man.

The increase in single-parent families has not been as swift in the 1980s as it was in the 1970s. However, a significant number of youngsters will spend part of their childhood in this family structure. Because of the deep-rooted problems experienced by women who head families, public policy must be concerned with ameliorating their deprivation and helping their children to enter the mainstream of American society.

Burdens
of the Black Female
Family Head

Part Three

FAMILY POLICIES:
SHORING UP THE HAVEN?

Chapter Seven

THE FAMILY IN THE WELFARE SYSTEM

> *Blanche Dubois:* I have always depended on the
> kindness of strangers.
> Tennessee Williams, *A Streetcar Named Desire*

PROBLEMS AND POLICIES

In the past, the family may not always have been the best haven from a heartless world, as Blanche Dubois discovered, but it was the main mechanism of support in times of trouble. However, economic and social changes in many cases have shifted responsibilities for individuals in need from the family to the state. Numerous families in the welfare system now depend on the impersonal kindness of strangers to help them cope and retain viable households.

Adjustments to dramatic economic and social changes never have been easy. During the initial wave of industrialization, workers may have obtained a higher standard of living, but at the cost of altered living and household arrangements. Older supporting mechanisms could not function in this new environment.

While industrialization created the conditions for rapid economic growth and rising living standards, it also brought new problems. The establishment of national markets and large urban factories made employment and wages highly dependent upon the vagaries of new economic forces; the unpredictable and invisible hand could stifle as well as uplift. Also, the factory system tended to depersonalize the relationship between employer and workers. Industrialization often reduced the skill level and social status of labor. A growing number of workers were required to uproot themselves and leave the land for jobs in the expanding factories located in urban centers.

Nuclear Families

The economic and social transformations fostered a rapid rise in the gross national product, but at a considerable toll. A growing urban poor population and the destruction of established household patterns were byproducts of these changes. Historians continue to debate how extensive the extended family was in American society, but the evidence is quite clear that the nostalgia for the extended family as a stabilizing social institution is greatly exaggerated.

When the United States was an agricultural society dotted with villages and small towns, it was not uncommon to find three generations all living under the same roof. But since relatively few people lived beyond the biblical threescore and ten (as late as 1920, life expectancy at birth was 54 years), three-generation families were not widespread. When they persisted it was by economic imperative rather than by choice. The extended family shouldered the responsibility for the care of its elderly members and other relatives who could not fend for themselves. The family filled the primary roles as provider of economic necessities and education. In addition to its varied functions, the family in effect was a social security system, but limited resources precluded families from fulfilling these responsibilities effectively or efficiently. Norman Rockwell's depiction of granddad going fishing with his grandchild is heartwarming, but if grandpa was still alive he was more likely to settle for a rocking chair than to indulge in physical exercise.

As the industrial revolution progressed, the family was overshadowed by other institutions in performing some of its earlier functions. Economic production moved from the household to the factory. New and expanding manufacturing industries required a mobile labor force, and people moved to where the jobs were. Beyond employment, the economic gains generated by the highly productive industrial sector provided the resources to create public education, health care, and other social welfare institutions. Before the New Deal in America—or Bismarck in Germany and Lloyd George in England—the destitute could only turn to meager private or public charity or to the poorhouse. Now, with a vast web of income transfer and in-kind programs, an individual has many more options. In providing basic education to all youngsters, the

"Our family is very secure, except for the possibility of death, illness, unemployment, separation or divorce."

government also supplanted a traditional family function that was performed very poorly in most households.

In short, most of the roles undertaken by the modern welfare system were at one time the major responsibility of the family. In framing the Constitution, the Founding Fathers did not assign the federal government any jurisdiction over family affairs. The various colonies had traditionally enacted legislation covering sexual behavior, marriage, responsibility for rearing children and divorce, and it was assumed that the federal government had no authority in the domain of family law.

While the extended family, even when it existed, was often not the wellspring of bucolic bliss depicted by some fertile romantic minds, it had several qualities that the more urban nuclear family could not match until the welfare system filled the gaps. Compared with the extended family, the nuclear family had a much higher potential of facing economic crises. Prior to the advent of the welfare system, families were playing a game of chance. If the breadwinner could hang onto a stable job with good pay, the household would be a winner compared with extended families or rural life. However, if the breadwinner died or had some mishap, then the members of the nuclear family could experience a wrenching form of destitution, since employment prospects for widows were extremely limited.

High mobility may have increased the possibilities for better jobs, but it has often reduced family and community ties and increased the sense of alienation and loneliness. As an indication of the rapid residential mobility within the population, the average American moves 12 times in his or her lifetime, and roughly one of five Americans moves each year. However, nearly two-thirds of all movers remain within the same county, and an additional fifth remain within the same state.

As mobility reduced the roles played by the family, the void was seldom filled by other private institutions, so the government established programs to shoulder some of the responsibilities once performed by the family. Most of these programs were designed to cure a specific social pathology—such as destitution among the elderly population—and no real thought was given to how a specific program would affect other family-related measures. The welfare system has become an integral part of our economy and society, dramatically influencing American family life and easing severe economic pressures.

Toward a Comprehensive Policy?

Although the champions of a comprehensive family policy (whatever that may mean) continue to be heard, the government has tended to intercede to address specific needs. Political candidates have rarely followed clarion calls for a comprehensive family policy with concrete proposals once in office. However, short of a comprehensive program, the government could take several important steps to enhance family life, including promoting child care opportunities; establishing parental leave policies for pregnancy, early infancy and family illnesses; and assisting families lacking adequate housing or health insurance.

Campaigning for the presidency in 1976, Jimmy Carter expressed a deep concern about the "loss of stability and the loss of values" within American society. The root cause of this problem was "the steady erosion and weakening of our families," he asserted.[1] The solution, Carter argued, was to design a strong "pro-family" policy that would encourage families to remain together. Such a policy would include a system of income transfers that would raise families out of destitution, encourage work, and provide the in-kind goods and services required to stabilize family life. Our lack of a formal, comprehensive family policy was the "same thing as an antifamily policy," he asserted. President Ronald

Reagan, on the other hand, believed that the federal government could be most helpful by minimizing intervention. Reagan's goal was to "return money from the federal budget to the family budget," and he declared that "there is no question that many well intentioned Great Society-type programs contributed to family breakups, welfare dependency, and a large increase in births out of wedlock." There was hope, however, for a White House report on the family declared, "Unlike Sweden . . . the mothers of America have managed to avoid becoming just so many more cogs in the wheels of commerce."[2]

Presidents Carter and Reagan touched on what appears to be a very sensitive theme; issues concerning the future of the American family have become highly controversial. But despite the rhetoric, neither president got around to drafting a policy statement on the family until close to the end of their respective administrations, and neither had any impact. Carter's 1980 White House Conference on Families degenerated into a noisy squabble between liberals and conservatives. At the time it was issued in December 1986, the main purpose of the Reagan administration's report on the family was to try to deflect attention from the brouhaha surrounding the administration's assistance to Iran and the rebels in Nicaragua. The report was quickly forgotten. President Reagan also issued an executive order in September 1987 requiring all federal agencies to attach a family impact statement to proposed regulatory and statutory changes, and paid lip service to the new rule in his 1988 State of the Union address.[3] But the order's vagueness will probably render it superfluous.

While some advocates call for the creation of new programs to improve family life, critics argue that the welfare system has contributed to the erosion of the work ethic and caused some of the difficulties experienced by American families. Welfare, the opponents charge, has not only led to family breakups, encouraging husbands to desert their wives and fathers to leave their children, but it has also made bearing children out of wedlock profitable. Charles Murray argues, "All the innovations of the huge, expensive programs of the mid-sixties and early seventies failed . . . I suggest you go to an inner-city neighborhood [to] get some sense for how much the world has flipped upside down for young people living in the most disadvantaged communities. . . . If I could make only one of my proposed changes in the welfare system, I would make it just about impossible for a youngster aged 15 to 25 to get any kind of welfare assistance."[4]

Another analyst has argued that the welfare system has created a new class of "helping professionals" who have taken over too many parental and family responsibilities. The new class of social engineers has allegedly expanded the scope of its activities into areas once left to individuals and their families, on the assumption that these helping professionals can do a better job than the one "wretchedly performed by most parents." But, instead of improving conditions, these social engineers have left families less able to cope in the world and even more dependent on the services provided by this new class. Just as the rural family became dependent upon a highly complex food distribution system, today's family must seek a growing list of supporting services outside the home. Despite good intentions, according to this formulation, the welfare system has weakened the family and forced it to turn to public resources.[5]

In a conservative era, a growing number of critics have questioned the efficacy and desirability of many government efforts. In fact, government activities affecting households were more a response to, than a cause of, changing living conditions. America does not appear to be alone in this trend, nor has it even been the leader. Most Western European countries have more extensive welfare programs, which antedate those of the United States. The decline of the extended family preceded the establishment of the social security system in the 1930s. Payments to the elderly may have given more senior citizens the chance to maintain households independent of their children, but this freedom of choice can have many social benefits for individuals and society. It is far easier to damn the growth of the welfare system than to fashion realistic social, political, and economic alternatives. Rather than having their in-laws move in with them, even most critics prefer the separate living arrangements made possible by the social security system. Given the radically unequal distribution of the total economic pie, American family life would deteriorate if the assistance provided by the welfare system were eliminated or vastly reduced. In most cases, government action was required because numerous families did not have the resources to cope with dire problems affecting their households. Far from leading to a weakening of family bonds, the welfare system enabled many families to remain together.

It would be more persuasive to argue that all too often the programs designed by the welfare system ignore the fact that most people live in families. For example, analyses of labor force measurements count individuals as employed, unemployed, or not in the labor force, too frequently ignoring the economic status of their families. The offical statistics treat an unemployed worker who is the sole support of a poor household no differently than one who lives in an affluent family. Economic hardship can only be understood when one considers not just the work experience of the individual but the total family income. Several major government social programs set their goals, collect data, and provide benefits on the basis of individual needs and do not consider the larger picture of household living conditions.

Despite their concern over mounting federal budget deficits, Americans still place a high priority on social welfare programs. A 1987 survey found that when asked whether they preferred reductions in defense spending or cuts in specific social and family-related programs (e.g., social security, health care, nutrition, education, and others) to reduce the deficit, a large majority of the American public indicated that defense should be cut.[6] Given Americans' longstanding love-hate relationship with government, it is understandable why calls to reduce government involvement in people's lives have coincided with a mounting effort to expand social programs.

It is easy to call for a coordinated pro-family policy on the campaign trail or during congressional oversight hearings. However, it is much more difficult to propose an acceptable package of programs that would win a consensus in a pluralistic society. Policymakers may agree on the desirability of "stabilizing" the family, but they differ sharply on the type of family that the government should stabilize. Some would tilt government policies in favor of households in which a husband is the sole breadwinner supporting a full-time housewife and several children. When the ethos was to move into suburbia and live the "good life," it appeared sound social policy to pass legislation favoring home ownership and a highway system that made suburban family life possible. Tax laws, social security, and other government benefits and obligations were structured in such a way that they encouraged household formations agreeing with this once-predominant social norm.

However, social norms have become highly diverse, and prospective changes in the structure of American families may increase this diversity. Husband-wife couples, who made up about 75 percent of all households in 1960, comprised 58 percent of the total by 1987. Even within husband-wife families there have been major changes, and more can be expected. By 1987 less than half of all married couples had children under 18 years of age in the house, compared with 57 percent in 1970.

With these changes in mind, should policies encourage a return to the family as some imagine it existed in the 1950s, or should they support and encourage currently diverse preferences? The appropriate answers are not at all clear. Some traditionalists view adjustment of our institutions—including education, social security, tax laws, and the health care system—to accommodate the new forces as fueling the fire that is destroying once widely held norms that they believe should be supported and sustained. Others believe that it is neither wise nor even possible to reverse the current trends in living arrangements, arguing that family policy should be neutral and even-handed to all types of household arrangements, thus avoiding the need to specify what type of family life the government is trying to stabilize. Still others want a family policy that is neither neutral nor protective of traditions; they advocate policies that would speed up the changes, or even would make it easier to split up a husband-wife family.

If strict neutrality sounds like a worthwhile goal in relation to household types, then the specifics must be considered. Should families that have children be expected to pay the same taxes as childless households that have the same income? Or should home-owning families receive favorable tax treatment vis-à-vis renting families? Strict neutrality may appeal in principle, but it would gore some favorite oxen.

Even if the ends could be agreed upon, questions would arise concerning the means of attaining these objectives. For example, how would fertility or divorce rates respond to specified shifts in the tax code? For that matter what legislative enactments change the basic trends that affect family life? Family allowances have failed to reverse falling fertility rates in Western Europe. Government actions do, of course, have a profound impact on many aspects of daily living within households, but there are limits to what can be realistically accomplished within constitutional constraints. And the experience with the proposed equal rights and abortion amendments shows the obstacles to achieving consensus by way of constitutional change.

What about Other Countries?

A comparison between several foreign countries' family policies and those of the United States demonstrates real differences in their approaches and programs. The Scandinavian countries are often cited as models of family policy. It would be difficult to duplicate similar programs in the United States. Some of the Scandinavian programs are not suitable for the American scene and may also have been inappropriate for the countries that tried them. However, the United States has been taking halting steps—even one or two during the Reagan years—to fit Scandinavian family programs to the American scene.

The major thrust of the initial Scandinavian family policies was to promote population growth. In Sweden, Gunnar and Alva Myrdal were among the first and most influential advocates of policies to increase the annual crop of babies. During the 1930s, Swedish economists and sociologists experienced dramatic changes in their views regarding demographic growth. Prior to the 1920s, social scientists in Sweden had believed that their country would be facing problems associated with overpopulation. Toward the end of the nineteenth century, the renowned Swedish economist Knut Wicksell had launched a major campaign that made Malthusian population theory a topic of household conversation. Wicksell was concerned that if their population continued to grow unchecked, Scandinavian countries would not be able to feed their citizenry and their per capita income would plummet, because population increases would vastly outstrip realistic prospects for economic growth. Initially Wicksell's views had received a cold reception, and he was threatened with the loss of his academic post for pressing his unpopular population theories. However, in time his views were accepted, and they became the dominant outlook.[7]

Sweden's population growth rate appeared to be out of control despite large-scale emigration. But within two decades the nation was equally alarmed by the possibility of a *declining* population. From 1920 to 1935 the birth rate dropped by nearly half, and in the latter year Swedish deaths exceeded births and the country had the lowest birth rate in the world. Population growth continued only because emigration had virtually ceased and the number of immigrants exceeded the emigrants.[8]

The situation raised deep emotional and ideological conflicts affecting all of society. Leading policymakers raised the specter of an "incessant and self-perpetuating liquidation of the people."[9] The outcome could not be left to chance or the market economy's "invisible hand," and active government policies were viewed as a necessity even by conservatives. Beyond national pride, the threat of depopulation posed other serious problems to the Scandinavian nations. The revolution in demographic thought coincided with the rising influence of Keynesian macroeconomic ideas. Declines in population could be a major force halting economic development, causing long-term economic stagnation, reducing demand for goods and services, and discouraging capital investment in new technology. It would also have the effect in the long run of producing dire labor shortages, and it could make a country more highly dependent upon other nations.[10]

Fears of depopulation and economic stagnation resulted in an expansion of the welfare system. The rationale behind reducing the financial costs of having and rearing children was that if the price of progeny were lowered, potential parents would have more children, just as they would presumably buy more of any other commodity if its price were marked down. A 1937 Swedish law provided free maternity care, obstetrical services, and child health care. The government also backed low-cost loans for home furnishings and other household items to newly married couples. In 1948 these efforts were expanded to include universal family allowances to support all children up to the age of 16, apparently with little consideration that the meager allowances could hardly encourage greater fertility. Later, the system was amended to include a rent allowance for households with children, and a supplemental formula was devised to provide a larger allowance to destitute families.[11]

Other Western European nations also provided family allowances to promote population growth. World War I and the uneasy peace that followed were an important stimulus. The loss of life was staggering, especially in France. Before the rise of more sophisticated weaponry, sufficient cannon fodder was a critical element in a nation's military strength. Currently, all of the developed industrial countries except the United States have family allowance systems providing some modest payments regardless of family income. Because the allowances are most often universal, the actual cash value has often remained small—typically between 5 and 10 percent of a country's median wage for the first child and slightly more for additional siblings.[12] France's program is the most generous. In the early 1980s, the annual allowance for an only child was equal to about $1,500 in 1986 U.S. dollars. Benefits are far more generous for additional children, and France augments the basic allowance by 24 other family benefit programs.[13]

Following World War II, the original justification for family allowance policies became less and less important, and the programs were integrated with other social welfare policies. Despite annual expenditures of 1 to 1.5 percent of GNP—the equivalent of about

$40–60 billion in the United States—Western European family allowances have failed to reverse declining fertility rates. By 1985, Ireland was the only Western European country with a fertility rate adequate to prevent a long-term population decline. In most of the countries, the fertility rate has been below the replacement level for the past 15 years, and the populations of West Germany, Denmark, and Austria have already begun to decline.[14]

Population policy advocates such as the Myrdals were interested not only in quantity but also in the quality of the next generation. Family planning support was provided to avert the birth of more unwanted children. Once the children were born, the next step was to improve the environment in which children were raised. The goal of the emerging welfare state was to assure that all goods and services deemed essential for parents and children would become either free or subsidized.

Family policy in Sweden in the 1970s branched out to consider other problems such as sexual equality in households. As in the United States, the Swedish tax code was based on the assumption of a household consisting of one male worker, a full-time housewife, and one or more children, but this model became less representative as women entered the labor force. To end what was, in effect, a marriage tax penalty, the Swedish tax code was revised in the 1970s to allow individual taxation for husband-wife families.

By the mid-1980s, Sweden had established a wide range of programs to assist parents in raising their children and to prevent unwanted conceptions and births. Contraceptives and abortion are generally provided free. Either parent has the right to take paid leave (with nearly full pay) for a year. In 1986, parents of one or two children received an annual allowance worth about $700 per child; benefits increased for additional offspring. The government has actively promoted child care opportunities since the 1970s. These family programs are augmented by generous retirement, health, unemployment insurance, and labor market programs available to all Swedes.[15] Thus, Swedish social welfare efforts were revised to better reflect the gradual replacement of the one-earner family by the two-breadwinner household.

Should the United States emulate this model of family policy? To be sure, some of its features could and should be included in American social welfare programs. For example, the inaccessibility of affordable child care undoubtedly impairs the labor market prospects of many American mothers, especially those who are single. However, the United States is far more heterogeneous than other democratic industrialized nations and appears to lack any specific central unifying principle, such as the former depopulation fears of other nations, which could unite American concerns in this area. Considering U.S. concerns about economic and environmental constraints on the nation's standard of living, it does not appear that pronatalist policies could provide the impetus to motivate an integrated American family policy. The emotions generated by the 1980 White House family conference—the last time a president attempted to establish a foundation for a comprehensive family policy—and some of the pronouncements of President Reagan on family policies are ample evidence of the obstacles that lie in the path of any attempt to formulate a consensus.

Instead of designing an explicitly coordinated family policy, the American welfare system has opted for a series of disparate programs that affect families. Avoiding a grand design, these programs have expanded gradually while adapting to changing needs. Most policymakers recognize that American families will remain in a period of transition and that the resulting society will continue to have highly pluralistic living arrangements. This view, however, is not universally accepted, and voices are raised exalting a puritanical or Victorian society that was not even suitable for its own time.

A policy that seeks to provide a basic living standard and essential services for all would ensure that children are not raised in deprivation; it would keep them dry, warm, and fed no matter what type of household they live in, and teach them the basic skills necessary to function effectively in the labor market and in society at large. A realistic approach to these problems would be, first, to examine the already existing social efforts in these areas, and then to determine what changes are desirable and attainable.

PROGRAMS AFFECTING FAMILIES

The United States may lack a coordinated family policy, but the government has instituted myriad programs that affect households. A 1980 study counted 270 different federal programs, administered by 17 different departments and agencies, that have a direct impact on American families; some of these have since been consolidated under federal block grants to the states.[16] The government's massive income transfer system touches most families in some way. Indeed, it seems almost impossible to establish policies that do not affect families. Like Molière's hero who spoke prose all his life but was oblivious to the fact, American public and private policymakers keep on designing new programs without recognizing their family implications. President Reagan's directive mandating family impact statements reflected a proper recognition of the problem, but his administration failed to advocate programs that would promote family stability.

The basic assumptions in programs concerning family life are often vague and obscure. Decisions that may have been responsive to societal needs during the 1930s may no longer reflect the shifting conditions and social mores that prevail today. Sometimes policymakers have ignored the ramifications of specific programs. Few politicians are on record as favoring policies that discourage marriage, but, as noted earlier, some programs may have such an impact.

Programs aimed at solving a specific problem unrelated to families may nevertheless have a tangential impact upon them. Reducing youth unemployment and retraining workers displaced by technological changes or imports have been the goals of several government efforts. That the alleviation of these problems could also have a beneficial impact on American family life cannot be denied, because workers with stable and sufficient earnings may be in a better position to lead stable family lives. However, family-related objectives often have not been explicitly considered in these programs, as their design or evaluation has tended to treat the target population only as individuals and not as members of household units.

Basic Needs

The state's concept of what constitutes basic needs has expanded during the past half-century to include food, income, health care, shelter, education, and social services. The welfare system has also responded to changing needs and conditions. For example, when the cost of fuel rose sharply during the 1970s, Congress added assistance for heating homes; in 1987, federal and state governments spent $2 billion for energy assistance. As the cost of maintaining a telephone rose, bills were introduced in Congress to subsidize telephone costs for low-income households. The Social Security Act of 1935 has been the cornerstone in federal social welfare efforts. In fashioning this legislation, the Roosevelt administration and Congress concluded that shifting economic and social realities had created conditions requiring federal intervention, because the then-existing arrangements of mutual aid—including family, private, and local assistance—could not meet the complex needs of an advanced industrialized society mired in a lengthy economic depression. In the early stages of drafting the proposal, some New Dealers advocated a social security system that included provision for family subsidies, health care, and maternity benefits. However, the final package was much less ambitious and limited to what were then considered basic necessities.

It remained for later generations to expand the definition of basic needs. Helping all families to obtain minimally adequate living conditions requires a sustained long-term effort. The problems faced by many households in need are due not so much to cyclical slumps in economic conditions as to deep-rooted structural problems within society. Efforts to provide basic needs for all households and to raise families out of poverty have met with some success. Deprivation and hunger have been significantly reduced, but not eliminated.

Despite conceptual and technical problems of measurement, the federal government has devised a poverty index that has gained wide acceptance. The index reflects the different consumption requirements of families based on size; the 1987 poverty thresholds follow:

Number of family members	Income
1	$5,776
2	7,399
3	9,056
4	11,612
5	13,743
6	15,534

The number of families in destitution declined significantly during the generation following World War II, but rose in the early 1980s owing to retrenchments in the welfare system, high inflation, and inordinately high unemployment. While more than one of every five families were poor at the start of the 1960s, this level had fallen to one of ten by 1980. Poverty rose again to one in eight families during the depth of the recession in 1982 before declining during the recovery to 10.9 percent four years later. The chances of being in poverty are highly related to family structure. A third of female-headed families are poor. Even more disturbing is the fact that one of five families with minor children lives in poverty (fig. 18).

FIGURE 18.

About one of five families with children lives in poverty.

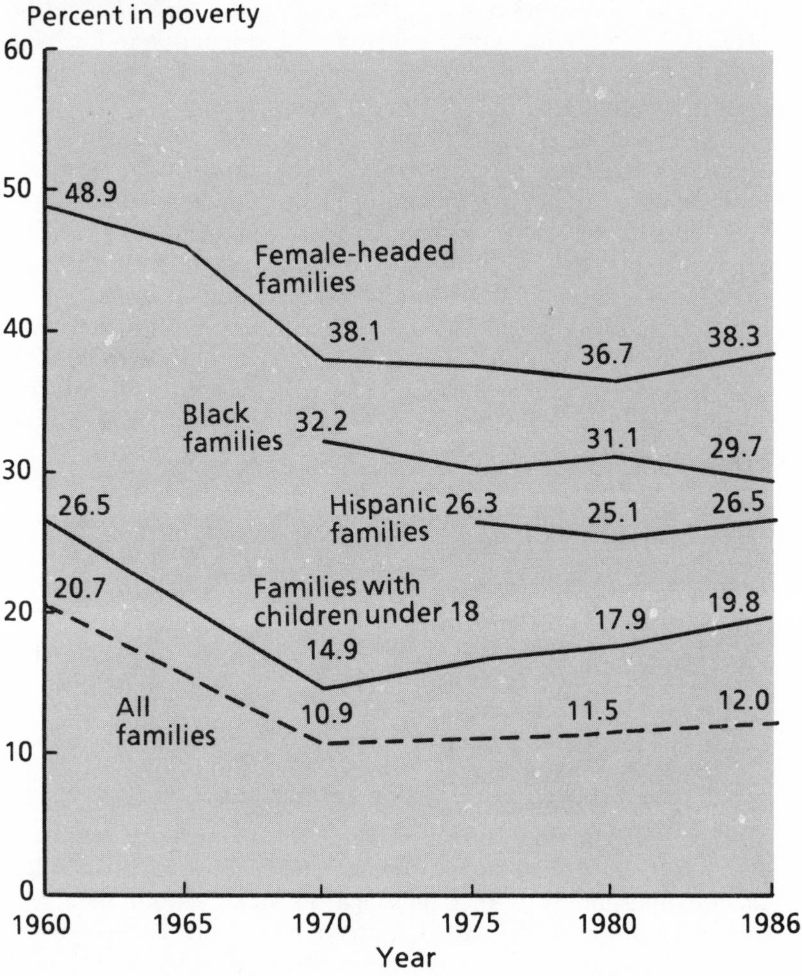

Percent in poverty
60
50
40
30
20
10
0
48.9
Female-headed
families
38.1
36.7
38.3
Black
families
32.2
31.1
29.7
26.5
Hispanic 26.3
families
25.1
26.5
20.7
Families with
children under 18
14.9
17.9
19.8
All
families
10.9
11.5
12.0
1960
1965
1970
1975
1980
1986
Year

Source: U.S. Department of Commerce, Bureau of the Census

The population of families in poverty also demonstrates other important differences in personal characteristics when compared with all American families. About one of six heads of poverty families has completed fewer than eight years of elementary school education, compared with only about one of fifteen for all family heads. Place of residence also affects the incidence of destitution. Rural families face a much higher chance of living in poverty than do urban households. Husband-wife families experience a lower poverty rate than other families. However, of the 7 million families classified in 1986 as living in poverty, 44 percent were husband-wife families, 51 percent were headed by females, and the remainder were male-headed with no wife present.

The principal economic support of almost 30 percent of all American families no longer comes from the earnings of a male head. In about 16 percent of families, there is no male head to provide any support. Also, with an increased percentage of wives in the workforce, their earnings plus earnings of other family members may exceed that of the traditional provider.[17]

Having an employed head may reduce the probability that a family will be in destitution, yet many heads are among the ranks of the working poor. A job for these working poor heads—even full-time employment—is no sure escape from poverty. About half of the heads of poverty households work during the year, and over 1 million of them work full time, full year.

Alternative definitions and concepts have a major impact on poverty estimates. In the absence of government transfer payments, about 18 percent of all American families would have been in poverty during 1986. However, government cash transfers are included in the official poverty index, and this inclusion reduced the proportion of destitute American families to about 12 percent. If the market value of medical benefits, subsidized housing, and food stamps were included, the percentage in poverty would be reduced even further, to 8 percent.[18]

Government programs may not have eliminated poverty within all families, but they have vastly reduced penury for almost all types of households. Destitution has been most highly reduced among households with heads age 65 and over. In 1986, over 700,000 families were headed by an elderly adult. Without government transfer payments, elderly couples in poverty would be six times as numerous, while the number of destitute families headed by females would have been 25 percent greater. While the free market has tended to reduce the proportion of families living below the official poverty threshold, many more households would have been counted among the poor in the absence of government intervention.

The welfare system has done very little, however, to aid the working poor, including two-parent families. Low-income families are frequently driven into poverty by the addition of family members (fig. 19). Indeed, family size and poverty are closely related, as half of families with five or more children are poor. A higher incidence of poverty among larger families is to be expected in a society where need is ignored as a factor in wage determination and where the lack of child care facilities often hinders the wife or female family head from earning needed income. As noted earlier, half the states deny AFDC to two-parent families.

In general, government policies to help the poor include four types of programs: (1) cash support; (2) direct provisions of necessities such as food, shelter, and medical care; (3) social services, including birth control assistance, child care, and compensatory and remedial education; and (4) the establishment of institutions—community action, legal services, and community development agencies—which enable the poor to address social, legal, and economic issues at the local level.

Various categories of families have different needs. Family heads and young people with their life's work ahead of them must have not only mere daily subsistence but also encouragement and support for acquiring the skills sought by employers. Children also need health care and basic education to promote opportunities in the future. For the aged and their families, medical care and nursing homes are of primary concern.

Government social welfare efforts and the system used to finance these efforts have a pervasive impact on family decisions. Government policies may affect the choice of a place of residence or the decision to purchase or rent shelter, and may have an impact on the determination to marry. The financial prospects of ending a marriage can be altered by government transfer payments and in-kind aid programs. Whether one enters the labor market could well depend in many cases on government child care policies. This is not to say that people just calculate economic costs and benefits before they make decisions regarding love, marriage, and family life. Any analysis that ignores the irrational and emotional aspects bound up in these decisions is likely to be off the mark. However, households cannot totally ignore the impact of government policies.

FIGURE 19.

Larger families face a greater risk of economic hardship (1986).

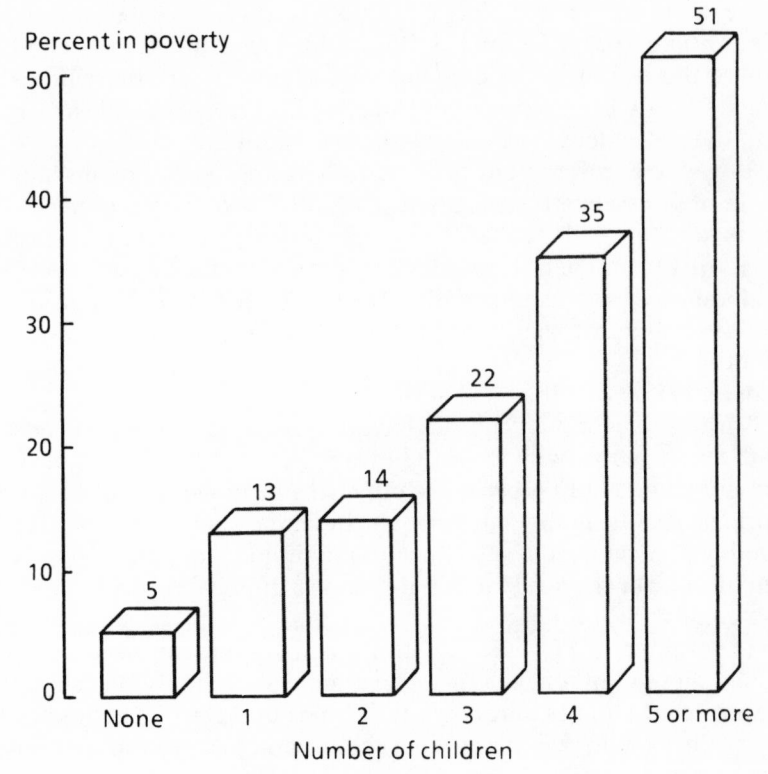

Source: U.S. Department of Commerce, Bureau of the Census

Realistic Goals

It is difficult to fashion social welfare efforts and the system to finance these programs without having an impact upon family life. A major problem underlying recent policies is that government interventions fail to pay adequate heed to changing family structures and attitudes about the diverse roles of families in modern society. The basic assumptions concerning the typical American family that prevailed during the 1930s, when some of the major current programs were initiated, no longer fit American family life. Furthermore, given the rapid changes that American families are experiencing, grand designs for a new comprehensive family policy are likely to be based on misleading assumptions or values that lack a consensus. Marginal changes in current intervention policies addressed to emerging problems are likely to be more productive.

Both Democratic and Republican administrations in recent years have shown a distinct propensity to oversell their proposals. The Johnson administration promised that the Great Society programs would "open the doors of learning . . . rewarding leisure . . . and opportunity . . . to everyone." The revenue-sharing system launched in the early 1970s was far less than the "second American revolution" touted by the Nixon administration. The "Reagan Revolution" has been equally oversold. After years of debate, numerous presidential proposals to combine welfare with work programs or requirements have failed to become law. A grand design of family policy is likely to meet a similar fate. While it may be far less dramatic, incremental reform of the already existing system provides the most realistic approach to helping families during this rough period of transition.

Chapter Eight

CASH SUPPORT AND MORE

> Each unhappy family is unhappy in its own way.
> Tolstoy, *Anna Karenina*

INCOME SUPPORT

Money does not necessarily buy happiness and love, as Tolstoy's picture of the wealthy Russian Karenin family clearly demonstrates. But statistical studies often indicate that lack of adequate financial resources can be a primary cause of family dissolution.

The Constitution entrusts the federal government with promoting the nation's general welfare. While efforts by the government cannot promise to bring bliss to all families, social programs can fill basic economic needs and thereby have an impact upon family structure and behavioral patterns. Since the New Deal, an expanding system of cash support and in-kind aid has been established to help families and individuals in need. The entire massive transfer payment and in-kind aid system is not neat and simple. Families with problems come in all shapes and sizes, and the vastly different household pathologies defy any one facile formula to provide all needed forms of aid.

Families and Cash Support

Inequality has been a problem in all societies. No system has distributed income evenly, nor necessarily should it. The reasons for this inequality of income are many, some desirable and others unconscionable. In the United States, family income distribution became slightly more egalitarian in the two decades following World War II, but in the next score years higher-income families obtained a larger share of the pie, as follows:

Income rank	Share of aggregate income		
	1947	1966	1986
Total	100.0%	100.0%	100.0%
Lowest fifth	5.0	5.6	4.6
Second fifth	11.8	12.4	10.8
Third fifth	17.0	17.8	16.8
Fourth fifth	23.1	23.8	24.0
Highest fifth	43.2	40.5	43.7

In 1986, when the poverty threshold for a family of three was $8,740 and $11,200 for a family of four, 12 percent of American families had an annual cash income of less than $10,000:

Income Level	Percentage
Below $5,000	4.6%
$5,000–$9,999	7.8
$10,000–$14,999	9.7
$15,000–$24,999	19.5
$25,000–$34,999	18.1
$35,000–$49,999	19.6
$50,000 and above	20.7
Median income	$29,458

In 1987, about one-third of all Americans received transfer payments from public programs amounting to $543 billion, mostly paid in cash. Government support programs are the mainstay of the typical poor family, which gets less than half of its income from wages, salaries, and self-employment (fig. 20). Transfer payments, equaling 17.1 percent of total disposable personal income in 1987, have become a significant source of income for many families— even some who exist well above poverty.

The Social Security Act, the product of over 50 years of evolution since its enactment in 1935, is the nation's most far-reaching public income maintenance program. The law's goal has been to protect families and individuals against the loss of earnings through two basic groups of programs: (1) social insurance programs—for the aged, the disabled, orphans, the temporarily unemployed, and veterans—which distribute payments on the basis of prior tax contribution or prior service; and (2) public assistance programs—for the elderly, the blind, the disabled, and families

FIGURE 20.

The sources of income of poor families differ significantly from those of all families (1986).

Income source

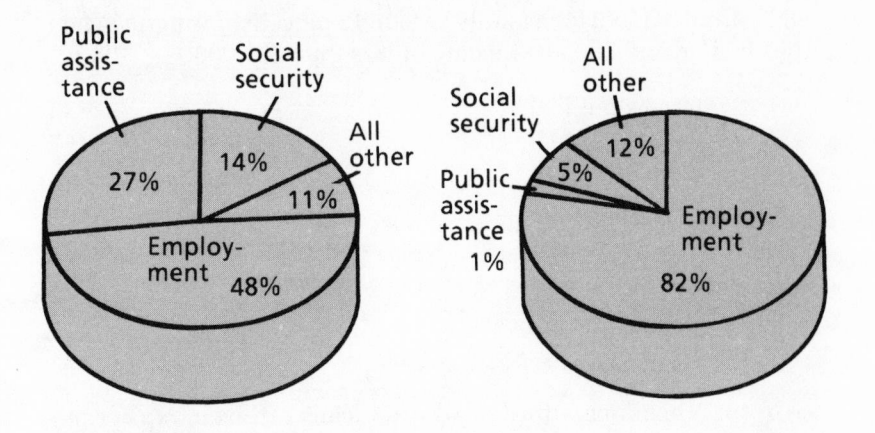

Poor families   All families

Public assistance   Social security   All other
27%   14%   11%
Employment 48%

Social security   All other
Public assistance 1%   5%   12%
Employment 82%

Source: U.S. Department of Commerce, Bureau of the Census

with dependent children—which provide income support on the basis of need alone.

The most comprehensive of the social insurance components is the Old Age, Survivors, and Disability program, popularly referred to as social security. OASDI primarily supports the older population, but 28 percent of beneficiaries are under 65 years of age, including 2.7 million minor children. Nearly one poor family in five receives these benefits. About 95 percent of all orphans would receive benefits if a parent were to die.

Old age insurance provides income to 95 percent of the aged population. The elderly accounted for about 21 percent of the nearly 90 million households in 1987. The proportion of all households and families made up by the elderly has increased in recent years, but far more gradually than is widely believed.

	Proportion over 64	
	1970	*1987*
Families	13.8%	15.9%
Households	19.5	21.3
Population	9.8	12.1 (1986)

This increase was due to economic and social changes, as well as demographic shifts. First, the relative number of individuals who live beyond age 64 expanded. Second, broader coverage and payments under the Social Security system gave many elderly Americans the financial means to run their own households. Accordingly, more and more of them have decided not to live with their children. The role of the extended family was declining even before the social security system was instituted in the United States, but federal insurance and private old age insurance have accelerated this trend.

Declines in the fertility rate have caused concern over the prospect of a vast increase in the ratio of dependent individuals to productive workers. Because OASDI, in effect, transfers income from the working population to the retired generation, some have expressed grave concern that the financial burden on workers will be too great. Current projections indicate that declines in the population below age 18 will more than offset the growing share of elderly through the year 2010. The "dependency ratio"—those under age 18 and above 64 for every 100 working-age persons (aged 18–64)—will fall from 63 in 1982 to 58 in 2010. However, the ratio of the elderly population alone for every 100 working-age persons is projected to grow rapidly thereafter, from 22 in 2010 to 37 in 2030. In the absence of further policy changes, this could place a significant strain on OASDI resources.

When workers retire, their initial benefits are calculated on their covered earnings, averaged over most of their working years, and indexed for inflation. The benefits formula is progressive, with a higher proportion of earnings replacement for lower paid workers. The average December 1986 monthly payment of $832 for a couple raised many retired workers above the poverty threshold. But benefits remain inadequate to raise some low earners above poverty. About 6 percent of aged persons 65 and over received supplemental security income payments, designed in part to reach those who receive minimal or no social security benefits. Three-fourths of elderly SSI recipients are women.

The original Social Security Act was designed to benefit retired workers; it aided their families only indirectly. However, the addition of dependents' and survivors' benefits in 1939 not only made social security a family program, it treated families much more advantageously than single workers. OASDI was designed to fit the needs of families as they were structured during the 1930s. The assumption was that in most cases the husband would be employed and the wife would remain at home to care for dependent children and therefore not qualify for social security on the basis of her own earnings. It was also assumed that, once married, a couple would stay together. Even at that time these assumptions were questionable, as nearly a third of women were in the labor force. But the equity of these formulas has been undermined now that a majority of adult women and wives are in the labor force and more marriages end in divorce.

One problem is that a wife's earnings result in higher total family benefits only if her entitlement exceeds the 50 percent spouse's benefit she receives based on her husband's earnings. In most cases, the two-earner couple pays far more into the system than a one-earner couple, but the added contribution and labor result in only minor benefit increases for the two-earner household. The proportion of women beneficiaries 62 or older who receive benefits only because they are the wife of a retired man dropped by half between 1960 and 1985, from 33 to 16 percent.[1]

The traditionalist family and gender assumptions embodied in the social security program were not challenged until the 1960s. Ironically, the catalyst for the initial changes was the program's unfairness to men. For example, the law provided survivors' benefits to widows but not to widowers unless they could prove their dependence upon their wife. During the 1970s, the courts struck down many discriminatory gender-based provisions, thereby increasing program costs.[2] Virtually all of the law's remaining gender-based distinctions were removed by the 1983 social security amendments.

Given the current benefits formulas and existing conditions within American labor markets, working wives' contributions to the OASDI fund frequently make a very small difference in benefits paid. If the assumption of the one-earner family were dropped, a payment formula could be devised to better reflect married women's significant role in the labor force. But any new formula is

likely to increase total outlays, and Congress is understandably reluctant to raise benefits.

The second problem concerning the equity of the social security
system grows out of changes that adjusted the initial assumption of
lifetime marriages to reflect a growing rate of divorce. Currently,
spouse benefits are paid to a worker's divorced wife, provided the
couple was married for at least 10 years. However, the benefits for
divorcees tend to be small—about $270 monthly for new retirees
in 1982, the latest information available. No distinction is made,
beyond the ten-year limit, for either the length of the marriage or
the wife's age at the time of divorce. According to a survey of new
beneficiaries in 1982, 7 percent of the women entering retirement
were divorced (about the same proportion had remarried after a divorce, but before 1984 these women were ineligible for benefits
based on their former husband's earnings). Although most of the
currently divorced women had been married for at least a decade,
only two-thirds of these women received benefits as the spouse of a
retired worker.[3] Current trends will both increase the proportion of
beneficiaries who are divorced women and make the inequities of
the program more egregious for these women. Currently, most marital breakups occur within a decade; these divorced women are not
entitled to benefits based on the earnings of their former husbands.

Two changes in the system could bring it into better alignment
with American family life today. One option would be to institute
homemaker credits for parents (usually mothers) who remain at
home to raise their children. These homemaker credits would be
paid without reference to need and would thus be tantamount to a
grant. Adoption of such a proposal would increase benefits and
therefore program costs. The idea has not received any serious consideration in Congress beyond occasional Mother's Day rhetoric.
The political reality is that in order to get the homemaker credit
adopted, it would have to be made so small that it would not alter
the problems of the one-earner versus the two-earner couple.

Another way to adjust the system would be through an earnings-
sharing principle. One form of earnings sharing might be to award
benefits to couples as individuals based on their own shared records. Besides providing greater protection to divorced homemakers, earnings sharing could equalize the benefits paid to one-
earner and two-earner couples. As Nancy M. Gordon has noted,
under earnings sharing social security records would become "another monetary asset accumulated during marriage," and the
shared records would, in effect, resemble joint property owned by

both partners.[4] Congress in 1983 required the Department of Health and Human Services and the Congressional Budget Office to propose options for implementing an earnings sharing system and to examine other proposals to better align social security with the contemporary family. The department's study made no recommendations but found that, unless current enrollees' benefits were guaranteed, all options would produce both winners and losers compared to the present program.[5] Of course, unless the reform would cut benefits, earnings sharing would increase social security costs.

On balance, the achievements of the social security system overshadow any inequities, real or apparent. The system has helped numerous families in what otherwise would have been difficult times. It has provided surviving beneficiaries, as well as older Americans, needed resources to remain financially independent and to maintain their own households. This does not mean that the benefit and contribution formulas should be rigid and not adjusted to reflect changes in American living patterns. Earnings sharing or other adjustments could be phased in over time without causing undue stress on the system, so that it would better reflect the record numbers of women in the labor force. Even with shifts in American household structure, the underlying objectives of the system make just as much sense today as they did when the act was passed in 1935.

In contrast to the social security program, which is federally administered, unemployment insurance is a federal-state program. It assists individuals who are laid off through no fault of their own. The states have established widely varying regulations affecting eligibility, including the level and duration of benefits. In 1987, the average beneficiary received $139 weekly for 15 weeks. With few exceptions, the maximum duration of benefits is 26 weeks. Only 11 states boost benefits for workers with dependents.[6] In three of these states, the maximum unemployment insurance benefit can be 50 percent higher for parents than for single persons.

Public Assistance

The Social Security Act also provides means-tested aid to families. The largest, costliest, and most controversial public assistance program is aid to families with dependent children (AFDC). Assistance is also provided to the aged, blind, and disabled through the supplemental security income (SSI) program.

AFDC is identified with "welfare" because it has accounted for most of the increase in means-tested income support since World War II. Despite these programs, over 60 percent of the families that receive public assistance income remain in poverty.

In 1987, there were 11 million AFDC recipients in an average month, including 7.4 million children, or one of every nine children. Direct care payments during 1987 totaled $16.5 billion. Though the federal government contributes more than half of the total cost of AFDC, it delegates administration of the program to the states, within broad federal guidelines. Most important, the states determine eligibility standards and the level of benefits. The grant paid to the recipient is based on need standards determined by each state, and varies widely among the states. The standard nominally reflects the minimal cost of rent, utilities, food, clothing, and other basic needs. In most states, however, monthly need standards fall far short of the federal government's poverty guideline for a three-person family, and the maximum state benefit is usually below the need standard, as follows:

	1987	Percentage of poverty line
Federal poverty guideline	$775	100%
Median state's need standard	428	55
Median state's maximum payment	354	46

In 1987, monthly payments per family averaged $360, or $123 per individual recipient, and ranged from $114 per family in Alabama to $533 in California and $571 in Alaska.

Fathers are "officially" present in only one AFDC home in 15. Over half of the AFDC families are members of minority groups. AFDC mothers have substantially lower educational attainments than other women of the same age level, and their work experience is also limited. Only 1.6 percent of AFDC mothers worked full time in 1986, while fewer than 5 percent worked part time or in some other capacity. Employed AFDC recipients earned an average of $276 per month in 1986.

Since World War II, AFDC has grown phenomenally, with the number of beneficiaries doubling each decade between 1947 and 1967 and again between 1967 and 1972, when the expansion virtually ceased (except for a mild increase during the recession in the mid-1970s), as the bulk of needy female-headed families qualified for assistance.[7] The reasons for the expansion of AFDC are many and complex. Not only did more people become eligible, but also benefits were increased and the stigma attached to welfare was reduced.

Population growth, especially among children, contributed to swelling the AFDC rolls. Federal legislation and judicial decisions also added to the welfare population by extending coverage to groups not previously eligible. In 1961, Congress allowed states to extend eligibility for AFDC assistance to families with an unemployed—but employable—parent, and 25 states have taken advantage of this provision. In 1968, the Supreme Court struck down the "man in the house" rule, which held that a man living in an AFDC house was responsible for the children's support even if he was not their father. The following year, the Court invalidated residency requirements for public assistance.

Numerous critics have charged that AFDC has significantly contributed to the breakdown of the family and undermined the work ethic of the poor. AFDC may be viewed as a response to economic and social conditions resulting from the rise of the single-parent family, but the program itself may induce families to modify their behavior in order to qualify for benefits. AFDC may encourage the phenomenon to which it is a response, by inducing a couple to beget children without getting married. It also may offer an incentive for an unemployed man to desert his family so that his dependents can be eligible for assistance in half the states, where families with unemployed fathers are ineligible for public assistance. Some critics have gone as far as to say that because of these negative impacts on families, welfare is doing more harm than good. Yet the data on these controversial and complex issues are far from unequivocal.

The evidence that the greater availability of welfare has contributed to marital breakups or has reduced the propensity to marry after conception is mostly anecdotal or conjectural.[8] There is little likelihood that AFDC has influenced the increase in single-parent families. In the decade after 1975, the proportion of children living with a single parent rose from 17 to 23 percent, while the proportion of all children receiving AFDC remained at 12 percent. It is possible that AFDC has influenced family formation and dissolution in the welfare population itself, but there is little evidence to support this claim. Contrary to popular impressions of large welfare "broods," the number of children in AFDC families has steadily declined. The proportion of welfare families with four or more children dropped from a third to a tenth from 1969 to 1986, and over the same period the average AFDC family size declined from four to three persons, mirroring the trend for the population as a whole. A formerly married woman who becomes a family head can expect a substantial drop in her level of economic well-being, even with public assistance.[9] The average maximum AFDC and food stamp benefit for a family of four with no income has declined in real terms by 19 percent since 1976, and half of female-headed AFDC families remain in poverty. Finally, a comparison of states with widely varying welfare payments shows little correlation between the amount of assistance provided and the incidence of single-parent families, out-of-wedlock births, or divorce.[10]

Another charge frequently leveled at AFDC is that the program undermines the work ethic of the poor. Although AFDC cash payments have trailed cost of living increases, a significant expansion in corollary programs (including food stamps, free school lunches, subsidized housing, medical care, and social services), on the one hand, and the decline in the value of the federal minimum hourly wage, on the other, have tilted the economic balance in favor of welfare over poorly paid jobs. A single mother with three children can, on average, obtain a higher income from AFDC and food stamps alone than she can earn by working full-time year-round at minimum wage rates, as follows:

	1972 (1987 dollars)	1987
AFDC plus food stamps	$9710	$7656
Minimum wage job	9049	6968

Moreover, the AFDC mother is automatically eligible for free medical care and does not face the day care costs borne by the working mother. In several states—for example, California and Connecticut—a single mother would need a full-time job paying nearly $6 an hour to match the value of the AFDC and food stamp grant alone. Despite the economic incentives of welfare, many recipients retain a strong attachment to the work ethic. However, many beneficiaries remain on the rolls for lengthy periods, which has prompted continued federal efforts to emphasize work over welfare.

Work and Family Welfare

Back in the 1930s, the AFDC program was viewed as aid to destitute widows who needed financial support in raising children. The female family head was not expected to work, but to be fully occupied in rearing her children. The social mores of the times did not encourage mothers with young children to become wage earners. Labor market conditions were not conducive to encouraging mothers to work outside their homes; there was a shortage of jobs even for married men, who were seen as more deserving of employment.

The demographic characteristics of AFDC recipients have changed radically during the past four decades. At present, only 2 percent of AFDC mothers are widows, and over half have never been married. Also, the number and proportion of nonwhite mothers on AFDC vastly increased. Meanwhile, the social norms regarding women and work changed significantly. As more mothers with infants entered the job market, a growing number of critics argued that welfare mothers should earn their living.

Prior to 1967, the benefits paid under AFDC were most often calculated as the difference between a client's own income and the maximum payment standard established by a state, although minimal work expenses were allowed. Benefits were reduced by whatever amount the family head earned. This "marginal tax rate" or benefit reduction of 100 percent created a disincentive to seek even part-time work. To overcome this disincentive, Congress in 1967 established a different means of treating the earnings of AFDC recipients. Welfare officials were required to disregard the first $30 plus one-third of the remaining monthly wages plus work-related expenses in computing benefits, even if this brought a family's total income (earnings combined with welfare) above a state's needs standard. This was viewed as an inducement to get AFDC family heads into the labor force and to encourage them to become economically self-sufficient. Yet the earnings level required—assuming jobs were available—to remove a family of four from AFDC is more than many AFDC mothers can command.

To complement the carrot of earnings incentives, Congress also required all AFDC recipients except those with children under age six to participate in a work incentive (WIN) program to gain work experience and to learn job search skills. Congress made few other work-related changes in the AFDC program until the 1980s, when the Reagan administration inaugurated a series of amendments. The most important was a stricter set of rules for counting a recipient's earned income. Previous administrations treated earned income leniently, both to encourage welfare recipients to seek work and to boost total income for poor families. In contrast, the Reagan administration equated any work with self-sufficiency, even if the job provided very low wages. The impact of the 1981 amendments was immediate and dramatic. In the following year, during the worst recession since the Great Depression, the number of families receiving AFDC declined by 8 percent—300,000 families. The General Accounting Office found that few of the individuals terminated later returned to the welfare rolls, despite sustaining substantial economic losses.[11] Ironically, the results of the administration's actions demonstrated employed AFDC recipients' commitment to the work ethic. Only a small minority quit their jobs to return to welfare, including some who could have economically profited by doing so.

Many recipients, however, remain on the rolls for years and could benefit by job search and training assistance. The median continuous length of time spent on AFDC is 2.2 years; however, because many leave the rolls for a period and then return, and because a few remain for a much longer duration, the mean total time on AFDC is 7 years for the average recipient.[12] Funding for WIN and other work-welfare programs—never very generous in the first place—has been cut by two-thirds during the 1980s.

An examination of changes in the welfare caseload over a period of longer than a decade shows that changes in family structure provide a better explanation of why individuals go on and off the rolls than do changes in earnings.

Reasons for entering and departing from AFDC

Entering	Distribution
Divorce or separation	45%
Unmarried woman gives birth	30
Drop in income	16
Other or unidentified reasons	10
Departing	
Marriage	35%
Increased earnings	26
Increase in transfer income other than AFDC	14
Children leave home	11
Other or unidentified reasons	14

In addition to the amendments affecting the earnings of AFDC recipients, Congress used other means to restrict access to the program. Since 1981, welfare administrators have been required to count the income of stepparents in ascertaining eligibility for AFDC. Three years later, Congress also required administrators to count the income of siblings living with a child who receives

AFDC. A third change liberalized AFDC somewhat by not counting the first $50 the family receives in child support payments from the father. The Congressional Budget Office estimated that these changes "saved" the federal government nearly $1 billion in 1986, when the federal contribution to AFDC was $9.5 billion.[13]

Amendments	Estimated impact on 1986 outlays (millions)
Tighten rules for counting earned income	−$330
Count stepparents income	−118
Count income of all family members living together	−140
Disregard first $50 of child support income	115
Impact of all AFDC amendments during the 1980s	−811

Welfare Reform

There are three basic strategies to replace or reform the existing AFDC system: (1) either a guaranteed income or a negative income tax; (2) child allowances; and (3) employment guarantees or wage subsidies. These approaches are not mutually exclusive and can be combined in a total package. While all three paths contain some benefits for improving family welfare, they also involve added costs and other drawbacks.

A negative income tax could, for example, guarantee a family of four an income equal to the poverty threshold (i.e., $11,200 in 1986). If a family with four members had an annual income of, say, $8,000, then they would receive a grant equaling $3,200. However, guaranteeing a poverty-level income would be expensive. Also, it might reduce the pecuniary incentives to work for millions of families, because their incomes would remain at the poverty threshold whether or not they held jobs. To counter this possibility, any workable plan must allow low-wage workers to keep at least a portion of their earned income. For example, half the earnings of low-income families might be exempt. Thus, a family of four with an income of $8,000 would count only $4,000 for tax purposes and obtain a total income of $13,200, compared with the $11,200 maximum paid to a family without a wage earner.

Finding consensus on a formula for a negative income tax has proven to be difficult. If the guarantee is set too low, it will leave many families and individuals in dire economic hardship. If it is set too high, then many families significantly above poverty will be able to claim benefits. Yet incentives must be attractive enough to induce able-bodied workers to contribute to their family's support. A low tax rate is of no help to those who cannot work, while a high benefit level may draw able-bodied workers out of the labor market. Combining a high benefit level with a low tax rate would qualify many middle-income families. Ever present as a constraint on benefits and incentives is the cost of such a program. Public debate about the efficacy of a negative income tax has been abandoned during the 1980s. Whether a negative income tax will be revived after the Reagan administration is doubtful considering the costs and potential side-effects of the plan.

During the early 1970s, the federal government financed a large-scale experiment to test the impact of a negative income tax. The families involved received a guaranteed income equal to 95, 120, or 140 percent of the poverty line, and within these groups a variety of tax rates were applied to the participants' earned income. Marital breakups increased compared to a control group, although this result is extremely puzzling. First, the *lowest* guaranteed income had the greatest impact on marital instability, with breakup rates increasing by 50 to 60 percent compared to the control group. In contrast, the most generous benefit slightly increased family stability. Second, guaranteeing an income equal to 95 percent of the poverty line was roughly equivalent to prevailing welfare benefits at the time (but much more generous than current benefits), which individuals in the control group received. If anything, the negative income tax recipients might have been expected to have more stable families, because unlike the welfare system, two-parent couples obtained more generous benefits. While inexplicable, the results indicate the many imponderables associated with the implementation of a negative income tax.[14]

Another method of providing cash assistance is to pay families with children an allowance to supplement their own income to meet some portion of the costs of childrearing. This proposal recognizes that the wage system alone distributes income inadequately, because wages are based on productivity or tradition rather than on need. The underlying justification for family allowances is that a child's well-being should concern society as a whole.

The United States, as noted, is the only advanced industrialized nation without a family allowance program. Except for adjustments in income tax deductions, the take-home pay for a bachelor is usually the same as for the head of a family with dependents in an identical job. The armed forces are unique in having traditionally adjusted compensation based on the number of dependents. In many countries nearly all children are eligible for subsidies, while in others no benefits are paid for the first or second child. Benefits are usually paid for children up to the age they would normally leave school, but they may be extended for further schooling, training, or apprenticeship. The allowance per child may also vary.

Family allowance programs are not a complete alternative to a guaranteed income because many people living in poverty do not have children: the 1986 poverty rate for unrelated individuals was 22 percent, higher than the rate for families with minor children. However, a program that would give benefits to all children probably would find broader political support than any other alternative. On the other hand, a meaningful family allowance plan would entail high costs. An examination of seven industrialized countries' allowance policies showed that these nations devoted about one percent of GNP to allowances—over $40 billion in 1986 U.S. dollars. But even the generous benefits offered in France compensated for only about a sixth of the cost of raising a child, according to one estimate, and to equal French allowances the United States would have to spend $60 billion annually.[15]

A third alternative strategy to reform welfare and assist poor families is either to create jobs or to subsidize wages. In the late 1970s the United States took several halting steps in this direction, but the effort was short-lived. Public job slots under the Comprehensive Employment and Training Act reached a peak of 750,000 in 1978. President Carter's unsuccessful welfare reform proposal envisioned doubling the number of public service jobs. Support for a full employment policy grew steadily during the decade. The Comprehensive Employment and Training Act provided for federal jobs when unemployment exceeded 4.5 percent, but succeeding Congresses as well as presidents Carter and Reagan ignored the law. Finally, in 1977 Congress provided a generous tax credit to employers who hired additional workers. The credit diminished revenue by over $4 billion in one year and was replaced in 1978 by the targeted jobs tax credit, which provides a tax break to employers who hire poor youth, young adults, and welfare recipients. The program will cost the treasury an estimated $300 million in 1988 to subsidize the hiring of over half a million individuals.[16]

Because poverty remains a persistent problem, any serious attempt to reform the welfare system would entail considerable costs. Employment and training programs, which emphasize the work ethic in addition to supplying needed income, are preferable to either a negative income tax or family allowances. However, tax and allowance measures targeted to the needy can play a useful supporting role in ameliorating family financial difficulties. The principle of the negative income tax is embodied in the current earned income tax credit, available to poor families with children. A realistic program would view work as complementing welfare and not force recipients to choose either work or welfare. The underlying justification would be the recognition that millions of Americans will remain among the working poor—even if they can find and keep a steady job.

Other programs such as general assistance, workers' compensation, and veterans' and private pensions are all part of a system designed to help households cope and to mitigate many different pathologies and social needs. The entire system is far from unified or simple, and it does not satisfy advocates of a comprehensive and integrated plan.

IN-KIND AID

It has been argued that a negative income tax, a family allowance system, and other cash support programs could replace in-kind goods and services provided to needy households by the government. However, families in need require in-kind goods and services as well as cash support. The view that all in-kind aid can be "cashed out" rests on several highly questionable claims. In many cases it is unrealistic to expect that the private sector will provide these essential goods and services, even if families are given added cash support. For many reasons, poor families face numerous handicaps, or roadblocks, in purchasing essential goods and services from private suppliers. A realistic public policy must include both cash support and in-kind aid.

To help the poor, the government has increasingly invested greater resources in in-kind rather than cash assistance. While the provision of goods and services accounted for only one-fifth of federal outlays to poor households in 1964, it increased to over half within four years and to 72 percent of all antipoverty outlays by 1986 (fig. 21). The growing reliance on providing goods and services can be traced, in part, to longstanding public skepticism concerning the moral character and reliability of poor households. The

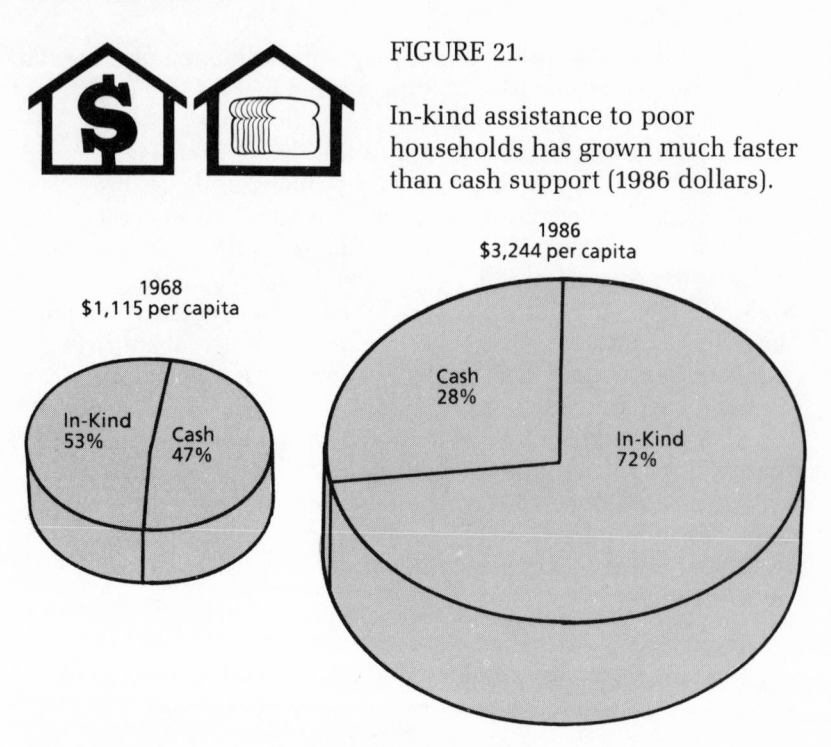

FIGURE 21.

In-kind assistance to poor households has grown much faster than cash support (1986 dollars).

1968
$1,115 per capita

In-Kind
53%

Cash
47%

1986
$3,244 per capita

Cash
28%

In-Kind
72%

Source: U.S. Library of Congress, Congressional Research Service

fear is that if only cash support were given, the funds would not be used to purchase food, shelter, and medical care. But because of the isolation of some needy families and shortcomings in the market mechanism, it has been recognized that more than cash is required. It is doubtful that all of these services, with the exception of food, would be provided to needy families by the private suppliers without some government efforts in these areas.

The Next Generation

Beyond coping with existing family-related difficulties, several government programs have aimed at preventing such problems. Assisting couples in keeping family size within their desires and means will aid the next generation to begin at less of a disadvantage. Providing care to preschool children can alleviate some family pressures and help family heads—and potential second wage earners—enter the labor force. Education policies can have a significant impact on family life.

Not only has there been a marked increase in the number of adults who use some form of birth control, but the types of methods they use have changed and improved in quality. The laws associated with birth control have also changed. In 1973 the Supreme Court struck down restrictive state laws regarding abortion, especially during the first three months of pregnancy.

National opinion research indicates vast changes in attitudes toward abortion. In 1968, about seven of eight adults opposed abortions based solely on the desire not to have another child, but by the 1980s the proportion had dropped to three of five.[17] Similarly, the percentage of adult Americans who believed that birth control information should be available to anyone who wants it rose from 73 in 1959 to over 90 by the end of the 1970s. The largest change in attitudes on this matter has occurred among Catholics. Attitudes toward premarital sex have also undergone radical change. In 1987, according to a Gallup poll, 46 percent of adults considered the practice wrong, compared with 68 percent two decades earlier.[18]

Changes in bedroom technology and law notwithstanding, unwanted and unplanned births remain a too frequent occurrence. The incidence of unwanted births is greater for lower income and poorly educated households. One study found that a woman with a college degree has only about an 8 percent chance of having an unwanted birth, but for women who have not completed a high school education this chance increases to roughly 33 percent.[19] The evidence is clear that limited access to birth control devices and family planning services has deprived many women unable to afford medical care of the same degree of choice open to more affluent women.

In 1985 about 5 percent of all females between the ages of 15 and 19 became pregnant, accounting for 470,000 births. Of this total, three-fifths were born out of wedlock. There is ample evidence that a teenage single mother is going to face many difficult problems. In many cases, both mother and child end up on welfare. In 1984, for example, 54 percent of all women receiving AFDC had been teenagers when they first became mothers.[20] Even if teenage parents do marry and support their offspring, their education is still likely to be interrupted and their job opportunities may be limited for life. There is also considerable evidence that early parenthood leads to larger families and a higher incidence of divorces, placing continuing economic and emotional burdens upon the household.

About 9.5 million poor and near-poor women were in need of organized family planning services in 1983, the latest year for which data are available. The cost of providing a patient with a gynecological examination and birth control devices is about $70 a year. While funding of birth control information and devices increased dramatically during the late 1960s and 1970s, it did not meet total potential demand. In the 1980s, federal and state funding for contraceptive services has declined by about 10 percent after adjusting for inflation. Estimated funding in 1987 was a little over $400 million, primarily from medicaid and the family planning program operating under Title X of the Public Health Service Act. Inadequacy of funds is endemic to social programs but appears less justified in the case of birth control efforts whose cost effectiveness is well proven. The increasing support for federal programs providing family planning services to women who need and desire them reflects the expanded consensus that fertility control is not only a valuable contribution to family life but also an effective measure in preventing poverty. Accordingly, all states participating in medicaid are required to provide such services. The goal is to expand services in areas with high out-of-wedlock birth rates.

The number of women served by organized programs rose from fewer than 900,000 in 1968 to 5 million 15 years later (fig. 22). Over four of five clients had incomes of less than 150 percent of the poverty level. However, nearly half of low-income women at risk of an unintended pregnancy did not receive subsidized family planning services. Public assistance recipients made up one-eighth of the women served by ongoing programs.[21]

Federal support of child care has remained an important political issue. Most child care arrangements are informal, either in the child's or the caretaker's home, although the number of licensed child care centers and nursery schools has risen rapidly since the 1960s. About 2 million children under age 5 participate in some form of preschool or formal out-of-home child care program. Government efforts and support have had a major influence on this growth. Various government social programs permit the use of at least a portion of the funds for child care, but several programs provide the bulk of the assistance. The Head Start program received $1.1 billion in 1987 to provide education and day care to about 450,000 poor children. Nearly a fifth of the social services program (Title XX of the Social Security Act), funded at roughly $5 billion from all levels of government in 1987, is devoted to child care. In

FIGURE 22.

The number of patients receiving organized family planning services has increased vastly during the past two decades.

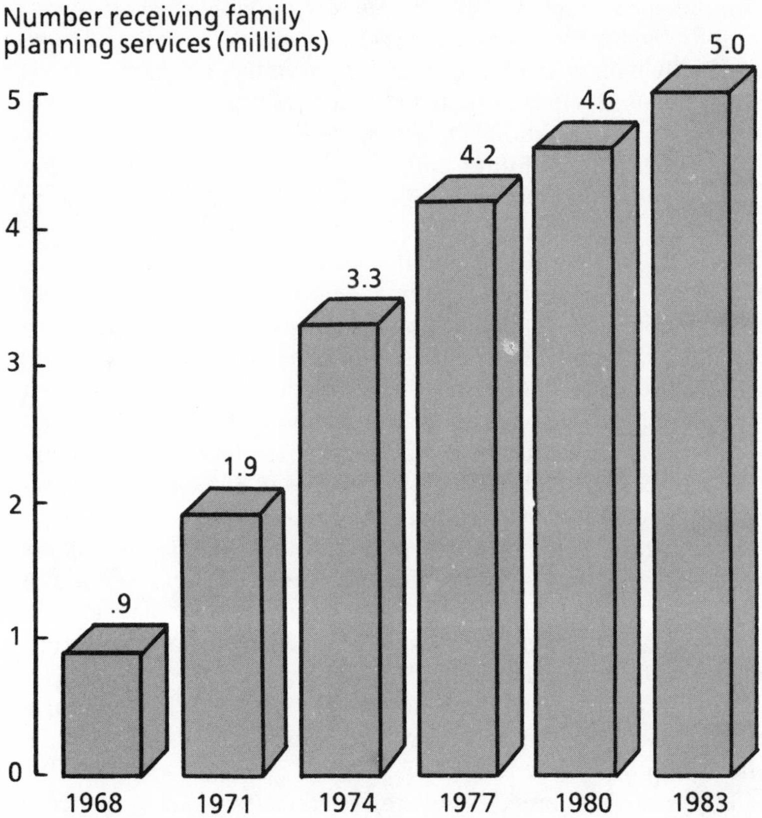

Number receiving family planning services (millions)

[Bar chart showing:
- 1968: .9
- 1971: 1.9
- 1974: 3.3
- 1977: 4.2
- 1980: 4.6
- 1983: 5.0]

Source: Aida Torres and Jacqueline Darroch Forrest, "Family Planning Clinic Services in the United States, 1983," *Family Planning Perspectives* (January/February 1985): 32–33

addition, the child care food program provided $537 million for meals for about 1.1 million poor children daily in day care centers in 1987.[22]

A federal tax credit is the most important federal child care subsidy for the nonpoor. Congress initially created a tax deduction in 1954 for employment-related child care expenses borne by low-income women, widowers, and divorced or separated men. Over the next two decades, Congress extended the deduction to tax filers with higher incomes. In 1976 the deduction was replaced with a tax credit, which made the tax break more accessible to low earners (who rarely itemize deductions) and more valuable to all filers. Tax credits are more generous than deductions because they reduce tax liability, while deductions merely reduce taxable income.

The congressional Joint Committee on Taxation estimated that in 1988 8.4 million filers will claim the child care credit, at a loss to the treasury of $3.5 billion—over five times the revenue loss a decade earlier. The credit is generally available only to single-parent families or to two working parents. Families with adjusted gross annual incomes of $10,000 or less receive a credit equal to 30 percent of their employment-related child care expenses up to $2,400 for one child and $4,800 for two or more children. The 30 percent credit is reduced by one percentage point for every $2,000 in increased annual income over $10,000, but not lower than 20 percent. Thus, families with adjusted gross incomes of $30,000 or more receive a 20 percent credit for their allowable child care expenses.

Despite the expansion of the child care tax break, it still benefits very few low-income families, who account for less than a tenth of filers using the credit. Since the 1986 tax reform law drastically reduced income taxes for poor families, the child care provision (unchanged by Congress in 1986) will be of even less benefit to the poor in future years. Another important reason why poor families have not benefited from the provision is that they tend to rely on free child care provided by relatives.

Child care combined with early education not only frees mothers to work outside the home but also helps improve the future school record of children from poor families. While expansion of child care combined with teaching the ABCs entails considerable costs, low fertility rates will help contain these outlays. The alternative costs that must be paid for not providing child care services should also be considered. Working mothers and their children would be well served by child care programs provided within the existing public school system. These programs would be open to all families on an equal basis and would avoid the segregation of children by race and class that is inherent in programs where participation is based on income. Federal guidelines and monitoring would be required to ensure proper care for all and to provide for the special needs of children from low-income families. Child care facilities remain relatively scarce, and proposals to expand such services remain high on the agenda of almost all family policy advocates.

Health Care, Food, and Shelter

Beyond programs for the next generation, in-kind aid has vastly reduced economic hardship by helping families meet their basic needs for health care, food, and shelter. However, shifting family conditions have affected several basic assumptions contained in these programs.

Although we do not practice it, under the current concept of the welfare system a basic minimal level of medical treatment is in theory viewed as a right not dependent upon the financial condition of an individual family. Since the passage of medicare and medicaid in 1965, the federal government has assumed the major responsibility as the provider of health care for the aged and the poor. Despite massive federal and state expenditures of over $150 billion annually, the deficit in health care remains startling, whether measured in life expectancy, infant mortality rate, or numbers of visits to physicians or dentists. In general, adults and children in husband-wife families experience fewer health problems than individuals in other household structures when the data are adjusted for differences including race, age, and other variables. However, it is not clear that a true cause-and-effect relationship exists between health problems and family structure. It could be, for example, that single-parent families have more health-related problems because they tend to have lower incomes than two-adult families. Whatever the path of causation, a higher proportion of children and adults in broken families have serious medical problems—and they have fewer resources to cope with these difficulties.

Medicare covers the bulk of short-term hospital and medical costs for elderly or disabled social security beneficiaries. All social security and railroad retirement recipients and others who meet special qualifications are entitled to medicare hospital insurance. In 1987 about 31 million persons were covered. Medicare provisions have helped a growing number of elderly Americans maintain their own households. It is a universal program designed to help the elderly regardless of their income. No doubt medicare has kept many near-poor elderly out of poverty, and it has eased the anxieties of those elderly whose life savings would have been wiped out. The medicare program spent $79.7 billion in 1987.

Despite medicare's importance, the program gave beneficiaries very little protection against catastrophic or long-term illnesses, providing only two months of free hospital care. As of January 1988 both houses of Congress had enacted separate bills expanding hospital coverage to a full year, and capped out-of-pocket costs for non-drug-related services to no more than $1,587 or $1,850 (depending upon the bill that is finally approved) in any given year. Nearly a million of the aged annually pay medical bills of at least this much. Under the separate proposals, medicare would also pay 80 percent of outpatient drug costs beyond either $500 or $600 a year. The proposed benefits are to be financed by phased-in premiums that will cost almost $8 monthly by 1993; higher income beneficiaries would pay increased premiums.[23]

Medicaid was launched in 1965 to replace a fragmented public health care system for the poor. Eligibility for medicaid is primarily linked to eligibility for AFDC and the federal supplemental security income program for the aged, blind, and disabled. However, each state sets its own rules within federal guidelines and regulations and may extend coverage to the nonwelfare poor. Federal and state governments spent $49.3 billion in 1987 to provide medicaid coverage to 23 million persons.

Medicare and medicaid account for the bulk of federal health expenditures, but the government spends tens of billions more to promote the health of current and former government employees (including active military personnel and veterans) and to subsidize medical research and the construction of medical facilities. A variety of smaller programs attempt to fill the gaps in coverage left by other health programs. State medical general assistance programs spend about $2 billion annually to aid the poor. Federal and state governments budgeted $1.4 billion for three health care block grant programs in 1987. Finally, the federal government appropriated $975 million in 1987 for the medical needs of Indians and migrant workers.

Apart from direct outlays, federal tax breaks for medical expenses have significantly promoted the health of American families. By not taxing fringe benefits, the federal government encourages employers to pay for employee health coverage, at an estimated 1988 cost to the treasury of $24.2 billion. The deduction for medical expenses, which tends to benefit higher-income families, has been increasingly restricted in recent years but is still expected to result in a tax expenditure of $2.3 billion in 1988.

Despite these efforts, further expansion of medical services remains a key part of programs favoring family policy. With rising medical costs, many families could face serious financial difficulties if one of their members required hospitalization, and some 37 million persons are not covered by any health insurance, including about 24 million workers and their dependents. While a nationalized medical system—similar to the United Kingdom's—has been repeatedly proposed but rejected by Congress, other policies could promote family stability. For example, universal comprehensive insurance against serious medical risks is one option. This type of universal insurance could be geared to provide nationally established minimum standards of benefits, with periodic upward readjustments reflecting changes in real incomes, medical costs, technology, and social standards.

The provision of food to low-income households has been another major expanding commitment of the federal government. While the federal food stamp program was in operation nationally from 1939 to 1943, the program was not revived until 1961. Several years later, the Johnson administration added school lunch, school breakfast, and special milk programs for children. After a slow beginning on these food programs in the 1960s, the following decade witnessed a massive growth in federal spending for food assistance, reaching almost $19 billion by 1986. Unlike most other social programs, federal food aid has kept pace with inflation since 1980. State governments contribute about another $1 billion for food assistance.

Over 90 percent of all benefits under these food programs are distributed on the basis of need. In 1987 about 21 million persons received monthly allotments of food stamps based on their household's income and size. The stamps can be exchanged in retail stores for food. The maximum monthly food stamp allotment for a family of four in the continental United States was $290 in 1988. This amount is reduced based on the family's income. For example, a family of four with a monthly income of $700 was entitled to receive $61 in food stamps. Benefit levels are adjusted annually to reflect changes in food prices.

The expansion of the program during the 1970s reflected wider eligibility for benefits, more generous formulas for calculating benefits, and higher unemployment rates. More than half of the households that received food stamps in 1985 were headed by a female, while one-fifth were headed by persons age 65 and over. The food stamp program remains one of the few federal initiatives that extends help to family heads who are active members of the labor force but are counted among the working poor, although 80 percent of the household heads who received food stamps in 1985 did not work at all. Food stamps account for two-thirds of government food assistance expenditures. School lunch and breakfast programs provide free or reduced-price meals to some 25 million youngsters daily, carrying an estimated price tag of $3.3 billion in 1987. The $1.6 billion special supplemental food program for women, infants, and children annually assists some 3.3 million pregnant women and children under age 5 who are poor and not receiving adequate nutrition. Several programs distributed food directly at an estimated 1987 cost of about $1 billion. Finally, a nutrition program specifically for the elderly spent a little over $600 million in 1986.[24]

Since the end of World War II, the federal government has assumed a major responsibility for helping families with their housing needs. These efforts have included mortgage guarantees, loans, subsidies, tax credits, and public housing. In 1985 almost two-thirds of U.S. households owned their homes, even if most still had mortgages.

Proportion of owner-occupied households

1930	47.8%
1940	43.6
1950	55.0
1960	61.9
1970	62.9
1980	64.4
1985	64.3

Stagnant income growth and rising housing prices and interest rates have halted progress in boosting home ownership rates. In 1970, the median price of a new or existing single-family house was $23,000; by late 1987, the median price of an existing house was over $85,000, and a new house cost nearly $110,000. During the same period, median monthly gross rents rose from $108 to over $350.[25] In the 1980s, housing costs have outpaced overall inflation increases. Rising rental costs—increasing at nearly twice the overall inflation rate since the end of 1982—have especially hurt low-income families. The General Accounting Office found that from

1975 to 1983, low-income families were devoting a rapidly growing share of their income to rent payments.[26]

Single-parent families are much more likely to be renters, and only a small portion of the families that experience a divorce are able to hold onto their homes because to divide property equitably during the settlement it is usually necessary to sell the house and divide the proceeds. Delinquency and foreclosure rates also indicate that female-headed families tend to face more shelter-related problems than other types of households. The share of total income allocated to shelter is inversely related to the level of a family's income. The share of family income devoted to housing rises substantially after divorce or separation for female-headed families. Few markets are as sensitive to changes in American family patterns as housing. The financial requirements for home buyers contributed to the influx of married women into the labor force. As the cost of financing housing mortgages or rentals mounted—and as family income growth stagnated—these pressures fostered growth in the number of multi-paycheck families.

Although housing problems have multiplied, the federal government in the 1980s reduced spending for shelter needs. Since 1981 the Reagan administration has cut subsidies for low-income housing by 60 percent, to $13.3 billion in 1986.[27] Federal construction of housing for the poor was virtually ended in 1981. One consequence has been increased homelessness.

One of the major federal subsidies for homeownership has been the tax provision permitting filers to deduct the interest charges on their mortgages from their taxable income. This deduction, expected to cost the treasury nearly $30 billion in 1988, is the second most expensive individual income tax deduction. The provision tends to benefit families with above-average incomes, who are more likely to itemize deductions than to use the standard deduction. The renting families who most need housing assistance receive no benefit at all from the mortgage interest deduction. The 1986 tax reform law left the housing tax deduction basically unchanged, although by lowering the overall tax rates Congress effectively reduced the value of the deduction. Consequently, shelter expenses will increase even more than they otherwise would have for many families.

As federal programs helping poor families expanded during the 1960s, Congress increasingly acknowledged the importance of social services in helping families. The scope of social services is so broad as to defy definition; they include services in the home, legal representation, temporary housing, psychological counseling, and protective services for abused or neglected children.

If the content of social services is somewhat amorphous, the cost certainly is not. Under a 1967 law authorizing open-ended federal matching funds (3 federal dollars for every state dollar) for social services to former, current, or potential welfare recipients, state requests for federal funds quickly ballooned to over $4 billion by 1972. In one year alone, federal social services spending doubled. In response, Congress capped federal spending for the Social Security Act's social services program at $2.5 billion annually. The ceiling was raised in the late 1970s to $2.9 billion. The Reagan administration and Congress lowered the cap to $2.4 billion and replaced the program with a social services block grant. The federal grant ceiling is now set at $2.7 billion annually, a reduction of nearly 40 percent since 1981 after adjusting for inflation. States and localities contribute roughly another $2 billion to social services block grant funding. Almost two-thirds of the program was devoted to the following services in 1985:[28]

Child care	17.7%
Foster or substitute care	14.9
Protective services for abused or neglected children	10.3
Home-based services (e.g., Meals on Wheels)	8.9
Mental health services	6.1
Health care	4.1
Assistance to the disabled	3.1

Two smaller social services programs have survived during the 1980s despite continual attempts by the Reagan administration to eliminate them. The community services block grant allocated $370 million in 1987 to local community action agencies that provide temporary or emergency food, shelter, and referral services to the poor.[29] The Legal Services Corporation, a government entity created in 1974 and funded at $306 million in 1987, offers legal assistance in noncriminal cases to the poor. A large part of the caseload involves assisting the poor in obtaining government benefits.

POLICY CONSTRAINTS

Government policy can have a beneficial impact upon families. Probably the most cost-effective and helpful policy is the provision of the necessary resources to prevent the birth of unwanted children. Public policy should, at a minimum, ensure that all children are provided a basic standard of living, and it has moved, albeit slowly, in this direction in the 1960s and 1970s, but the 1980s witnessed a reversal of this trend.

A comprehensive and grand family policy may be superficially appealing, but has been rejected by the public on closer scrutiny. Besides budget constraints, most Americans will continue to prefer pluralism to having families fitted to any one procrustean bed.

Full employment, a man on the moon, energy independence, and the strategic defense initiative—all have served as slogans and objectives in other fields, but there is no similar rallying cry in family matters. It is popular to favor a stronger American family, but what does this mean? Does this mean making it more difficult to obtain a divorce, outlawing abortion, reinstating prayer in public schools, installing a full-time wife in the home, and boosting the average number of children per family? Others would view a stronger family as one having equal partners, no roadblocks to obtaining a divorce and starting over, or even the right of homosexuals to marry and adopt children.

In essence, public policy can be used to ease the buffeting American families are experiencing. But public policy will not be able—nor should it attempt—to "fine tune" families into fitting any one paradigm or norm.

Chapter Nine

CHANGING INSTITUTIONS AND FINANCIAL ARRANGEMENTS

> My lofty ideals—which I now have well under
> control—prevented me from seeing the workings of the
> social machinery; I was compelled to see it in the end
> by bumping against its wheels, knocking into its shaft,
> getting covered with its grease, and hearing the
> constant clatter of its chains and fly-wheels.
>
> Honoré de Balzac, *Lost Illusions*

PAID WORK AND FAMILY RESPONSIBILITIES

After several unsuccessful efforts to change what
he viewed as hypocritical Parisian customs, Balzac's young hero,
Lucien, is eloquently told that he cannot fight city hall. Lucien
heeds this advice given by an older friend, and by the end of the
story he not only has conformed to the social institutions of the day
but also has learned how to turn them cynically to his own advantage. Ever idealistic and optimistic, Americans tend to reject Lucien's cynicism. Despite bumping into the wheels and knocking
into the shafts, millions of Americans have continued to adapt family life to the ever-changing social machinery.

Beyond income support, family policies should consider the relationship between the family and other basic institutions. How labor markets function, or fail to function, can have a strong influence on families. The courts and the tax system also have a major
impact on family life. The interrelationships between public institutions and the home have become increasingly complex.

174

Labor Markets

Millions of family heads fail, or are being failed, in labor markets. Lack of work is an obvious reason, but finding a job is no guarantee that it will pay enough to raise the worker's family out of poverty. Altogether, some 3.5 million heads of families who work during a year remain in destitution, and these include 1 million who work at full-time, full-year jobs. Over one-fifth of families headed by working women were poor in 1986, and 5 percent of all husband-wife families with an employed householder experienced similar economic hardship.

Besides unemployment and low wages, discrimination has been a major cause of hardship among families headed by females, blacks, Hispanics, and other minority groups. Title VII of the Civil Rights Act of 1964 and a series of other laws have sought to ban discriminatory employment practices. However, significant wage and promotion differences based on sex and race persist, even when data are adjusted for education, job seniority, part-time work, and other variables. Discrimination in the labor market remains very real and has a serious negative impact on the earnings of female- and minority-headed families.

Family environment has a significant impact on the types of remedial training required and the effectiveness of these programs. It is difficult to counteract in a brief training course the influence of living, say, 18 years in a neglectful household, and limited human resource investment may be too little and too late, or have only a marginal effect. Given the recent structural shifts in American family trends, greater attention will have to be given in the earlier years of an individual's development and his or her household living conditions. It may be that greater returns would be obtained if more resources were allocated for career education and training prior to the time when individuals are expected to support themselves or form their own families. The trustees of the Committee for Economic Development, consisting of some 225 business executives and a sprinkling of major university presidents, concluded in a 1987 policy statement:

> Each year's class of dropouts costs the nation more than $240 billion in lost earnings and forgone taxes over their lifetimes. Billions more will be spent on crime control and on welfare, health care, and other social services. Every $1 spent on early prevention and intervention can save $4.75 in the costs of remedial education, welfare, and crime further down the road.[1]

Family background apparently has a very strong influence on one's work life. One study estimated that almost half the occupational advantage and three-fifths of the earnings advantage of people who hold good, well-paying jobs appear to be due to their family backgrounds.[2] Through both the laws of supply and demand and custom, American labor markets are highly cognizant of an individual's family history.

To help individuals who have failed or are being failed in the labor market, the government has sponsored a number of employment and training programs. Since 1973 many of these efforts have been consolidated under the Comprehensive Employment and Training Act (CETA) and its successor, the Job Training Partnership Act (JTPA), while other programs operate separately from JTPA.[3] All welfare recipients are automatically eligible for employment and training assistance. At its peak, more than 40 percent of CETA's public service employment positions were held by family heads, and 30 percent of enrollees had two or more dependents when they entered employment and training programs.[4] However, the Reagan administration terminated CETA's public jobs component in 1981. JTPA, enacted the following year, operates on a budget that is only a fraction of CETA's funding. JTPA enrolls about 2.2 million persons annually and is funded at $3.7 billion in 1988. Nearly all enrollees have low incomes and receive limited occupational training or job search assistance. The work incentive (WIN) program, established in 1967, is designed to provide employment assistance for household heads receiving AFDC, but its budget was cut sharply to $133 million in 1987—a third as much money after adjusting for inflation as the program received at the start of the decade.

American society still appears to revere the work ethic, but seems willing to pay only a low price for fostering it. In 1986, almost 7 million workers were employed at or below the minimum wage, which has stood at $3.35 per hour since 1981. If the minimum hourly wage had kept pace with inflation, it would have been a third higher in 1988. During 1986, the hourly wage of 8.9 million workers was less than $4. Without a wage floor that is adjusted for changing living costs and growth in productivity, the income gained from welfare too frequently outpaces the rewards obtained from work for millions of families. Welfare then becomes an increasingly rational alternative to work for a growing number of households. For these reasons, a minimum wage is needed as a floor to encourage those with low skill and educational levels to enter the labor force as well as to meet basic income needs when

they find a job. Edward Gramlich concluded that female workers may be helped the most by a wage floor.[5]

Family policies in a welfare system that tries to encourage more household members to enter the labor force require a wage floor that will help a full-time worker escape poverty. By 1988, consumer prices had risen by a third since the minimum hourly wage was last increased. Indexing the minimum wage to half the average private sector wage rate, an increase of over a dollar an hour above the current $3.35 standard, would restore the minimum wage to the value it held during the 1960s and raise millions of families above the poverty line.

Alternative Work Schedules

Rigid work schedules are an obstacle to employment and can create family strains for both working couples and single family heads. As many working wives have discovered, a majority of women do not exchange the role of housewife for paid worker. Instead, they are expected to fill both jobs. Or, as one TV jingle advertised:

> I can put the wash on the line, feed the kids
> Get dressed, pass out the kisses
> And get to work by five to nine
> Cause I'm a wo-man.

Instead of conforming to the older norm of a woman's role, today's woman is expected to be a tireless companion for the man, or men, in her life; a devoted mother for her children; and a perfect housekeeper, along with pursuing a career in the workplace. This new vision is, in many ways, harder to live up to than the older and simpler standard. It is quite difficult for many working parents to fit into the standard 40-hour workweek. Alternatives to worktime rigidities, including flexible work schedules and worksharing, would make it easier for more parents to have productive and sane lives both on the job and at home. Such policies would recognize the unique problems many parents face in balancing household and job-related demands. It could also ease the transition experienced by families as either a wife or a female family head enters the labor force. Alternatives are emerging, but the standard workweek remains remarkably resilient. Nearly 70 percent of all employed Americans continue to work 40 hours or more per week.

Part-time work is the most common alternative work schedule. In 1987, a monthly average of nearly 20 million people worked on part-time schedules (1 to 34 hours per week), or more than one of every six employed persons. Almost two-thirds of these worked short hours because they did not want, or were unavailable for, full-time jobs. Another 27 percent worked part-time for economic reasons such as slack work or the inability to find a full-time job, while the remainder worked short hours because of illness, vacations, or other reasons.

Although most working women are not part-time employees, most part-time workers—nearly two-thirds—are women. Married women account for more than one in three part-time workers, contributing greatly to the financial well-being of their families. The poverty rate among married couple families with a part-time employed wife was 5.7 percent in 1985. Without the earnings of these wives, the rate would nearly have doubled, to 9.8 percent.

Despite the promise of part-time employment as a way to balance work and family responsibilities, reduced hours remain an unsatisfactory solution for many working parents. The vast majority of part-time jobs offer low pay, few if any fringe benefits, and second-class employee status. In 1987 the median part-time worker earned $4.42, compared with $7.43 for a full-time worker. While nearly 8 of 10 full-time workers receive health insurance subsidized or fully paid by their own employers, only 3 in 10 part-time workers receive direct medical benefits. Similarly, nearly 60 percent of full-time workers but less than 20 percent of part-timers obtain pension coverage on the job. Finally, part-time employees have little job security or opportunity for promotion. Some companies using a skilled workforce have offered limited part-time openings to attract and keep quality employees. However, many firms use part-time employment to reduce wage, benefit, and job security commitments rather than to satisfy employee desires.[6]

Alternative work arrangements such as flexible scheduling, in contrast, are designed to meet the needs of workers. Flexible scheduling enables full-time workers to choose workday patterns other than the traditional "nine to five" shift. For example, an employer can establish a core period of working hours in the middle of the workday, when workers must be on the job. Then workers would have the option of picking periods in the morning, afternoon, or evening to make up the rest of their scheduled hours.

The data and evidence are still too scanty to draw firm conclusions, but it does appear that many working parents are helped by these programs. When given a chance, many workers opt for flexitime systems.[7] Flexitime is widespread in several European nations. However, flexitime or other schedules enabling workers to vary the start and end of their workday are available to only 12 percent of full-time American workers.[8]

An alternative to flexitime is jobsharing, whereby work schedules remain unchanged but a single job is shared by, say, two persons, each working half-time. In addition, worksharing sometimes is used as an alternative to layoffs. For example, if a firm must cut the total hours worked by 30 percent during an economic slump, it reduces the hours of all employees equally instead of laying off workers. Employees might be compensated through unemployment insurance for a part of the wages lost because of reduced hours. A major benefit of worksharing is that the work experience and skills gained by the workers with least seniority, who are most often laid off during a recession, are not lost. As a result, both employers and workers benefit. Ten states have enacted worksharing laws to minimize layoffs. Where implemented, the programs have generally been well received by both employers and workers, but few firms have instituted worksharing schemes. Evaluations have been few, but Motorola, one of the largest corporate users, claimed that worksharing produced significant net savings.[9]

While worksharing and flexitime may produce benefits for society and individual families, these plans may also carry a cost. From the employer's standpoint, instituting alternative work schedules may raise labor costs more than using more standard methods of adjusting total hours (i.e., layoffs to reduce hours or overtime to increase them). This is true because rising overtime may hold down expenditures for fringe benefits and other fixed labor costs.

The interrelationship between families and the labor market indicates that issues regarding worktime will not go away. The postwar baby boom, combined with the increasing costs of rearing children and a persistent yearning for a rising standard of living, has induced many households to trade potential gains in leisure for more income. Declines in real income among young adults during the past 15 years have reinforced the preference for more money over more leisure in an effort just to keep real family income constant. Analyses that take into account changes in the number of children and the costs of rearing them, the level of schooling, and rates of inflation can explain why the workweek of full-time workers has not dropped significantly.

However, some of these very same forces—especially lower fertility rates—are now exerting far different influences and can be expected to continue in the same vein in the near future. As Juanita Kreps has noted, the growth in married women's labor force participation rates could tilt the family's leisure-income trade-off in the direction of leisure, because a good portion of the time that economists call "leisure" really is spent on household work.[10] Such a shift in the income-leisure decision probably will not be massive, but even a small change can have an important cumulative impact. Because of the changing composition of the labor force, more workers are likely to prefer shorter hours.

During the post–World War II period, labor markets accommodated some of these preferences. Employment growth in the service and retail sectors, which have used a major proportion of part-time workers, including wives, increased faster than the rest of the labor force. But the continuing treatment of part-timers as marginal workers makes reduced schedules unattractive to workers. Although part-time employment is growing rapidly, 60 percent of the increase in the 1980s has been involuntary. Government intervention is necessary to make alternative schedules attractive to employees and employers. The wider introduction of flexitime and worksharing will require federal policies that reduce the costs of adopting these alternatives. One example would be changing the rules regarding unemployment insurance so that it can be used for worksharing compensation, as a fifth of the states have already done on a modest scale. Similarly, a higher minimum wage and an expansion of employee benefits such as health insurance would make part-time employment a more viable option.

Parental leave is also a problem for many working couples. As noted earlier, several European states have comprehensive policies regarding maternity, and even paternity, leave. Little progress has been made on this front in the United States, although Congress is demonstrating increased interest in the idea and some companies have provided for maternity leave.[11]

FAMILIES AND THE LAW

Marriage and families have had a special legal standing in our society. The law reflects long-held attitudes, but also changes in response to shifting social mores regarding families. Too frequently, however, lawmakers and judges have failed to anticipate the impact their decisions will have.

Income Tax

The federal income tax codes are a prime example of how legislative enactments have been slow to adapt to or even consider changing family needs. When the tax was reintroduced in 1913 after its emergency use during the Civil War, individuals were taxed on their personal income regardless of marital status. An individual paid the same tax on adjusted gross income whether the person was married or single.

However, different property laws in the various states affected the individual's final tax liability. A few states had "community property" laws stipulating that the income of a married couple belonged equally to both spouses. Married residents of these states reduced their total federal tax payments by claiming that each spouse was legally liable for the income tax due on 50 percent of the couple's total income, thereby escaping the rising progressive liability. In the rest of the states—the "common law" property states—the taxable income of an individual was unaffected by marital status. Suppose a working husband earned $25,000 a year and his wife remained outside the workforce. In a "community property" state, the couple could have filed two individual returns for $12,500. However, in a "common law" property state, the working husband would have had to file a return covering the full $25,000. In 1930, the Supreme Court ruled (*Poe v. Seaborn*) that the residents of "community property" states could take advantage of this different tax treatment.

Eighteen years later, Congress allowed all married couples the benefits of income splitting, creating a national marriage subsidy in cases where the couple had disparate incomes. By 1969, a single person could pay as much as 40 percent more in taxes than a married couple with the same income. To ameliorate this "singles penalty," Congress in 1969 created a special tax rate schedule for married individuals choosing to file separate returns, prohibiting them from using the schedule for single persons. The new schedule was calibrated to ensure that a single person's taxes could be no more than about 20 percent above those of a married couple with the same income. However, in the process of reducing the singles penalty Congress inadvertently created a marriage penalty in cases where both spouses had earnings, a situation that was becoming increasingly prevalent. By the late 1970s, the marriage penalty had become increasingly controversial. President Carter denounced the tax system for encouraging couples to live in sin, and according to one estimate the added tax liability of 16 million married couples in 1979 exceeded $8 billion.[12]

Consequently, Congress in 1981 created a special tax deduction for working couples which reduced but did not eradicate their marriage tax burden. The marriage penalty controversy subsided and received scant attention during the debate leading to the 1986 tax reform law. Although the new law repealed the 1981 deduction for working couples, the estimated net effect of the reform is to allow couples with less than $30,000 in annual adjusted gross income a small tax advantage, while retaining the marriage penalty (or fee license) for higher earners (fig. 23).[13]

Ideally, the law might strive to achieve three basic household-related objectives: to retain progressive rates, to treat the family as a taxpaying unit, and to establish "marriage neutrality." By being neutral toward marriage, the total tax bill would not be affected by household status. Any two of these goals can be attained simultaneously, but all three cannot be achieved at the same time.

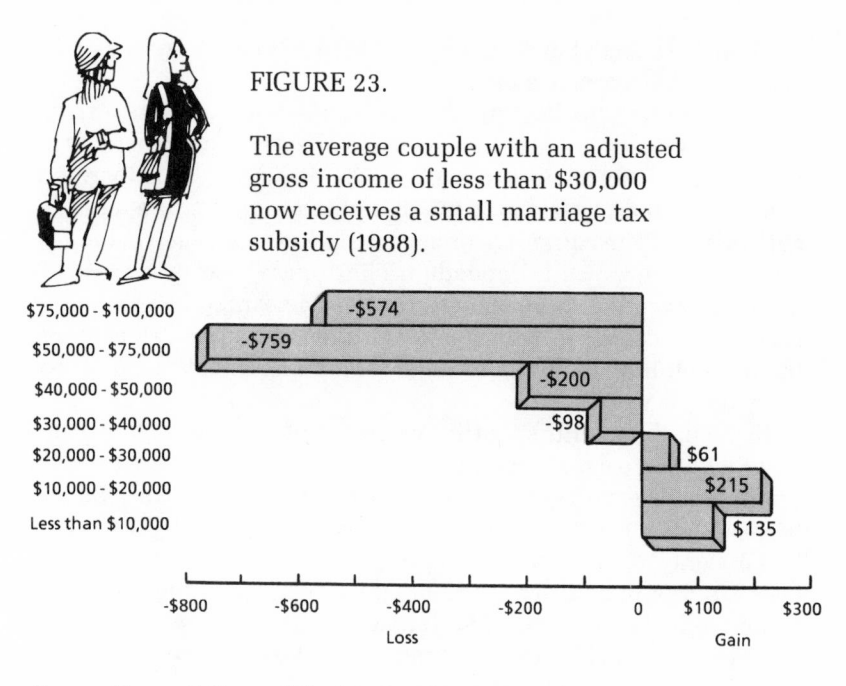

FIGURE 23.

The average couple with an adjusted gross income of less than $30,000 now receives a small marriage tax subsidy (1988).

Source: Harvey F. Rosen, "The Marriage Tax Is Down but Not Out" (Cambridge, Mass.: National Bureau of Economic Research, May 1987)

Congress first provided a tax exemption for children in 1917, but until 1940 the exemptions for adults were at least double those for children. Despite periodic increases, the exemption fell far behind the pace of inflation until the passage of the 1986 tax law; the 1986 exemption of $1,080 was over $1,700 below the real value of the 1946 exemption. The antifamily bias of the code became a major issue during the 1986 tax reform debate, when Congress raised the exemption to $1,900 for 1987 and $2,000 for 1989, and indexed it for inflation thereafter.

By granting exemptions, Congress attempts to mitigate to some extent the fact that wage scales normally ignore family needs. The amount of the exemption is far too small to subsidize the cost of raising children, and some advocates, including the Reagan administration, favored at least doubling the value of this tax break.[14] However, enactment of such a provision would raise the federal deficit by nearly $20 billion annually and increase family income only by about $300 per child.[15] The new law's reduction of tax rates has had the effect of making exemptions and deductions less valuable than they were formerly.

An important tax benefit for low-income families is the earned income tax credit, introduced in 1975 to offset rising social security payroll taxes. Tax credits reduce liability directly and are therefore worth more than tax exemptions or deductions, which reduce taxable income. The earned income credit is in fact a negative income tax. Low earners with dependent children whose tax credit exceeds their tax liability receive a rebate. The earned income credit is only applicable to working parents, and it attempts to encourage the work ethic by denying eligibility to parents whose major source of income is welfare.

In 1988, the credit is worth 14 percent of an eligible taxpayer's first $6,260 in earned income, for a maximum of $880. This maximum credit remains in effect for adjusted gross earnings of $6,260 to $9,850. For every subsequent dollar earned the credit is reduced by ten cents, effectively eliminating the credit for parents earning over $18,610. In addition, the 1986 tax law indexed the earned income credit for inflation. The impact of the credit is expected to increase dramatically in three years, as follows:[16]

	1985	1988 (est.)
Families receiving credit (millions)	6.5	11.3
Amount (billions)	$2.1	$6.1

For working parents earning less than $10,500 in 1988, the earned income credit more than compensates for their direct social security payroll tax burden. The credit could be made even more effective by adjusting it for family size, because poor families with more than one child receive no additional benefit, and by awarding the credit on a monthly basis rather than in a lump sum annually.

The 1986 law will drastically reduce the poor's overall tax burden (including income as well as payroll taxes), which had risen from 1.8 to 10.4 percent from 1979 to 1985 for a family of four with poverty-level earnings (fig. 24).[17]

The tax system and social welfare efforts may induce the institutionalization of family members who could be taken care of in the home. For example, a larger portion of a medical bill may be paid by public programs if the ill person is placed in a hospital rather than treated at home. More liberal financial assistance for home treatment might send fewer people to hospitals and nursing homes if the family were able—and willing—to have these relatives remain at home. Tax credits can also better reflect the added burden

Tax rate
(federal income plus
payroll taxes)

FIGURE 24.

The 1986 tax reform greatly reduced
the tax rate for a poor family of four
with poverty-level earnings, but the
tax burden remains higher than it
was a decade earlier.

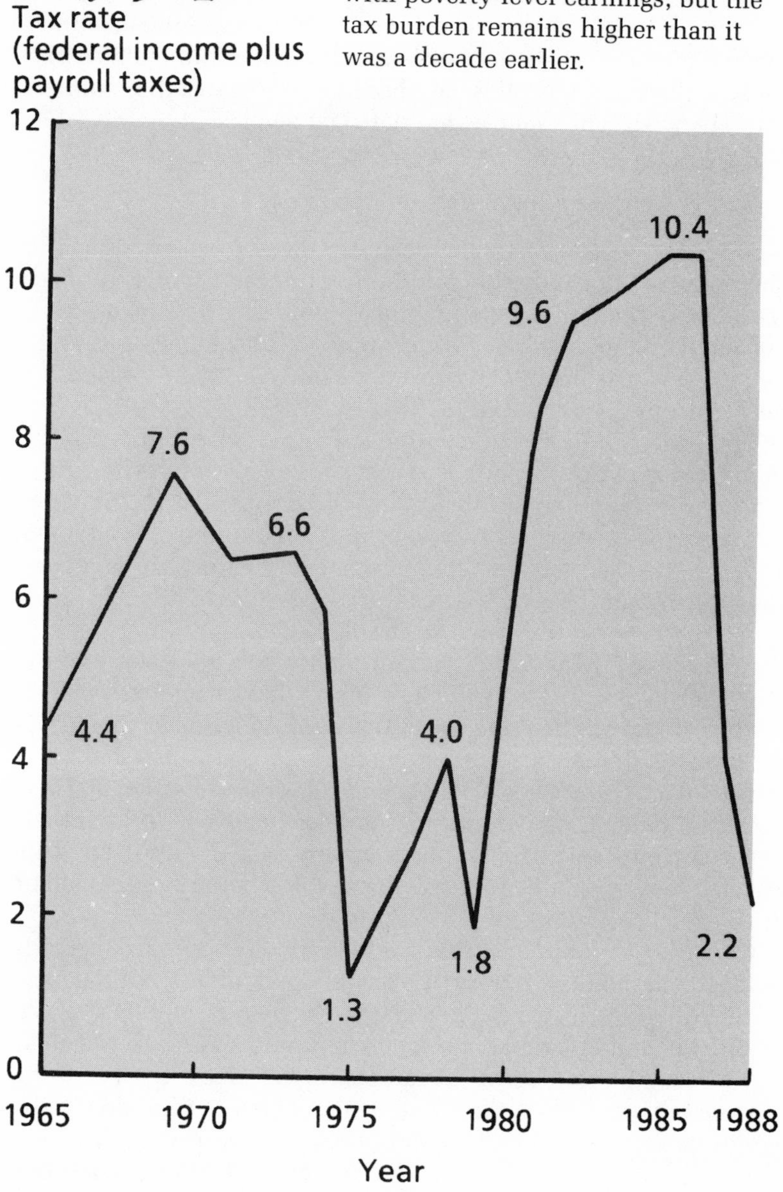

12

10.4

10

9.6

8

7.6

6.6

6

4.4

4

4.0

2

1.8

2.2

1.3

0

1965   1970   1975   1980   1985 1988

Year

Source: same as note 17

caused by home treatment for family members with these difficulties. Not only are added costs involved, but some adults also
may have to forgo full-time employment because of a seriously ill
child or relative. Public policy—in the form of both social services
and the tax code—should be more sensitive to this situation. It is a
sad commentary on our society if people are institutionalized only
because the financial scales have been skewed in that direction, despite the wishes of a family and personal needs.

Regulating Family Behavior

The law is undergoing rapid transformations reflecting structural and economic family changes. Divorce, property
settlements, and child custody proceedings have occupied a growing amount of judicial attention. Automobile accident cases represent the majority of suits in court, but family-related cases are currently running a close second.

The word *family* is not mentioned in the Constitution, and the
framers unquestionably believed that family law was the domain of
the states. Almost no family law cases came before the Supreme
Court during the first century after the Constitution was adopted,
and, despite the increased involvement of the Court in family issues during the past quarter-century, only five family law cases
were argued before the Court in its 1985–86 term.[18]

Consequently, the foundation of family law has been built by
state legislatures and courts. State family laws constitute an odd
mixture of the modern and the antiquated. As one legal expert put
it, "In family law, as perhaps nowhere else, the accumulated experience of our culture has a weight and standing of its own."[19] However, the National Conference of Commissioners on Uniform State
Laws has in recent years proposed a number of model statutes applicable to specific areas of family law which have been enacted by
many state legislatures.

Overall, state and federal law and court decisions have greatly
reduced the family's authority to control its affairs, although in
some important respects the state has bolstered the family as an
institution and enhanced the rights of families vis-à-vis the state.
Government policy during the last century has reflected a continuing tension between regulation and laissez-faire. A hundred years
ago, Supreme Court Justice Field noted (*Maynard v. Hill*), "Marriage . . . having more to do with the morals and civilization of a
people than any other institution, has always been subject to the

control of the legislature." A half-century later, Justice William O. Douglas (*Skinner v. State of Oklahoma*) characterized marriage and procreation as two of the "basic civil rights of man." The federal income tax and numerous social welfare programs impelled the federal courts to promulgate national legal policy in many areas that might otherwise have remained the preserve of the states.

The legal relationship between parents and children has undergone the greatest change. Parental—especially paternal—authority over children was virtually unchallenged in nineteenth-century America, but education and child labor and child abuse laws have radically altered parental authority. Instead of working in or around the home, children are subject to compulsory state education laws, which regulate much of their daytime activities between ages 5 or 6 and 16. Although parents may technically have the right to educate their offspring, they generally face a difficult hurdle in proving that home instruction would meet state standards.

Children's work is also governed by strict government regulation. The 1938 federal Fair Labor Standards Act bars the employment of children under 14 in most occupations, and from age 14 to 16 children may not work in positions that interfere with their schooling. Youth under age 18 are barred from working in occupations considered dangerous, such as mining or construction. All states have enacted child labor laws, which augment the federal statutes. On the other hand, with few exceptions parents retain control over their children's earnings.

What society once regarded as necessary disciplinary measures are now unequivocally considered child abuse. The laws of the American colonists required corporal punishment of disobedient children, and whipping was common. Current laws proscribe discipline that causes children serious injury, and proof of child abuse is one of the more common grounds for terminating parental rights by removing the child from the home.

Apart from circumscribing parental rights, the modern state requires parents to adequately feed, clothe, shelter, and provide health care for their children, and the government assists parents who lack the resources to support their children. The Supreme Court and Congress have acted to strengthen the family by applying this principle to the parents of children born out of wedlock. As late as 1973, when the Court overturned the practice, Texas denied out-of-wedlock children the right to support from their fathers.

Currently, about one of five states has accorded children born out of wedlock the same rights as other children. However, stepparents are generally not obligated to support their stepchildren.[20] Until 1971, parents generally possessed the legal duty to support, and the authority to supervise, their children until the age of 21. However, with the ratification of the Twenty-sixth Amendment to the Constitution, which allows 18-year-olds to vote, nearly all states reduced the age of majority to 18.

State power has also been used to augment parental authority. Shortly after the turn of the century, when the first juvenile courts were established, the states enacted "status" offenses. Unlike criminal laws, which proscribe specific actions, status offenses encompass ambiguously defined behavior such as "incorrigibility," "associating with undesirable company," "bad habits," and disobeying parents. These statutes are known as "children in need of supervision laws," and allow parents to use the police and the court system to compel filial obedience, and even to incarcerate children in a reform school in instances of serious or repeated misbehavior.

State laws governing marriage have undergone far less evolution than other family laws, but the Supreme Court has overturned two longstanding state practices. The first to fall, in 1967, were state prohibitions of interracial marriages. Six years later the Court struck down laws that set different marital age requirements for men and women. However, state laws proscribing the marriage of individuals under 16 or requiring parental permission for youngsters below age 18 have withstood court challenges. Stipulations that marital applicants be of sound mind remain on the books but are rarely enforced. One of the earliest Supreme Court family law decisions prohibited polygamy, and homosexuals have not won the right to marry. About half the states proscribe marriages between first cousins.

Despite common usage of the phrase *marriage contract*, the matrimonial institution has traditionally had little in common with other legal contractual relationships. Until recently, only in exceptional cases could the parties mutually dissolve the contract through divorce. The courts are becoming more inclined to accept premarital contracts, provided financial agreements are accompanied by full fiduciary disclosure and make fair provision for the spouse (what is considered fair may differ widely from one judge to another, even within the same state). Judges generally will not enforce agreements concerning the religious or educational training of children, and are loathe to interfere in an ongoing marriage.[21]

But when the question is one of gender discrimination, judges have demonstrated no such caution.

Marriage law has come a long way since William Blackstone wrote on the subject two centuries ago. According to Blackstone, the legal rights of the woman were, in effect, suspended during marriage and passed on to the husband. This meant that in the case of a divorce, the father had the right to take custody of the children. All the wife's real and personal property was under the legal control of the husband. Under British common law, a husband had the right to beat his wife moderately as long as he used a stick no wider than his thumb.

The concept of a common law marriage has increasingly fallen out of legal fashion, and today only about a quarter of the states continue to recognize them. The legal ambiguities that formerly beset the common law marriage now afflict an increasing number of cohabitors, many of whom live without the blessings of state and church, partly to avoid the legal and financial consequences of divorce. In a highly publicized case a dozen years ago, a woman sued the late Lee Marvin, with whom she had lived for nearly six years, for half of the actor's earnings during their cohabitation. The California Supreme Court, in a decision that must have struck terror in the hearts of rich playboys across the nation, held that not only could the courts enforce explicit property agreements between cohabitors, judges should also ascertain whether the cohabitors' conduct "demonstrates an implied contract." Only Oregon has attempted to follow California into this potential juridical swamp, and even in California Marvin's former mate came away empty-handed after the case was remanded to a lower court. Despite continuing interest in the concept by lawyers and judges, few courts have shown an inclination to bestow a quasi-marital legal status upon cohabitation.

A high incidence of violence within the family has come to light in recent years: over 1 million children are neglected or abused each year, and probably over 2 million wives experience violence at home. It is not clear whether incidents of family violence are rising or whether the recorded data reflect a heightened social concern for these issues.[22] Having one separated or divorced parent kidnap a child from the other parent has become all too frequent.

The Office of Domestic Violence in the federal Department of Health and Human Services estimated that about one of four couples will undergo serious family violence during the course of a marriage or cohabitation. Nearly 16 percent of all homicides in

1986 involved family members, and half of these murders were committed by spouses.

The old image of the presiding judge in juvenile and family courts, according to one legal scholar, was that of a wise and benevolent Solomon who could cut through all the legalisms and offer sage advice and counsel, as well as judgment. But times and mores have changed. The judge's maturity and wisdom are now most often expressed to a family's lawyer rather than directly to the offending child. At one time, family or juvenile courts may have been viewed as an implicit extension of social welfare agencies, but recently they have "rapidly become real courts of law."[23]

LAGS

All too often the effects of legislative enactments have not been examined for their impact on households. Families do not exist in isolation from other social institutions; labor markets, welfare legislation, tax regulations, and the legal system influence household structures. The recent trend has been to look at "compelling state interests" and individuals' rights in judicial reviews of family laws. Few hard and fast rules have emerged, but, in general, if courts have not found very compelling interests, they have struck down the regulations.

Public policy can have a positive impact on families, although households are likely to respond slowly to legislative mandates, and institutions tend to adapt their practices at a snail's pace to evolving family needs. Progress toward equality and equity can be steady, if deliberately pursued. There is no reason for following the course taken by Balzac's young hero and giving up on altering the social machinery as it affects families.

Part Four

THROUGH A MURKY LOOKING GLASS

Chapter Ten

THE QUEST FOR FULFILLMENT

A man's worst difficulties begin when he is able to do
as he likes.

—Thomas Huxley

Freedom and discipline are indeed handmaidens;
without the discipline of genuine love, freedom is
invariably nonloving and destructive.

M. Scott Peck, *The Road Less Traveled*

DOUBTFUL UTOPIAS

If Huxley was correct, the removal of many social
constraints on individual behavior during recent years bodes trouble for our society. Choice in household and sexual arrangements is
far wider today than in the recent past, replacing established societal rules and accepted constraints.

Interest in exploring alternative or utopian family structures is a
long and honorable tradition. Titillating sex stories have commanded universal appeal from time immemorial, and the art of
picturing ideal family structures that could enrich human relationships is a close runner-up, going all the way back to Plato. Sir
Thomas More's *Utopia* contains such an alternative vision, and
H. G. Wells's *A Modern Utopia* shows how the subject continues to
fascinate both writers and readers.

Not surprisingly, notions of the structure and role of families in
utopian society have differed widely throughout the history of
Western civilization. Plato's *Republic* is the earliest recorded vision of utopia. The ideal society would consist of three classes: the
common people, the soldiers, and the guardians, mostly a heredi-
tary elite. *The Republic* is concerned mostly with the elite class.
Their sons and daughters would receive the same education, and
both men and women would serve as guardians. Male guardians

would share not only common houses and meals but also the women, and no man "will have a wife of his own." Procreation would be decided by lot sufficient to maintain a stable population. Recognizing that some parents are more equal than others, however, superior men would be afforded greater opportunity to sire children. Infants were to be brought up by the state without knowledge of their parents, who were prohibited contact with their progeny.

Some two millennia later, Thomas More had an entirely different vision of the family's place in his *Utopia*. As in Plato's *Republic*, private property is inimical to the utopian society, but current advocates of a traditional family structure would find many of More's ideas to their liking. He envisioned strictly monogamous families and proscribed premarital sex. Married men and women were to work together six hours a day, but the workday would be shortened if there were a surplus of necessary goods because an accumulation beyond essential needs should be discouraged. More would hardly receive a stamp of approval from modern-day feminists. Although he advocated gender equality in the workplace, the family would be dominated by a patriarch, and only learned men would be eligible to govern utopia.[1]

In this century, H. G. Wells's *A Modern Utopia* is probably the best-known vision of the future family. Despite his reputation as an "advanced thinker," Wells's utopian family would also hardly serve as a model for today's feminists. Premarital relations would require licensing in advance, and either party could dissolve the temporary union. To tie the knot in the old-fashioned manner, the couple must have "acquired a minimum education," and the man "must be in receipt of a net income above the minimum wage." Once "properly" married, the mother would be entitled to a stipend for the support of each child, but children produced out of wedlock or as a result of an extramarital affair would not be entitled to government support.[2]

It would seem that past notions of the family in utopia would hardly fit today's aspirations. But visions of utopian family forms have had a continuing appeal to fiction writers, science or conventional. Aldous Huxley, in *Island*, portrays a society composed of adoptive families that coexist with biological families in order to provide surrogate parents, alternative role models, and richer life experiences for children. His *Brave New World* did away with the family altogether. In B. F. Skinner's *Walden Two*, men and women are equal and entirely free.

Science fiction writers have been among the vanguard in portraying experimentation in household structures and romantic relationships. Robert A. Heinlein's hero, Michael Smith (*Stranger in a Strange Land*), is a prime example. He is conceived by two Earthlings during an interplanetary expedition to Mars. The entire crew perishes except, of course, Smith. In a new twist on an old plot, Mike is raised in Martian society and returns to Earth as a young man. Since Martian culture was well beyond the level of technology and ethics demonstrated by earthlings, Mike finds himself in the role of a prophet to a war-torn, restless, and unhappy Earth. The heart of the matter, Mike believes, is that human problems are caused by the way Earthlings have handled sexual and family relationships. In contrast, Martians have achieved perfect union between man and woman, and that accounts for their blissful existence.

The solution, according to Mike, is to allow men and women to realize their potential by "the joining of bodies with merging of souls in shared ecstasy, giving, receiving, delighting each other." Following Martian patterns, this includes establishing "nests," which are to replace conventional families. A nest is supposedly one big happy family in which sex is free among all members and in which jealousy is viewed as the ultimate vice. Similar to early Christian communities, a number of nests are formed as the good news spreads. But they are driven underground by the rest of society, and the young man from Mars is killed by a vengeful mob.

If the dreams or nightmares of science fiction authors and utopians remain just that, scientists have fostered technologies that once would have been considered equally fanciful. Artificial insemination and in vitro fertilization enable women to procreate without physical contact with a male partner. As the *National Journal* observed:

> Today, a child can have up to five people claiming to be its parents: a sperm donor, an egg donor, the woman providing a womb for gestation and the couple raising the child can all call a child theirs. And that's before any stepparents get involved.[3]

The Quest Continues

While past generations may have been thinkers, it could be argued that this generation is filled with doers. Instead of dreaming about achieving a blissful existence, people in this era are actively exploring what new forms and relationships can be created in reality. However, a closer examination indicates that the wisdom of Ecclesiastes holds true also in this era: "There is nothing new under the sun." Students of family history have noted how often modern utopian visions of the family are only old wine in new bottles. As Jessie Bernard has noted, the newer writers may fill their stories with computers and rocketships, but their underlying models of households and sexual relationships most often have been borrowed from writers of previous ages. These alternatives have been on the scene for a long time, and they are not peculiar to this age.

Still, applying the old adage that where there is smoke, there is fire, the constant battery of the family may lead to the conclusion that today's conditions are unique. Jumping to the conclusion that the family is on the verge of collapse ignores all sense of historical perspective. Even when it comes to being doers and not just talkers, the people living in this age are not unique. The nineteenth century was full of experimental communities that explored new family forms. Members of John Humphrey Noyes's Oneida Community, one of the most successful and lasting of the utopian experiments, believed that Scripture should be taken literally when it commanded men and women to love one another. Sexual exclusiveness was abolished within the community. Not only was traditional marriage contrary to the Bible, Noyes and his followers believed, but it was also not in harmony with human nature. In contrast, the communes of the 1960s that were the staple of Sunday supplements two decades ago had relatively short lives and have all but disappeared.

Granted that alternative family structures have always existed, it has been argued that a growing number of individuals are availing themselves of these opportunities. Even this point is debatable. For example, while there has been a vast increase in the reported number of couples living together without the blessings of state or church, it is quite difficult to know how much of this shift is really a new trend. With diminished social pressures to follow any one pattern, a good portion of the reported increase in this behavior may represent only the increased willingness of people to be open about what has always taken place. "Swinging," which was presumably popular a mere decade ago, is probably one of the oldest indoor sports known to humanity, as even a casual reader of the Bible would find. The current dread of AIDS may make the old virtues fashionable again, however, and yuppies may believe that they have discovered monogamy.

The evidence does not indicate that this era is buying into radical new family visions at any greater rate than in the past. True, family life has changed in many ways in recent years, and society has displayed greater tolerance, if not acceptance, for living arrangements that depart from the norm. Public reaction to the unsuccessful nomination of Robert Bork to the Supreme Court showed a massive outpouring of support for the right of individuals to practice behavior in private that may not be acceptable to the majority.

The current situation of these radical alternative family forms has much in common with the economist's notion of "effective demand." What keeps factories busy, workers employed, and taxes paid are not so much human desires, which may be insatiable, but the willingness and ability of consumers to purchase goods and services. Daydreaming and window shopping in front of a Rolls Royce dealer's showroom do not create jobs or enhance a country's gross national product. There appears to be quite a bit of daydreaming about alternatives to current family structures, but the effective demand remains very small.

The Israeli kibbutz is often pointed to as an example of an alternative form that has withstood the test of time. However, even in Israel the kibbutz model has attracted only a few people, remaining constant at about 3 percent of Israel's population. Also, the role of the nuclear family in the kibbutz has tended to expand in recent years. Kibbutz children are spending an increasingly significant amount of time with their parents, and many household tasks that were once the community's responsibility are now being returned to the family. For example, there has been a significant trend in having children sleep in their nuclear family's living quarters. Despite the vast interest in the kibbutz movement, being raised in this communal fashion is the exception rather than the rule in Israel.[4]

Even if alternatives to the nuclear family are not the wave of the future, this does not mean that family life will not continue to evolve and change in many subtle ways. It does mean that there will be a continuum with the past instead of a radical break.

Current family forms are not the only, or probably not even the best, modes of living that the human mind and the economy could establish. History indicates that households have existed under numerous and different structures. Recent changes have been extraordinarily rapid, but most Americans continue to seek spouses and desire children. In most cases, divorced adults—even those who spend several years experimenting—still return to more conventional family patterns, and cohabitation arrangements often have proven to be a way station en route to the altar or a transitional period rather than a preferred style of life for the long run. A study sympathetic to the presumed new order found that some cohabiting couples followed conventional practices of allocating household work, while other couples who had a marriage license demonstrated more true sexual equality and freedom. The authors concluded that whether or not a marriage or relationship was "open" or "closed" depended much more on its participants than on its legal standing.[5]

Yet the evidence does indicate departures from conventional family forms compared with the 1950s, changes that will present serious challenges to the stability of American society if they persist. While the increased trading of partners cannot be equated with renouncement of marriage and families, the changed rules not only have dire consequences for children born out of wedlock and their mothers, but also are the source of persistent and growing societal tensions.

MARXIST THEORY AND SOVIET PRACTICE

The most sweeping, but short-lived, modern social experiment in family relations and marriage has taken place in the socialist countries. The results indicate that the family is much more than a bourgeois institution that is no longer required once the government has taken control of the means of production. The initial policy expressed by the Russian Bolsheviks was deeply hostile toward families and conventional marriage.

As a result of party policies, family bonds in the U.S.S.R. weakened, creating troublesome conflicts for the new rulers. Family disintegration was hindering other social goals such as rapid industrialization and the rearing and socialization of the next generation. As a result, the party line changed to incorporate stable family structure as an integral part of the progress toward socialism. Not only were the slogans changed, but Soviet family law shifted almost 180 degrees. The Soviet experiment indicates that modern society, however ruled, has not found a substitute for the family to rear and socialize children.

Karl Marx and Friedrich Engels realized that their views of the family would evoke even more hostility than their calls to tear down capitalism. Yet they boldly called for the "abolition of the family," recognizing that this would be regarded as "the most . . . infamous proposal of the Communists." Denouncing "the bourgeois clap-trap about the family," they charged that "as a result of modern industry, all family ties among the proletarians are torn asunder."[6]

Marx spent much effort in a blistering analysis of existing family institutions rather than explaining what household life would be like, comes the revolution. He argued that capitalist industrialization had destroyed—or corrupted—family bonds among workers. Long hours, child and female labor under exploitative working conditions, unemployment, alcoholism, and prostitution were all making a mockery of middle-class family mores. Even for the bourgeoisie, marriage was often reduced to nothing more than a legal arrangement to keep property and pass it down to the next generation.[7]

Engels continued to flesh out the Marxist theory of the family's role in the Communist scheme. Within the patriarchal family, he found "in miniature the same oppositions and contradictions as those in which society has been moving."[8] Under socialism the patriarchal family would be destroyed, and society would return to "pairing relationships." The interests of private property caused males to control females' sexual behavior, he insisted, in order to guarantee that their wealth would pass on to their offspring. However, marriages of convenience led to adultery and vice. He also argued that the strongest upholders of the traditional patriarchal family were the very same groups that had the largest vested interest in upholding the capitalist state.

Once private property was abolished, the need for the patriarchal family would disappear. Although marriage is entered into by a contract, it becomes a legal status in the eyes of the state. In many other types of contracts, the parties can tear up the agreement without the approval of the state. But even under modern no-fault divorce laws, the state must sanction the severance of marriage bonds. Under socialism, Engels asserted, the state would not intervene in decisions affecting marriage or the wishes of couples to terminate their union. Early Communists saw (or conveniently misinterpreted) Engels's notions of "pairing relationships" as the equivalent of "free love."

Within weeks of the revolution, Lenin signed a decree taking marriage and divorce completely out of the hands of the church. In line with the concept of pairing relationships, Lenin felt that the authority of the state should be limited to recording marriages, births, deaths, and divorces. Under the first Soviet family code, issued in 1918, even unregistered marriages had equal validity with registered marriages in the eyes of the law. In line with Engels's ideas, Lenin sensed that strong family ties could block the road toward developing a socialist state, and the role of families in the new Soviet society was downgraded. A divorce was easy and inexpensive to obtain. Even if only one party wanted the divorce, the marriage would be declared ended without a court hearing. In fact, at one point all that was required was for either the husband or wife to mail in a preprinted "divorce" postcard.

Under these regulations, Soviet divorce rates climbed (although hard data are difficult to come by), and party officials became alarmed about the social instability that they believed was caused by family dissolution. Besides creating problems for raising the next generation, it was also felt that family instability had a negative spillover effect on productivity in the workplace. Starting in the 1930s, Soviet family policy dramatically shifted, culminating in a 1944 law that ended easy divorces. The state resumed the authority to pass regulations controlling the dissolution of marriage, just as in decadent capitalist nations. With regard to child support responsibilities, Soviet courts tended to be even stronger enforcers than their Western counterparts. Significant declines in the fertility rate of ethnic Russians led Soviet officials to adopt policies that would ease the financial burden of having children. Stalin and the party press praised the virtues of a strong family as a basic building block in a healthy socialist state. Two American observers noted: "The wheel had turned full circle. The Soviet Union had been one of the easiest countries in the world in which to secure a divorce. Now it was one of the hardest."[9]

The stringent legal obstacles kept Soviet divorce rates low until the mid-1960s, when the government again relaxed divorce procedures. Between 1964 and the end of the next decade, the divorce rate more than doubled to 3.6 divorces per 1,000 population before dropping slightly to 3.4 by 1985. The Soviet divorce rate is exceeded only by the U.S. rate of 4.8 per 1,000 persons. Housing shortages frequently mean that divorced couples must continue to live together after the breakup.

Marxist social scientists have tried to explain the vast change in official attitudes toward the family as the logical development of a

socialist state, although the events of the past 70 years do not necessarily support their speculations or theories. When the Bolsheviks
came to power in 1917, and when other Communist parties took
control of other Eastern European nations following World War II,
the family institutions were highly sexist, male dominated, and
often used as a means of passing power and privilege down to succeeding generations. Also, some of the strongest advocates of the
traditional family were religious and conservative opponents of the
new system. In this context, the defense of the "family" often was a
code word used to rally opposition to building a socialist society.
Once the antisocialist forces were purged, the family could become
a useful institution in obtaining the party's goals. At first the family
was viewed, according to one Eastern European analyst, as "the
stronghold of private life and individualism, diverting attention
and energy from public concerns and weakening the collective
values." But as these "retrograde features" were removed, the family's "stability, its well-being, and the prevention of its malfunc-
tioning or disruption were [seen as] extremely important."[10]

In reality, this neat exposition does not conform with—or explain—all the evidence or reasons for the shift in Soviet family policy. Despite government efforts and inducements, many ethnic
Russian couples have chosen to have only one child, and the U.S.
Census Bureau projects that the proportion of ethnic Russians will
drop below half of the Soviet population by the early 1990s. Long
before Western women's liberation movements encouraged women
to enter the labor force, the typical Soviet wife and mother worked
outside the household. But the bulk of low-paid Soviet workers are
women, and sexual equality in the workforce is still a distant goal.
Even in the professions, female workers hold a significant chunk of
the lower paid teaching and medical jobs. For example, women
constitute 85 percent of medical personnel but only half of all chief
physicians and executives of medical institutions. All predomi-
nantly female occupational groups in the U.S.S.R. have below-
average earnings, and despite their work experience Soviet
women's average wages are only two-thirds of men's, about the
same ratio that exists in the United States.[11]

Gender equality within the Soviet household also has not been
realized. The burden of shopping and housework falls dispropor-
tionately on working Soviet women. These responsibilities are
more burdensome for Soviet than American women, as they regularly must stand in long lines to purchase consumer goods and
often do not possess advanced household technology to perform

chores. According to Soviet estimates, the average working woman spends over four hours a day on domestic chores, and nearly two hours shopping. As in the West, Soviet women often defer, and play a secondary role, to the men in their lives. The tradition of the extended family (three generations) is still a strong Russian institution. Even with the reputation of cradle-to-the-grave welfare, many Soviet families prefer to take care of their own younger and elderly members. Or, as Hedrick Smith of the *New York Times* noted, "Paradoxically at both ends of life—in childhood and old age—the system's deficiencies are strengthening the importance of the family."[12]

Russian family policies represent the most far-reaching modern efforts to redesign the role of the family. The Soviet experience supports the thesis that family stability is an essential ingredient in the achievement of social stability. Even in a vast welfare system, the family has been required to perform many functions that a collectivist state could not provide. It is ironic that American conservatives and Soviet leaders have been equally vociferous in advocating "pro-family" sentiments. In both cases, the stability and authority of the family are seen as necessary for upholding and carrying out radically different societal goals.

CONFLICTING ASPIRATIONS

Marxists have not cornered the market in predicting the demise of the family. Respected establishment analysts also have predicted its deterioration. Joseph Schumpeter, a leading conservative economist, predicted the "disintegration of the bourgeois family" because "the capitalist process, by virtue of the psychic attitudes it creates, progressively dims the values of family life and removes the conscientious inhibitions that an old moral tradition would have put in the way toward a different scheme of life."[13]

Walter Lippmann noted that the "family is the inner citadel of religious authority and there the churches have taken their most determined stand." But in this area, as in others, he stated, the churches have lost their authority. Religious leaders "have lost the exclusive right to preside over marriages. They have not been able to maintain the dogma that marriage is indissoluble."[14] Many Western religious and moral leaders have been very concerned that society could be debased by the shifts in family trends. As one theologian put it, American marriage mores have broken away from the biblical idea of "covenant" to one of just "contract." A contract can always be broken, but a covenant means that individuals exist under a higher order, which they are not free to dissolve.[15]

The Old Testament is tolerant of divorce and provides for the legal dissolution of marriage.[16] But Christ spoke out against this view. When asked by the Pharisees about divorce, Jesus responded: "What therefore God hath joined together, let no man put asunder. . . . Whosoever shall put away his wife, and marry another, committeth adultery against her. And if a woman shall put away her husband, and be married to another, she committeth adultery."[17]

The Roman Catholic church has followed this injunction. However, some marriages may be annulled—for specific causes, such as nonconsummation or adultery. Religious authorities have always provided a safety valve—no matter how limited—for dissolving certain unions. The Catholic view is still that marriage "is effected by Divine power," although the grounds for annulment have been more liberally interpreted in recent years. Protestant theology tends to view marriage as a "holy estate," but one that can be terminated.[18]

Historical circumstances, in part, led to Protestant views concerning divorce. The immediate cause of the founding of the Church of England was in large measure a royal divorce. However, during the seventeenth and eighteenth centuries, legal divorce and remarriage in England was only for the very rich—the poor followed folk customs. For the vast majority, the dire social stigma and the high costs involved precluded divorce. More recently, most Protestant as well as Catholic countries enacted civil divorce acts that expanded the grounds on which a marriage could be ended. Christian theologians often found themselves in the position of conceding to the new powers of the civil authorities, and biblical justifications were found for shifting views on divorce.[19]

Other religions have recognized the right of divorce. Muhammad countenanced divorce only as a last resort. Although he admonished his followers that nothing displeased God more than the disruption of marital vows, the Koran makes provision for divorce. The traditional Jewish marriage contract contains clauses providing the wife with certain financial means and assets if the marriage is ended.

With a diminution of the hold of religious authority, new freedoms—if not new disciplines—have emerged as religious and social regulations and controls over marital behavior have declined. While a calculus for defining and measuring happiness is yet to be designed, some evidence indicates that the new-found freedoms have not always led to an increased sense of serenity. A growing number of individuals experiencing family dissolution find that they have rejected old codes of behavior without devising new rules to fill the vacuum. Or as one researcher of shifting sexual and family mores put it, "The freedom to cross the frontiers is of no value to people immobilized by anxiety and inadequacy."[20]

The rejection of old codes raises the question whether the traditional family model remains suitable for a modern free democratic society that places pluralism and individualism on a pedestal. Totalitarian or theocratic societies have one official ideology—or state religion—and countenance little dissent, suppressing individual aspirations. In trying to bottle up change, they render their societies more unstable in the long run. In free societies, the price of new sexual and household freedoms is constant debate and conflict. American society is searching for new rules to reestablish a stable family structure (including the rearing of children), but without subjecting individuals to past sanctions. It is the old conflict of desiring to have the cake and eat it too; we can't do both.

The family is likely to remain a minority of households. Living arrangements will demonstrate a higher degree of diversity, which will require a greater degree of flexibility in public and private policies to cope with the varied needs of different households. The United States is not alone in undergoing these family changes; other industralized nations are experiencing a similar pattern.

Freud noted the inevitable antagonism between an individual's aspirations or instincts and the strictures civilization places on the individual. He concluded that civilization is made possible only by individual renouncement, and that a sense of guilt shapes civilized society. While society provides many benefits for the individual, it also produces a series of discontents. A similar process characterizes family life. Families entail repression of certain actions and desires in exchange for other rewards.

Underlying the current uneasiness and debate about the role of the family is a conflict between striving for social and personal stability versus individual freedom. The older pattern may have been dominated by sexism and lives of quiet desperation, but it did provide society and individuals with a sense of security. The new living arrangements, including frequent dissolution of family ties and the failure to initiate such ties prior to bringing children into this world, are bound to produce their own anxieties. They also frequently place insurmountable obstacles to attaining self-sufficiency. To some it may appear that families are falling apart with nothing to take their place. The scars of a broken home may be difficult to heal, but the pressures within many traditional families are also strong enough to create neurotic personalities. However, despite these discontents, the institution appears to have more strength and resilience than it is often credited with.

Joseph Fletcher, an Episcopalian theologian, noted that "free love is an ideal. Unfortunately, it is an ideal of which very few of us are capable."[21] Yet the important question seems to be: Is the ideal of real equality between husband and wife possible in a growing number of homes? This problem is not just a matter of concern to Western societies. Communist nations, including the Soviet Union and China, demonstrate that sexual inequality in the home and on the job is pervasive and not just a feature of capitalism. Can men and women share power, responsibilities, and opportunities in a far greater way than in the past? If the answer is affirmative, then the families that will emerge from this wrenching period will tend to be based on stronger foundations than in previous eras. Ibsen's Nora will not have to leave home—or her dollhouse—and turn her back on family life. Instead, she and others like her will be able to find a rewarding and self-fulfilling life within the family. All this assumes that parents will accept responsibility for their offspring.

UNRAVELING FAMILY TIES

A review of past developments may suggest what the future holds for the American family. Predictions of the future are always fraught with difficulties, yet turning the clock back to an older family system does not appear to be in the offing. The American family has undergone three periods of rapid change in this century. The first two were tied to pervasive economic and political events: the collapse of the economy during the Great Depression, and World War II followed by prolonged expansion. However, the extraordinary changes that have occurred since the mid-1960s are not so easily understood.

In some respects, it is the immediate postwar period rather than the last quarter-century that is atypical. With occasional diversions, divorce rates had been rising since the Civil War. Legal, religious, and social impediments to the dissolution of marriage had long been thought unjustly cruel by many people, a theme that has been abundantly espoused during the past century in American literature. Indeed, it is surprising that the floodgates of divorce remained closed as long as they did. The historical trend toward lower fertility and smaller households has been evident since the birth of the Republic. The notion that women had no place in the workforce rests upon an artificial distinction between work in or outside of the home, which was not drawn until the nineteenth century.

Whatever the impetus for the dramatic unraveling of the traditional family structure during the 1960s and 1970s, the apparent stabilization during the 1980s offers limited cause for satisfaction. Divorce and child poverty rates remain at near record heights, and the proportion of out-of-wedlock births continues to rise sharply. Families headed by single parents constitute one of the most serious social dilemmas facing the country. Prior to World War II, most single mothers were widows; currently, separation and divorce are the principal causes, but out-of-wedlock births are fast becoming a primary factor in creating female-headed families.

Other familial changes have brought more positive effects, although the rapid transition to new family forms has unquestionably been jolting. Men and women raised to believe that a woman's place was at home have had to adapt themselves to a world where most women labor outside the household. Rigid traditionalists rail against this development, ignoring its voluntary nature and the fact that it has helped women lead more fulfilling lives and raise the living standards of their families.

There is also concern about the unprecedented low fertility rates. Some analysts have raised the specter of a declining population that will diminish America's influence in the world and bankrupt the social security system. These concerns are premature and probably exaggerated. First, the predicted dire consequences are based on the assumption that recent fertility rates will continue into the next generation. Few demographers anticipated either the baby boom or the subsequent baby bust. There is no guarantee that the next generation will not decide to raise larger families. Second, population size has little relation to global influence, as England demonstrated in the nineteenth century and as India, with a population triple that of the United States, does today. Third, an increasing proportion of elderly citizens will put pressure on the social security program but will also diminish the tax burden of financing, for example, school systems for the young. Lower fertility also reduces the number of mouths younger families will have to feed, leaving more discretionary income that could be allocated to the social security system.

The increasing proportion of individuals living outside the family structure is partly a reflection of American affluence and individual preferences. Most of those who live alone are older Americans who prefer independent living; and, in contrast to their parents' generation, social security, private pensions, and savings enable them to do so. Grandparents show no sign of cutting their ties with their children and grandchildren, and in fact their rising affluence enables them to assist descendants far more effectively than grandparents of the past. Grandparents are an important source of child care for many working mothers who cannot afford day care centers. However, the converse is also becoming increasingly a problem. As the grandparents continue to live longer and their infirmities increase, they are becoming a burden to their progeny.

Despite the rapid changes undergone by the family during the last quarter-century, there is no indication that Americans have abandoned family ideals, even if they don't realize them. Most individuals still seek a lifetime spouse and look forward to raising children, even if they prefer smaller families.

SHORING UP THE STRUCTURE

Government assistance is no substitute for the family, but it is an effective means of addressing serious family problems. The expansion of the welfare system has been more a reaction to than a cause of family difficulties. A compassionate and affluent society should ensure that children are not denied basic goods and services because of their household structure. This could prove to be one of the most cost-effective and rewarding investments society can make.

The top priority should be the prevention of births to unmarried women. The government should ensure that family planning services, including the provision of birth control devices, are easily accessible to all adults, and free to those who cannot afford it. Providing birth control information or devices at or near high schools has been extremely controversial, but high-school-age women account for less than one in four out-of-wedlock births.

Wanted or unwanted, children deserve a decent standard of living. Prime responsibility rests, of course, with the parents, but two-thirds of absent fathers fail to provide for their offspring. Despite repeated federal prodding, state governments and the fathers themselves have failed to meet their responsibilities. The federal government should establish adequate child support criteria and effective means of guaranteeing timely payment. But although requiring absent fathers to support their offspring would measurably improve the economic well-being of millions of children, many such fathers earn too little to raise their children out of poverty.

When parents are unable to provide basic necessities for their children, further government assistance is necessary. Helping parents earn an adequate living is the first line of defense. The reintroduction of a public jobs program, abolished in 1981, would provide employment to individuals otherwise unable to find work. However, work alone is insufficient, as nine million Americans remain impoverished despite their work effort. A livable wage is especially important to young adults starting families, but since 1973 the earnings of 20- to 24-year-old men not in school full-time have declined by a fourth after adjusting for inflation. More young women are working, and although the gender gap has narrowed, women's average wages are still significantly below men's. In the 1960s and most of the 1970s, the minimum wage yielded full-time workers who were single parents with two dependents an annual income that raised them above the poverty threshold, but in 1987 the minimum wage provided for less than 80 percent of that standard. In addition to raising the minimum wage, the current earned income tax credit should be amended to consider family size in providing support for low earners.

Lack of affordable child care is a serious impediment to employment for many mothers, particularly single women. Finding affordable care is becoming increasingly difficult because grandmothers and aunts are likely to be either working or living too far away to watch their kin's children. Federal and state governments have to date provided insufficient resources to subsidize child care for parents who cannot afford it, but in late 1987 there are signs of revived interest in boosting federal child care support. Successive administrations and Congresses have ignored this issue since President Nixon vetoed a bill authorizing federal appropriations for child care.

Beyond employment and income assistance, renewed federal efforts to meet the basic health and shelter needs of American families are necessary. Some 37 million Americans have no health in-

surance coverage. Congress has devoted considerable attention and resources to the medical problems of the elderly, but virtually none to the working poor or near-poor and their children. A new federally subsidized health insurance system or an extension of medicaid could fill this gap.

In two short decades following World War II, Americans—with substantial government assistance—moved from being home renters to homeowners. However, the proportion of households owning homes peaked in the late 1970s and has declined slightly in the 1980s. Rental and owning costs in the 1980s have continued to exceed the pace of inflation. Consequently, poorer families must devote larger shares of their budget to shelter costs, and one result has been increased homelessness. The Reagan administration virtually ended construction of housing for low-income families in 1981, and sharply reduced housing outlays. The provision of shelter for low-income families should be another pressing item on the federal agenda.

The role of the government is essential in helping families adjust to the changing social environment. But whatever the government does, most families will continue to do what they have always done—cope as best they can in the face of shifting challenges. When Freud referred to families as the germ cells of civilization, his frame of reference was a traditional family. The direction of the type of society and economy we envisage and, in fact, create will depend in large measure on how this basic institution functions and evolves. Meeting these challenges, and not singing funeral dirges for the family, will provide our greatest opportunities and our greatest hope.

NOTES

CHAPTER ONE: FAMILY MATTERS

1. M. Rostovtzeff, *A History of the Ancient World*, 2 vols. (Oxford: Clarendon Press, 1927), 2: 364.

2. Robert L. Heilbroner, *An Inquiry into the Human Prospect* (New York: W. W. Norton and Co., 1974), p. 15.

3. Bertrand Russell, *Marriage and Morals* (New York: Horace Liveright & Co., 1929), p. 173.

4. François Raveau, "Future Family Patterns and Society," in *The Family and Its Future*, ed. Katherine Elliott (London: J. & A. Churchill, 1970), pp. 43–44.

5. Gary S. Becker, "A Theory of Marriage," in *Economics of the Family: Marriage, Children, and Human Capital*, ed. Theodore W. Shultz (Chicago: University of Chicago Press, 1973), p. 299. See also Robert J. Willis, "What Have We Learned from the Economics of the Family?" *American Economic Review* (May 1987): 68–81.

6. Margaret Mead, "The Impact of Cultural Changes on the Family," in *The Family in the Urban Community* (Detroit: Merrill-Palmer School, 1953), p. 4.

7. Victor R. Fuchs, *The Service Economy* (New York: Columbia University Press, 1968), p. 11.

8. Department of Health, Education, and Welfare, "Formulating National Policies on Child and Family Development" (1978, mimeographed), p. 7.

9. Roper Organization, *The American Dream: A National Survey by the Wall Street Journal* (Princeton, N.J.: Dow Jones Company, February 1987), pp. 46–47.

10. Arthur Norton, "Current Trends in Marriage and Divorce among American Women," *Journal of Marriage and the Family* (February 1987): 8–9.

11. Larry L. Bumpass, "Children and Marital Disruption: A Replication and Update," *Demography* (February 1984): 71–82.

12. Richard E. Leakey and Roger Lewin, *People of the Lake: Mankind and Its Beginnings* (Garden City, N.Y.: Doubleday & Co., 1978), p. 121.

CHAPTER TWO: LOVE AND MARRIAGE

1. Amitai Etzioni, quoted in White House Working Group on the Family, *Preserving America's Future*, 2 December 1986, p. 13.

2. Roper Organization, *The American Dream: A National Survey by the Wall Street Journal* (Princeton, N.J.: Dow Jones Company, February 1987), pp. 50–51.

3. Research and Forecasts, *The Ethan Allen Report: The Status and Future of the American Family* (Danbury, Conn.: Ethan Allen, 1986).

4. Ibid.

5. Alexander W. Astin et al., *The American Freshman: National Norms for Fall 1986* (Los Angeles: University of California at Los Angeles Higher Education Research Institute, December 1986).

6. Roper Organization, *The 1985 Virginia Slims American Woman's Opinion Poll* (New York: Virginia Slims, 1985).

7. Philip J. Greven, Jr., *Four Generations: Population, Land, and Family in Colonial Andover, Massachusetts* (Ithaca, N.Y.: Cornell University Press, 1970), p. 121.

8. National Center for Health Statistics, "Advance Report of Final Marriage Statistics, 1984," *Monthly Vital Statistics Report*, 3 June 1987, p. 3.

9. Paul C. Glick and Arthur J. Norton, "Marrying, Divorcing, and Living Together in the U.S. Today," *Population Bulletin* 32, no. 5 (1979): 6.

10. Roper Organization, "The Social Impact of AIDS," *Public Pulse*, April 1987, pp. 1–2.

11. Arthur Norton, "Current Trends in Marriage and Divorce Among American Women," *Journal of Marriage and the Family* (February 1987): 3–14.

12. Victor R. Fuchs, *How We Live* (Cambridge, Mass.: Harvard University Press, 1983), pp. 140–44.

13. Gary S. Becker, "A Theory of Marriage," in *Economics of the Family: Marriage, Children, and Human Capital*, ed. Theodore W. Schultz (Chicago: University of Chicago Press, 1973), pp. 301–4.

14. Eleanor D. Macklin, "Nontraditional Family Forms," in Marvin B. Sussman and Suzanne K. Steinmetz, eds., *Handbook of Marriage and the Family* (New York: Plenum Press, 1987), p. 320.

15. Council of Europe, *Recent Demographic Developments in the Member States of the Council of Europe* (Strasbourg, France: Council of Europe, 1987), p. 71; United Nations, *1976 Demographic Yearbook* (New York: UN, 1977), pp. 646–55.

16. Paul C. Glick and Sung-Ling Lin, "Recent Changes in Divorce and Remarriage," *Journal of Marriage and the Family* (November 1986): 737–47.

17. Anthony M. Casale, *USA Today: Tracking Tomorrow's Trends* (Kansas City, Mo.: Andrews, McMeel & Parker, 1986), p. 108.

18. Organization for Economic Cooperation and Development, *Living Conditions in OECD Countries* (Paris: OECD, 1986), pp. 23–24.

19. Mary Jo Bane, *Here to Stay: American Families in the Twentieth Century* (New York: Basic Books, 1976), p. 30, appendix A-6.

20. Arland Thornton and Deborah Freedman, "The Changing American Family," *Population Bulletin* (October 1983): 7.

21. Norval D. Glenn and Michael Supancic, "The Social and Demographic Correlates of Divorce and Separation in the U.S.: An Update and Reconsideration," *Journal of Marriage and the Family* (August 1984): 563–76.

22. M. F. Nimkoff, *The Family* (Boston: Houghton Mifflin, 1934), p. 446.

23. Elizabeth Peters, "The Impact of State Divorce Laws on the Marriage Contract: Marriage, Divorce, and Marital Property Settlements," *American Economic Review* (June 1986): 437–54.

CHAPTER THREE: BE FRUITFUL AND MULTIPLY

1. Alan L. Otten, "Birth Dearth," *Wall Street Journal,* 18 June 1987, p. 1; Ben J. Wattenberg, *The Birth Dearth* (New York: Pharos Books, 1987), parts 2 and 3.

2. Ansley Coale and Melvin Zelnick, *New Estimates of Fertility and Population in the United States* (Princeton, N.J.: Princeton University Press, 1963), p. 36.

3. Richard A. Easterlin, "The American Population," in *American Economic Growth: An Economist's History of the United States,* ed. Lance E. Davis et al. (New York: Harper & Row, 1972), pp. 123–27.

4. Charles F. Westoff, "Marriage and Fertility in the Developed Countries," *Scientific American,* December 1978, p. 51.

5. Thomas Malthus, *Population: The First Essay* (Ann Arbor, Mich.: University of Michigan Press, 1959), p. 5.

6. Richard A. Easterlin, Michael L. Wachter, and Susan M. Wachter, "Here Comes Another Baby Boom," *Wharton Magazine* (Summer 1979): 29–30.

7. William P. Butz and Michael P. Ward, *Countercyclical U.S. Fertility and Its Implications* (Santa Monica, Calif.: RAND Corporation, 1978), pp. 9–10.

8. Howard N. Fullerton, Jr., "Labor Force Projections: 1986 to 2000," *Monthly Labor Review* (September 1987): 25.

9. Andrew J. Cherlin, *Marriage, Divorce, Remarriage* (Cambridge, Mass.: Harvard University Press, 1981).

10. Stanley K. Henshaw, Jacqueline Darroch Forrest, and Jennifer Van Hart, "Abortion Services in the United States, 1984 and 1985," *Family Planning Perspectives* (March/April 1987): 63–70; Stanley K. Henshaw, "Characteristics of U.S. Women Having Abortions, 1982–1983," *Family Planning Perspectives* (January/February 1987): 5–9.

11. Kingsley Davis, Mikhail S. Bernstam, and Rita Ricardo-Campbell, eds., "Below-Replacement Fertility in Industrial Societies," *Population and Development Review,* suppl. to vol. 12 (1986): 43.

12. William F. Pratt, William D. Mosher, Christine A. Bachrach, and Marjorie C. Horn, "Understanding U.S. Fertility," *Population Bulletin* (December 1984): 22.

13. Stanley K. Henshaw and Susheela Singh, "Sterilization Regret among U.S. Couples," *Family Planning Perspectives* (September/October 1986): 238–40.

14. Stephen L. Isaacs and Renee J. Holt, "Redefining Procreation: Facing the Issues," *Population Bulletin* (September 1987): 10, 15–16, 24; William D. Mosher, "Reproductive Impairments in the United States, 1965–1982," *Demography* (August 1985): 415–30.

15. Greg J. Duncan, "Educational Attainment," in James N. Morgan et al., eds., *Five Thousand American Families: Patterns of Economic Progress* (Ann Arbor, Mich.: Survey Research Center of the University of Michigan, 1974–77), 1:317–20.

16. Peter H. Lindert, "Sibling Position and Achievement," *Journal of Human Resources* (Spring 1977): 209.

17. Russell Hill and Frank Stafford, "Time Inputs to Children," in Morgan, *Five Thousand American Families,* 2: 333–36.

18. Russell Hill and Frank Stafford, "Allocation of Time to Preschool Children and Educational Opportunity," *Journal of Human Resources* (Summer 1974): 339.

CHAPTER FOUR: THE CARE AND FEEDING
OF CHILDREN

1. Louis Harris, *Inside America* (New York: Vintage Books, 1987), p. 90; Anthony M. Casale, *USA Today: Tracking Tomorrow's Trends* (Kansas City, Mo.: Andrews, McMeel & Parker, 1986), p. 111.

2. Thomas J. Espenshade, *Investing in Children* (Washington, D.C.: Urban Institute, 1984), pp. 3, 26–27, 106; estimates were updated for inflation in accordance with Espenshade's recommendation.

3. House of Representatives, *U.S. Children and Their Families: Current Conditions and Recent Trends, 1987* (Washington, D.C.: Government Printing Office, March 1987).

4. Willard Waller, *The Old Love and the New* (New York: Horace Liveright & Co., 1930), pp. 22–23.

5. William J. Goode, *Women in Divorce* (New York: Free Press, 1965), pp. 317–18.

6. Sheldon Glueck and Eleanor Glueck, *Unraveling Juvenile Delinquency* (Cambridge, Mass.: Harvard University Press, 1950), p. 91; idem. *Delinquents and Nondelinquents in Perspective* (Cambridge, Mass.: Harvard University Press, 1968), p. 88.

7. Lee Burchinal, "Characteristics of Adolescents from Unbroken, Broken, and Reconstituted Families," *Journal of Marriage and the Family* (February 1964): 48–50.

8. F. Ivan Nye, "Child Adjustment in Broken and Unhappy Unbroken Homes," *Marriage and Family Living* (November 1957): 360–61.

9. Judson T. Landis, "Social Correlates of Divorce and Nondivorce among the Unhappy Married," *Marriage and Family Living* (May 1963): 179; Benjamin Schlesinger and Eugene Stasiuk, "Children of Divorced Parents in Second Marriages," in *Children of Separation and Divorce*, ed. Irving R. Stuart and Lawrence Edwin (New York: Grossman, 1972), pp. 21–22.

10. Judson T. Landis, "The Trauma of Children When Parents Divorce," *Marriage and Family Living* (February 1960): 10–11.

11. Joan B. Kelly and Judith S. Wallerstein, "Children of Divorce," *Principal* (October 1979): 55.

12. William G. Bowen and T. Aldrick Finegan. *The Economics of Labor Force Participation* (Princeton, N.J.: Princeton University Press, 1969), pp. 397, 411.

13. Albert Rees and Wayne Gray, *Family Effects in Youth Employment*, National Bureau of Economic Research (Cambridge, Mass., 1979, processed), p. 8.

14. Alvin L. Schorr, *Public Policies and Single Parents* (Cleveland: Case Western Reserve University, 1979), p. 12.

15. June O'Neill, *Determinants of Child Support* (Washington, D.C.: Urban Institute, 1985), pp. 8–9.

16. House Committee on Ways and Means, *Background Material and Data on Programs within the Jurisdiction of the Committee on Ways and Means* (Washington, D.C.: Government Printing Office, 6 March 1987), WMCP: 100–4, pp. 467, 485.

CHAPTER FIVE: THE FAMILY AND WORK
GO TOGETHER

1. *New York Times,* 12 September 1976, p. 1.

2. Howard Hayghe, "Rise in Mothers' Labor Force Activity Includes Those with Infants," *Monthly Labor Review* (February 1986): 43–45; Roper Organization, *The 1985 Virginia Slims American Women's Opinion Poll* (New York: Virginia Slims, 1985), p. 86; Research and Forecasts, *The Ethan Allen Report: The Status and Future of the American Family* (Danbury, Conn.: Ethan Allen, 1986), p. 197.

3. Judith Ann, "The Secretarial Proletariat," in *Sisterhood Is Powerful,* ed. Robin Morgan (New York: Vintage Books, 1970), p. 100.

4. Roper Organization, *Virginia Slims Poll,* table 3.2, p. 35.

5. Eleanor Flexner, *Century of Struggle: The Women's Rights Movement in the United States* (New York: Atheneum Publishers, 1968), p. 9.

6. Don D. Lescohier, "Working Conditions," in *History of Labor in the United States,* 4 vols., ed. John R. Commons et al. (New York: Macmillan Co., 1935), 3: 36–37.

7. Cited in Elizabeth Faulkner Baker, *Technology and Women's Work* (New York: Columbia University Press, 1964), p. 6.

8. William H. Chafe, "Looking Backward in Order to Look Forward: Women, Work, and Social Values in America," in *Women and the American Economy: A Look to the 1980s,* ed. Juanita M. Kreps (Englewood Cliffs, N.J.: Prentice-Hall, 1976), pp. 6–7.

9. Robert L. Heilbroner, *The Economic Transformation of America* (New York: Harcourt Brace Jovanovich, 1977), pp. 38–40, 134; Daniel T. Rodgers, *The Work Ethic in Industrial America, 1850–1920* (Chicago: University of Chicago Press, 1978), p. 196.

10. "Prefatory Letter from Theodore Roosevelt," in Mrs. John Van Vorst and Marie Van Vorst, *The Woman Who Toils* (New York: Doubleday, Page, & Co., 1903), p. 2.

11. Ben Wattenberg, "The Birth Dearth: Danger Ahead?" *U.S. News & World Report,* 22 June 1987, p. 61, and *The Birth Dearth* (New York: Pharos Books, 1987), p. 8.

12. Walter Houghton, *The Victorian Frame of Mind* (New Haven, Conn.: Yale University Press, 1957), p. 343.

13. Christopher Lasch, *Haven in a Heartless World: The Family Besieged* (New York: Basic Books, 1977), pp. 5–6.

14. Bureau of the Census, *Historical Statistics of the United States: Colonial Times to 1957* (Washington, D.C.: Government Printing Office, 1960), p. 72.

15. Francine D. Blau, "The Data on Women Workers: Past, Present, and Future," in *Women Working: Theories and Facts in Perspective,* ed. Ann H. Stromberg et al. (Palo Alto, Calif.: Mayfield Publishing Co., 1978).

16. National Commission on Employment and Unemployment Statistics, *Counting the Labor Force* (Washington, D.C.: Government Printing Office, 1979), p. 43.

17. Elizabeth Brandeis, "Labor Legislation," in Commons et al., *History of Labor,* 3: 511–12.

18. Tony Tanner, *Adultery in the Novel: Contract and Transgression* (Baltimore: Johns Hopkins University Press, 1979), p. 373.

19. Victor Fuchs, *How We Live* (Cambridge, Mass.: Harvard University Press, 1983), p. 134.

20. William G. Bowen and T. Aldrich Finegan, *The Economics of Labor Force Participation* (Princeton, N.J.: Princeton University Press, 1969), p. 28.

21. Fuchs, *How We Live*, pp. 152–88; Jacob Mincer and Solomon Polachek, "Family Investments in Human Capital: Earnings of Women," in *Economics of the Family: Marriage, Children, and Human Capital*, ed. Theodore W. Schultz (Chicago: University of Chicago Press, 1973), p. 397.

22. Sar A. Levitan, Peter E. Carlson, and Isaac Shapiro, *Protecting American Workers* (Washington, D.C.: Bureau of National Affairs, 1986), pp. 66–69.

23. Bureau of the Census, *Male-Female Differences in Work Experience, Occupation, and Earnings: 1984* (Washington, D.C.: Government Printing Office, August 1987), Household Economic Studies, Series P-70, no. 10, pp. 6–10; Barbara F. Reskin and Heidi Hartmann, eds., *Women's Work, Men's Work* (Washington, D.C.: National Academy Press, 1986), p. 123.

24. Laurie Hays, "Pay Problems: How Couples React When Wives Out-Earn Husbands," *Wall Street Journal*, 19 June 1987, p. 23.

25. Isabel V. Sawhill et al., *Income Transfers and Family Structure* (Washington, D.C.: Urban Institute, 1975), p. 3.

26. F. Ivan Nye, "Husband-Wife Relationship," in *Working Mothers*, ed. Lois Wladis Hoffman and F. Ivan Nye (San Francisco: Jossey-Bass, 1974), pp. 205–6.

27. AP/Media General Poll conducted 3–11 April 1986, Media General Inc.; Fabian Linden, "Women's Work Is Almost Never Done," *Across the Board*, June 1987, pp. 5–6; Selwyn Feinstein, "Labor Letter," *Wall Street Journal*, 3 November 1987, p. 1.

28. Sandra L. Hofferth and Kristin A. Moore, "Women's Employment and Marriage," in *The Subtle Revolution: Women at Work*, ed. Ralph E. Smith (Washington, D.C.: Urban Institute, 1979), pp. 113–15; Frank P. Stafford, "Women's Use of Time Converging with Men's," *Monthly Labor Review* (December 1980): 57–58.

29. Bureau of the Census, *Who's Minding the Kids? Child Care Arrangements: Winter 1984–85* (Washington, D.C.: Government Printing Office, May 1987), Household Economic Studies, Series P-70, no. 9, table 1, p. 13.

30. Bureau of the Census, *After School Care of School-Age Children: December 1984* (Washington, D.C.: Government Printing Office, January 1987), Special Studies Series, P-23, no. 149.

31. *Ethan Allen Report*, p. 7.

32. "OEO Child Care Program; Veto Sustained in the Senate," *Congressional Quarterly Almanac* (Washington: Congressional Quarterly, 1971), p. 504.

33. Louis Harris, *Inside America* (New York: Vintage Books, 1987), p. 19.

CHAPTER SIX: FEMALE-HEADED FAMILIES

1. Arthur W. Calhoun, *A Social History of the American Family: From Colonial Times to the Present*, 3 vols. (New York: Barnes & Noble, 1945), 3: 184.

2. Department of Labor, Office of Policy Planning and Research, *The Negro Family: The Case for National Action* (Washington, D.C.: Government Printing Office, 1965), pp. 5, 29, 35, 39, 47.

3. William Ryan, "Savage Discovery—The Moynihan Report," in *The Black Family: Essays and Studies*, ed. Robert Staples (Belmont, Calif.: Wadsworth Publishing Co., 1971), p. 58.

4. Robert B. Hill, *The Strengths of Black Families* (New York: National Urban League, 1971), pp. 6, 9, 31.

5. Irwin Garfinkel and Sara S. McLanahan, *Single Mothers and Their Children* (Washington: Urban Institute, 1986), p. 8.

6. Transcript of CBS Report, "The Vanishing Family—Crisis in Black America," in the Senate *Congressional Record*, 29 January 1986, pp. S. 393–403.

7. Betty Friedan, "Feminism Takes a New Turn," *New York Times Magazine*, 8 November 1979, pp. 40, 92; Carol F. Steinbach, "Womens' Movement II," *National Journal*, 29 August 1987, p. 2145.

8. Garfinkel and McLanahan, *Single Mothers and Their Children*, pp. 1, 8, 47.

9. Douglas Besharov and Karl Zinsmeister, "Unwed Moms Are White, Too," *Washington Post*, 3 May 1987, p. B5.

10. Council of Europe, *Recent Demographic Developments in the Member States of the Council of Europe* (Strasbourg, France: Council of Europe, 1987), p. 67.

11. Dirk J. van de Kaa, "Europe's Second Demographic Transition," *Population Bulletin* (March 1987): 35; Organization for Economic Co-operation and Development, *Living Conditions in OECD Countries* (Paris: OECD, 1986), pp. 23–24.

12. William Julius Wilson and Kathryn M. Neckerman, "Poverty and Family Structure," in Sheldon H. Danziger and Daniel Weinberg, eds., *Fighting Poverty* (Cambridge, Mass.: Harvard University Press, 1986), pp. 233–34; Willard L. Rodgers and Arland Thornton, "Changing Patterns of First Marriage in the United States," *Demography* (May 1985): 265–79.

13. Barbara Ehrenreich, *The Hearts of Men* (Garden City, N.Y.: Anchor Press, 1983).

14. Gordon Berlin and Andrew Sum, "Toward a More Perfect Union: Basic Skills, Poor Families, and Our Economic Future," 21 September 1987 (mimeo draft); 1986 data provided by Andrew Sum.

15. House Select Committee on Children, Youth, and Families, *U.S. Children and Their Families: Current Conditions and Recent Trends, 1987* (Washington, D.C.: Government Printing Office, March 1987), p. 68; Garfinkel and McLanahan, *Single Mothers and Their Children*, pp. 28–33.

16. Barbara Heyns, "The Influence of Parental Work on Children's School Achievement," in Sheila B. Kamerman and Cheryl D. Hayes, eds., *Families That Work* (Washington, D.C.: National Academy Press, 1985), pp. 229–67.

17. Sandara L. Hofferth, Joan R. Kahn, and Wendy Baldwin, "Premarital Sexual Activity among U.S. Teenage Women over the Past Three Decades," *Family Planning Perspectives* (March/April 1987): 46–53.

18. Stanley K. Henshaw, "Characteristics of U.S. Women Having Abortions, 1982–1983," *Family Planning Perspectives* (January/February 1987): 8.

19. Cheryl D. Hayes, ed., *Risking the Future* (Washington, D.C.: National Academy Press, 1987), p. 61.

20. House Select Committee on Children, Youth, and Families, *Teen Pregnancy: What Is Being Done?* (Washington, D.C.: Government Printing Office, December 1986), Report 99-1022, p. 13.

21. General Accounting Office, *Teenage Pregnancy* (Washington, D.C.: GAO, July 1986), PEMD-86-16BR, p. 11.

22. Arthur Campbell, "The Role of Family Planning in the Reduction of Poverty," *Journal of Marriage and the Family* (May 1968): 236.

23. Martha R. Burt, "Estimating the Public Costs of Teenage Childbearing," *Family Planning Perspectives* (September/October 1986): 221–26; Hayes, *Risking the Future*, pp. 126–28, 134–38; Marian Wright Edelman, *Families in Peril* (Cambridge, Mass.: Harvard University Press, 1987), p. 32.

24. Richard Lingeman, *Small Town America* (New York: Putnam, 1980), as cited by Walter Clemons, "of Sleepers and Swings," *Newsweek*, 28 July 1980, p. 65.

25. Don Colburn, "The Politics of Abortion," *Washington Post*, 8 September 1987, Health section, pp. 12–14.

CHAPTER SEVEN: THE FAMILY IN THE WELFARE SYSTEM

1. Jimmy Carter, "The American Family: A Campaign Statement in Manchester, N.H." (processed), 3 August 1976.

2. Presidential radio address, 3 December 1983; White House Working Group on the Family, *The Family: Preserving America's Future*, 2 December 1986, pp. 6, 31.

3. The White House, "Executive Order: The Family," 3 September 1987.

4. Charles Murray, "Poverty and Welfare: Are We Losing Ground?" *Cato Policy Report* (November/December 1984): 10.

5. Christopher Lasch, *Haven in a Heartless World: The Family Besieged* (New York: Basic Books, 1977), p. 100.

6. Louis Harris, *Inside America* (New York: Vintage Books, 1987), pp. 345–46.

7. Gunnar Myrdal, *Population: A Problem for Democracy* (Cambridge, Mass.: Harvard University Press, 1940), p. 74.

8. Franklin D. Scott, *Sweden: The Nation's History* (Minneapolis: University of Minnesota Press, 1977), pp. 370, 438.

9. Alva Myrdal, *Nation and Family: The Swedish Experiment in Democratic Family and Population Policy* (Cambridge, Mass.: M.I.T. Press, 1941), p. 27.

10. Gunnar Myrdal, *Beyond the Welfare State* (London: Methuen & Co., 1960), p. 24.

11. Rita Liljestrom, "Sweden," in *Family Policy: Government and Families in Fourteen Countries*, ed. Sheila B. Kamerman and Alfred J. Kahn (New York: Columbia University Press, 1978), pp. 25–26.

12. Sheila B. Kamerman and Alfred J. Kahn, "Europe's Innovative Family Policies," *Trans-Atlantic Perspective* (March 1980): 10.

13. Alfred J. Kahn and Sheila Kamerman, *Income Transfers for Families with Children* (Philadelphia: Temple University Press, 1983), pp. 202–5.

14. Dirk J. van de Kaa, "Europe's Second Demographic Transition," *Population Bulletin* (March 1987): 19.

15. National Social Insurance Board, *Social Insurance Statistics: Facts 1986* (Stockholm: National Social Insurance Board, December 1986).

16. The Family Impact Seminar of George Washington University, "Recommendations to the White House Conference on Families" (processed, 1980), p. 4.

17. Laurie Hays, "Pay Problems: How Couples React When Wives Out-Earn Husbands," *Wall Street Journal*, 19 June 1987, p. 23.

18. Bureau of the Census, *Estimates of Poverty Including the Value of Noncash Benefits: 1986* (Washington, D.C.: Government Printing Office, July 1987), Technical Paper 57, pp. 8, 13; General Accounting Office, *Noncash Benefits* (Washington, D.C.: GAO, September 1987).

CHAPTER EIGHT: CASH SUPPORT AND MORE

1. Barbara A. Lingg, "Women Social Security Beneficiaries Aged 62 or Older, 1960–85," *Social Security Bulletin* (May 1987), table 4, p. 39.

2. Edmund T. Donovan, "Goldfarb and Mathews: Legal Challenges to the Dependency Test for Spouse's Benefits," *Social Security Bulletin* (December 1984): 22–27.

3. Virginia P. Reno, "Women and Social Security," *Social Security Bulletin* (February 1985): 14, 22–23.

4. Nancy M. Gordon, "Institutional Responses: The Social Security System," in *The Subtle Revolution: Women at Work*, ed. Ralph E. Smith (Washington, D.C.: Urban Institute, 1979), pp. 239, 245.

5. House Committee on Ways and Means, *Report on Earnings Sharing Implementation Study* (Washington, D.C.: Government Printing Office, 14 February 1985), WMCP: 99-4; Congressional Budget Office, *Earnings Sharing Options for the Social Security System* (Washington, D.C.: CBO, January 1986).

6. Margaret M. Dahm and Phyllis H. Fineshriber, "Examining Dependents' Allowances," in U.S. National Commission on Unemployment Compensation, *Unemployment Compensation: Studies and Research* (Washington, D.C.: Government Printing Office, July 1980), 1: 77–80 (updated).

7. Patricia Ruggles and Richard C. Michel, *Participation Rates in the Aid to Families with Dependent Children Program* (Washington, D.C.: Urban Institute, April 1987), p. 37.

8. Charles Murray, *Losing Ground* (New York: Basic Books, 1984), pp. 156–62.

9. Greg J. Duncan and Saul D. Hoffman, "Economic Consequences of Marital Instability," in Martin David and Timothy Smeeding, eds., *Horizontal Equity, Uncertainty, and Economic Well-Being* (Chicago: University of Chicago Press, 1985), pp. 437, 468.

10. David T. Ellwood and Lawrence H. Summers, "Poverty in America: Is Welfare the Answer or the Problem?" in Sheldon H. Danziger and Daniel H. Weinberg, eds., *Fighting Poverty* (Cambridge, Mass.: Harvard University Press, 1986), pp. 94–97.

11. General Accounting Office, *An Evaluation of the 1981 AFDC Changes: Final Report* (Washington, D.C.: GAO, 2 July 1985), PEMD-85-4, pp. iii–vi.

12. House Committee on Ways and Means, *Background Material and Data on Programs within the Jurisdiction of the Committee on Ways and Means* (Washington, D.C.: Government Printing Office, 6 March 1987), WMCP: 100-4, p. 444.

13. Ibid., pp. 449–50.

14. SRI International, *Final Report of the Seattle-Denver Income Maintenance Experiment* (Menlo Park, Calif.: SRI International, 1983), 1: 357–58.

15. Alfred J. Kahn and Sheila Kamerman, *Income Transfers for Families with Children* (Philadelphia: Temple University Press, 1983), p. 203; Dirk J. van de Kaa, "Europe's Second Demographic Transition," *Population Bulletin* (March 1987): 51.

16. Sar A. Levitan and Frank Gallo, "The Targeted Jobs Tax Credit: An Uncertain and Unfinished Experiment," *Labor Law Journal* (October 1987): 641–49.

17. *Public Opinion* (November/December 1986): 34.

18. "Opinion Outlook," *National Journal*, 12 September 1987, p. 2296.

19. James Cramer, "Births, Expected Family Size, and Poverty," in *Five Thousand American Families: Patterns of Economic Progress*, 5 vols., ed. James N. Morgan et al. (Ann Arbor: Survey Research Center of the University of Michigan, 1974–77), 2: 285–86.

20. House Select Committee on Children, Youth, and Families, *U.S. Children and Their Families: Current Conditions and Recent Trends* (Washington, D.C.: Government Printing Office, March 1987), p. 87.

21. Aida Torres and Jacqueline Darroch Forrest, "Family Planning Clinic Services in U.S. Counties, 1983," *Family Planning Perspectives* (March/April 1987): 55; phone conversation with Lisa Kaeser, Alan Guttmacher Institute, 26 October 1987.

22. House Select Committee on Children, Youth, and Families, *Federal Programs Affecting Children, 1987* (Washington, D.C.: Government Printing Office, 31 July 1987), Report 100-258, pp. 55–58, 73–74, 81–82.

23. U.S. Senate, *Congressional Record* (daily edition), 27 October 1987, pp. 15086–15183.

24. Library of Congress, Congressional Research Service, *Cash and Noncash Benefits for Persons with Limited Income* (Washington, D.C.: CRS, 10 September 1987), 87-759 EPW, pp. 80–105.

25. George Sternlieb and James W. Hughes, "Demographics and Housing in America," *Population Bulletin* (January 1986): 9.

26. General Accounting Office, *Changes in Rent Burdens and Housing Conditions of Lower Income Households* (Washington, D.C.: GAO, 23 April 1985), RCED-85-108, pp. 1–3.

27. "In Search of a Housing Policy," *Ford Foundation Letter*, October 1987, p. 6.

28. Phone conversation with Toshio Tatara, American Public Welfare Association, 29 October 1987.

29. General Accounting Office, *Community Services* (Washington, D.C.: GAO, May 1986), HRD-86-91, pp. 12–15.

CHAPTER NINE: CHANGING INSTITUTIONS AND FINANCIAL ARRANGEMENTS

1. Committee for Economic Development, *Children in Need* (Washington: CED, 1987), p. 15.

2. Christopher Jencks et al., *Who Gets Ahead? The Determinants of Economic Success in America* (New York: Basic Books, 1979), p. 81.

3. Sar A. Levitan and Frank Gallo, *A Second Chance: Training for Jobs* (Kalamazoo, Mich.: W. E. Upjohn Institute for Employment Research, 1988).

4. Department of Labor, *Continuous Longitudinal Manpower Survey* (January 1980), report no. 10, tables 5–9.

5. Edward M. Gramlich, "Impact of Minimum Wages on Other Wages, Employment, and Family Incomes," *Brookings Papers on Economic Activity* 2(1976): 442–43; Sar A. Levitan and Isaac Shapiro, *Working but Poor: America's Contradiction* (Baltimore: Johns Hopkins University Press, 1987), pp. 49–59.

6. Sar A. Levitan and Elizabeth Conway, "Part-time Employment: Living on Half Rations," *Challenge* (May/June 1988).

7. Sar A. Levitan and Richard S. Belous, *Shorter Hours, Shorter Weeks: Spreading the Work to Reduce Unemployment* (Baltimore: Johns Hopkins University Press, 1977), pp. 66, 68, 70.

8. Paul O. Flaim, "Work Schedules of Americans: An Overview of New Findings," *Monthly Labor Review* (November 1986): 3; Dana E. Friedman, *Family-supportive Policies* (New York: Conference Board, 1987), p. 38.

9. Frank W. Schiff, "Short-Time Compensation: Assessing the Issues," *Monthly Labor Review* (May 1986): 28–30.

10. Juanita M. Kreps, "Some Time Dimensions of Manpower Policy," in *Jobs for Americans*, ed. Eli Ginzberg (Englewood Cliffs, N.J.: Prentice-Hall, 1976), p. 186.

11. Sheila B. Kamerman and Alfred J. Kahn, *A Workplace for People* (New York: Columbia University Press, 1987); Helen Axel, *Corporations and Families: Changing Practices and Perspectives* (New York: Conference Board, 1985), pp. 31–36; Cathy Trost, "Best Employers for Women and Parents," *Wall Street Journal*, 30 November 1987, p. 23.

12. Isabel V. Sawhill, talk before the White House Conference on Families, Baltimore, 5 June 1980.

13. Harvey S. Rosen, *The Marriage Tax Is Down but Not Out* (Cambridge, Mass.: National Bureau of Economic Research, May 1987), Working Paper no. 2231.

14. White House Working Group on the Family, *The Family: Preserving America's Future*, 2 December 1986, p. 45.

15. Thomas J. Espenshade and Joseph J. Minarik, "Demographic Implications of the 1986 U.S. Tax Reform," *Population and Development Review* (March 1987): 115–27.

16. Joint Committee on Taxation, *Estimates of Federal Tax Expenditures for Fiscal Years 1988–1992* (Washington, D.C.: Government Printing Office, 27 February 1987), JCS-3-87, p. 22; Internal Revenue Service, "Selected Statistical Series, 1970–1987," *Statistics of Income Bulletin* (Spring 1987): 77.

17. Testimony of Peter Gottschalk and Sheldon Danziger, Institute for Research on Poverty, before House Committee on Government Operations, Employment and Housing Subcommittee, *Work and Poverty: The Special Problems of the Working Poor* (Washington, D.C.: Government Printing Office, 12 December 1985), p. 22; House Committee on Ways and Means, *Background Material and Data on Programs within the Jurisdiction of the Committee on Ways and Means* (Washington, D.C.: Government Printing Office, 6 March 1987), pp. 657–58.

18. Doris Jonas Freed and Timothy B. Walker, "Family Law in the Fifty States: An Overview," *Family Law Quarterly* (Winter 1987): 443.

19. Harry D. Krause, *Family Law* (St. Paul, Minn.: West Publishing Co., 1977), p. 40.

20. Alan Sussman and Martin Guggenheim, *The Rights of Parents* (New York: Avon Books, 1980), p. 56.

21. Harry D. Krause, *Family Law in a Nutshell* (St. Paul, Minn.: West Publishing Co., 1986), pp. 77–85.

22. Murray A. Straus and Richard J. Gelles, "How Violent Are American Families?" in G. T. Hotaling et al., eds., *New Directions in Family Violence Research* (Beverly Hills, Calif.: Sage Publications, 1988, forthcoming), and "Societal Change and Change in Family Violence from 1975 to 1985 As Revealed by Two National Surveys," *Journal of Marriage and the Family* (August 1986): 465–79.

23. Sanford J. Fox, *Juvenile Courts* (St. Paul, Minn.: West Publishing Co., 1977), p. 17.

CHAPTER TEN: THE QUEST FOR FULFILLMENT

1. Bertrand Russell, *A History of Western Philosophy* (New York: Simon & Schuster, 1945), pp. 111–16 and 518–22.

2. H. G. Wells, *A Modern Utopia* (Lincoln: University of Nebraska Press, 1967), pp. 191–92.

3. "The Numbers Game," *National Journal,* 10 October 1987, p. 2574.

4. Marjorie Honig and Nira Shamai, "Israel," in *Family Policy: Government and Families in Fourteen Countries,* ed. Sheila B. Kamerman and Alfred J. Kahn (New York: Columbia University Press, 1978), pp. 407–8.

5. Nena O'Neill and George O'Neill, *Open Marriage: A New Life Style for Couples* (New York: M. Evans & Co., 1972), p. 52.

6. Karl Marx and Friedrich Engels, *The Communist Manifesto* (Chicago: Henry Regnery, 1954), p. 31.

7. Karl Marx, *Capital: A Critique of Political Economy,* 3 vols. (London: George Allen & Unwin, 1949), 1: 469–71.

8. Friedrich Engels, *The Origin of the Family, Private Property, and the State* (New York: International Publishers, 1969), pp. 58–59.

9. David Mace and Vera Mace, *The Soviet Family* (Garden City, N.Y.: Doubleday & Co., 1964), p. 221.

10. Zsuzsa Ferge, "Hungary," in Kamerman and Kahn, eds., *Family Policy,* pp. 72–73.

11. James Cracraft, ed., *The Soviet Union Today* (Chicago: University of Chicago Press, 1988), p. 334; Paul R. Gregory and Robert C. Stuart, *Soviet Economic Structure and Performance* (New York: Harper & Row, 1981), pp. 206–7.

12. Leonard Schapiro and Joseph Godson, eds., *The Soviet Worker* (London: Macmillan Press, 1982), p. 100; Hedrick Smith, *The Russians* (New York: Ballantine Books, 1977), pp. 186–87.

13. Cited in Victor Fuchs, *How We Live* (Cambridge, Mass.: Harvard University Press, 1983), p. 221.

14. Walter Lippmann, *A Preface to Morals* (New York: Macmillan Co., 1929), p. 88.

15. Charlotte Saikowski, "A Time for Families," *Christian Science Monitor,* 25 July 1980.

16. Deut. 24:12.

17. Mark 10:9–12.

18. Arthur W. Calhoun, *A Social History of the American Family: From Colonial Times to the Present,* 3 vols. (New York: Barnes & Noble, 1945), pp. 286–87.

19. Lawrence Stone, *The Family, Sex, and Marriage in England: 1500–1800* (New York: Harper & Row, 1977), pp. 41, 503.

20. Derek Bowskill, *All the Lonely People* (New York: Bobbs-Merrill Co., 1973), p. 146.

21. M. Scott Peck, *The Road Less Traveled* (New York: Simon & Schuster, 1978), p. 159.

INDEX

About the Authors

Sar Levitan is research professor and director of the George Washington University Center for Social Policy Studies. The author of some forty books, he is especially noted for his classic *Programs in Aid of the Poor,* also published by Johns Hopkins.

Frank Gallo is a research associate at the Center. Other books he has coauthored include *A Second Chance* and *One Thousand Days: The Reagan Record.*

Richard Belous is currently senior research associate and labor economist with the Conference Board. Formerly, he was a research associate at the Center for Social Policy Studies.